Landscapes
with Figures

THE NONFICTION OF PLACE

Edited and with an introduction by

ROBERT ROOT

University of Nebraska Press • Lincoln

Acknowledgments for the use of copyrighted
material appear on pages 293–94,
which constitute an extension
of the copyright page.

© 2007 by the Board of Regents of
the University of Nebraska
All rights reserved
Manufactured in the
United States of America

Library of Congress Cataloging-
in-Publication Data
Landscapes with figures : the nonfiction of
place / edited and with an introduction by
Robert Root.
p. cm.
ISBN-13: 978-0-8032-5983-6 (pbk.: alk. paper)
ISBN-10: 0-8032-5983-2 (pbk.: alk. paper)
1. American essays—21st century. 2. American
essays—20th century. 3. Autobiography.
4. Traveler's writings, American. 5. Setting
(Literature). I. Root, Robert L.
PS689.L36 2007
814'.5408—dc22   2006028349

For Anne Root, Fran Van Kirk, and June Root,
who know about place—and family

And for Deborah Tall, who contributed so much
through her teaching, her writing, and her life

Contents

Acknowledgments

The core of this book grew out of proposals I made for panels on place at academic conventions with some of the people in this book and the subsequent roundtable on place in nonfiction I moderated and edited for the journal *Fourth Genre*. I'm grateful to Kim Barnes, Lisa Knopp, Simone Poirier-Bures, Natalia Rachel Singer, and Deborah Tall for keeping company with this project through its various incarnations. I'm grateful as well for the willingness of the other authors I approached, roundtable in hand, who were eager to join this conversation: Alison Hawthorne Deming, David Gessner, Barbara Hurd, John Hanson Mitchell, and Scott Russell Sanders. Elizabeth Dodd and Reg Saner gave keynotes on writing for a conference, "Mapping Nonfiction: Inspiring a New Sense of the Terrain," which Susan Schiller and I coordinated with the support of the Assembly for Expanded Perspectives on Learning. I'm grateful for their participation and Susan's logistical and personal support throughout the conference. My affiliation with *Fourth Genre* has been a productive and rewarding one, thanks to friends and editors Mike Steinberg and David Cooper, whose support for the Roundtable on Place was instrumental in the development of this book. I'm especially grateful that my wife, Sue, who knows what doing this kind of project is like, still encourages me to do it.

Introduction

Locating the Nonfiction of Place

Place. Nonfiction. In daily parlance few words could be less precise, less allusive, less descriptive. How then can the words in combination refer to a specific body of literature? A nonfiction of place. How can we define such a term? How can we describe its features for a reader who wants to recognize it when he sees it? for a writer who wants to know it when she creates it?

The nonfiction of place is nonfiction in which the evocation of setting is central to the development of theme or character or action. It has the ability to evoke in the reader who is familiar with the setting recognition of the accuracy and insight of the re-creation. Even if some readers disagree with the essayist's interpretation of life in that setting, they should still be able to say, "Yes, I know this place; this account is true to the place where I live." It also has the ability to trigger in the reader who is unfamiliar with the setting a similar sense of having been there, of being able to dwell within the textual place. This is, after all, what armchair travelers are seeking to achieve, a sense of having lived in a space they have never inhabited except vicariously. In the most successful nonfiction of place, both kinds of readers, insiders and outsiders, feel they are in the same space, feel they would know the space again if they visited it.

In the nonfiction of place, setting—the landscape of the work, the backdrop against which events take place—is often foregrounded to such an extent that it is the primary focus of the work. We might think of this in terms of painting, where a landscape is generally a portrait of a specific terrain, with human beings often only providing a sense of scale rather than being the center of attention. Think of Chinese hanging scroll paintings, particularly those that hang vertically, in which only close examination reveals a tiny temple or dwelling or a path through the landscape traversed by tiny figures; Guan Tong's *Travelers at a Mountain Pass* or Fan Kuan's *Travelers among Mountains and Streams* evoke such scenes in their titles. Think of Pieter Brueghel's *Hunters Coming Home in the Snow*, a winterscape in which the hunters occupy the trees on a snow-covered bluff at the bottom left of the picture while the landscape stretches off across a valley to mountains in the distance and frozen ponds filled with tiny skaters occupy the center of the image. Think of Caspar David Friedrich's *Wanderer above a Sea of Mist*, in which a single individual stands on a promontory overlooking mountaintops and intervening cloud-filled valleys. Think of Claude Monet's painting of the Palazzo Dario in Venice, three buildings and a gondola across choppy canal waters, or Gustave Caillebotte's painting *Paris Street, Rainy Day*, with its glistening stone streets and chilly atmosphere. The nonfiction of place may be the literary equivalent of a landscape painting, and like a landscape painting it may be put to any number of purposes or reflect any number of perceptions and perspectives.

The nonfiction of place includes literary works in which setting has such a presence in its impact upon characters or events or atmosphere that specific place is inextricable from everything else in the work—the story cannot be transposed casually from one setting to another; the narrator cannot be easily confused with someone from a different part of the country; the events cannot be imagined as being enacted elsewhere. The nonfiction of place is never about generic locations—think of all the movies you've rented in which you had no real sense of where the story was taking place, in which Toronto or Vancouver (where the films were made) stands in for some vague, unnamed metropolis or a universal suburb. As homogeneous as our towns and cities may have become, it's impossible to create a nonfiction of place that is set everywhere and nowhere. Films and novels may often have generic locations, but I also have read some nonfiction that left me with no sense of place—a family memoir nominally set in Nova Scotia that didn't present a distinct coastline or forest, a travelogue taking the narrator kayaking to Timbuktu that didn't make the Niger River distinguishable from any other river or the city, archetypal for its remoteness, individual or idiosyncratic. Something more has to happen with setting to create a sense of place.

The literary works that make up the nonfiction of place include flat-out, up-front explorations of particular locales, pilgrimages to special sites, tours of specific terrain, narratives of travel or residence or investigation—indeed, any nonfiction form in which the reader comes away with a powerful sense of place, a vicarious sense of having been there, perhaps in addition to whatever else the book provides. The nonfiction of place, then, encompasses any number of subgenres and forms. It can be an essay like E. B. White's "Once More to the Lake" or Scott Russell Sanders's "Cloud Crossing," a memoir like Ivan Doig's *This House of Sky* or Patricia Hampl's *A Romantic Education*, a travel narrative like Robert Louis Stevenson's *Travels with a Donkey in the Cévennes* or André Aciman's "In Search of Proust," a scientific meditation like Chet Raymo's *Honey from Stone* or Loren Eiseley's *The Immense Journey*, literary reportage like John McPhee's "The Search for Marvin Gardens" or Susan Orlean's *The Orchid Thief*, personal cultural criticism like Jane Tompkins's "At the Buffalo Bill Museum" or John Elder's *Following the Brush*. To offer as compressed and exemplary an assortment as I can—beyond the table of contents for this very collection—I'd single out the following: *A Walker in the City* by Alfred Kazin, not only a great American memoir of growing up Jewish in the 1920s but also a vivid evocation of New York City, recreating an era; *Christ Stopped in Eboli* by Carlo Levi, a record of his internal exile to a remote region of Italy during Mussolini's regime and his discovery of its landscape and its people's lives; *All But the Waltz* by Mary Clearman Blew, collecting essays about family history that are also recreations of life in Montana; *The Outermost House* by Henry Beston, the nature classic about a year spent on the beach on Cape Cod; *This Cold Heaven* by Gretel Ehrlich, recounting her immersion in the landscape of Greenland; and *Trieste and the Meaning of Nowhere* by Jan Morris, the final travel book by a prolific travel writer. A host of other titles come to mind even as I type, but these should at least suggest the range of works that compose the nonfiction of place.

Writers approach place, generally speaking, from the perspective of either an insider or an outsider. The insider's story is often about observation, a narrative of close examination of landscape and locale expressing what time and repetition of experience teach the dweller about place. The outsider's story is often about discovery, a narrative of entering into landscape and locale and learning either how the sojourner passes through it or how to become a dweller in it oneself. The insider is an inhabitant, a denizen, a dweller; the outsider is a transient, a traveler, an *inter-loper* (in the sense of one *loping*—or striding—*through* unfamiliar terrain). The inhabitant's advantage is the ability to let understanding accumulate, to have unasked questions answered almost by osmosis rather than by confrontation or direct investigation; he or she has rehearsed the explanation of experience by thinking or talking about it over time, so that the words that emerge in the writing about place come from a deep, broad pool of familiarity. The interloper's advantage is to be able to see things afresh, to ask questions that the inhabitant doesn't think to ask because the answers are so familiar as to become transparent; he or she draws instinctively on experiences of other places in order to understand the one under consideration, so that the words that emerge in the writing allow insights prompted by conscientious scrutiny and candid questioning to surface. Both intimacy and distance have advantages.

Thoreau wrote about Walden Pond as an inhabitant. We know, of course, that he built a cabin on Emerson's woodlot a little distance from the pond, lived there two years, and kept a journal all the while, which he later relied on heavily for much of the early draft of *Walden*. His inhabitant position was one he might claim by simply being in place for so long—he had visited the pond often over the years as he grew up in Concord and continued to tramp around it after he ceased to live there—but without his habit of close observation and thoughtful, prolific journalizing, he might not have been able to represent that inhabitant position in his text.

Thoreau was relentlessly observant as well as thoroughly experienced in the space he moved through. He had a great deal of stored knowledge, both collected and innate, to draw on in his writing about the pond. *Walden* is permeated by his sense of place, in part because Thoreau's sense of place permeates him. For example, in his vivid account of an evening walk he reveals his feeling for place:

> This is a delicious evening, when the whole body is one sense, and imbibes delight through every pore. I go and come with a strange liberty in Nature, a part of herself. As I walk along the stony shore of the pond in my shirt sleeves, though it is cool as well as cloudy and windy, and I see nothing special to attract me, all the elements are unusually congenial to me. The bullfrogs trump to usher in the night, and the note of the whippoorwill is borne on the rippling wind from over the water.

The passage, written in the lyrical or simultaneous present tense, establishes a sensation of place, the feeling that is excited in someone by moving through this particular terrain. It gives us the idea that the writer has been—or at the moment both of his writing and our reading actually *is*—in this location.

In other passages Thoreau writes with the scientific detachment of a surveyor and naturalist, as when he says of the pond that it "is a clear and deep green well, half a mile long and a mile and three quarters in circumference, and contains about sixty-one and a half acres; a perennial spring in the midst of pine and oak woods, without any visible inlet or outlet except by the clouds and evaporation." In a later chapter he includes a map of the pond complete with locations for depth soundings, and measurements of area, circumference, and length.

Thoreau's depth of familiarity with the place as well as his thoroughness of observation emerges most clearly in those passages in which he reveals the various angles and seasons of his viewing. At one point he writes: "Walden is blue at one time and green at another, even from the same point of view. . . . Viewed from a hill-top it reflects the color of the sky, but near at hand it is of a yellowish tint next the shore where you can see the sand, then a light green, which gradually deepens to a uniform dark green in the body of the pond." This conscientious, thorough examination extends to a number of details that the casual visitor might easily overlook or observe without particular notice or curiosity. In talking about the paths around the pond, Thoreau not only notes their presence but also reflects on their origins:

> I have been surprised to detect encircling the pond, even where a thick wood has just been cut down on the shore, a narrow shelf-like path in the steep hill-side, alternately rising and falling, approaching and receding from the water's edge, as old probably as the race of man here, worn by the feet of aboriginal hunters, and still from time to time unwittingly trodden by the present occupants of the land. This is particularly distinct to one standing on the middle of the pond in winter, just after a light snow has fallen, appearing as a clear undulating white line, unobscured by weeds and twigs a quarter of a mile off in many places where in summer it is hardly distinguishable close at hand. The snow reprints it, as it were, in clear white type alto-relievo.

The comparison at the close of the passage is particularly good at making the image come alive for a reader, but only someone who has been constantly or repeatedly in a certain locale would begin to distinguish features such as this. Thoreau brings to his description of the pond not only his skills as a naturalist and a surveyor but also the advantage of long association with place. Dwelling in his native ground is not only his motive for making sense of it but also his means. Granted, *Walden* is not simply about physical place or about natural history in a specific locale, but on a certain level it could be said to be about developing an intensive sensitivity to place. A sense of place suffuses the entire book, perhaps because a sense of place suffuses the writer.

Insiders or inhabitants write about place out of a need to understand their relationship to it; outsiders or interlopers write about place as a way of remembering and responding to and reflecting upon locales that affect them somehow, that move them to write about them. Barry Lopez has written that it took him a long time "to see that a writer's voice had to grow out of his own knowledge and desire." He advised a man whose young daughter wanted to be a writer that "if she wants to write well, she will have to become someone. She will have to discover her beliefs, and then speak to us from within those beliefs. If her prose does not come out of her belief, whatever that proves to be, she will only be passing along information, of which we are in no great need." Inhabitants and interlopers alike find that writing about a place not only makes them pay more attention to it, it also brings to the surface associations only the writer can make, juxtapositions that arise because they happen to be stored in that writer's memory or to be part of that writer's experience. A writer's reflections are idiosyncratic, unique to the writer, and valuable precisely because they raise our awareness of other ways of looking at a specific locale. One little book, *A Place on Water*, is a good example of this. Composed of three essays about the same place, Drury Pond in Maine, the essays were written by three essayists—Robert Kimber, Bill Roorbach, and Wesley McNair—who know and visit each other on the pond and give the reader shifting perspectives on both the place and the friendships that center there.

Reg Saner, whose essay in this collection, "Mesa Walk," is focused on a site close to home, observes in his commentary about the piece that "where we are interacts reciprocally with who we are, what we are." Deborah Tall's essay, "Memory's Landscape," is set in unfamiliar terrain, Krakow, the site of family history. She points out in her accompanying comment, "The lens through which we look at the world is unavoidably both cultural and personal." These ideas complement one another, reminding us that, whether insider or outsider, the writer of place has to wrestle not only with the representation of place but also with the comprehension of how the writer is perceiving the place. One contributor to this book who consistently writes as an explorer to new terrain is Elizabeth Dodd, who says in her commentary that "something I've been trying to work toward in my writing [has been] to put the personal narrative of my individual life into a physical and intellectual habitat . . . of larger scope."

In an essay titled "Cahokia," originally published in the *Southwest Review*, Dodd writes about the prehistoric mounds across the Mississippi River from St. Louis. She not only helps the reader to imagine what this archaeological site looks like but also links the life that scientists and historians believe was lived there with the life she sees around her as a sojourner in St. Louis. She relies in part on powers of description generated by close observance of her unfamiliar surroundings. After her teaching job in Kansas ends for the semester, she rejoins her husband to spend the summer in St. Louis, where he is in graduate school.

> Here we have no air-conditioning, no laundry facilities in the apartment. A grid of clotheslines crisscrosses the cement plaza at the building's rear and today I carried wet clothes there from the washer in the basement, passing up the single drier in the windowless, musty room to the ample space out back, although I met no one else while at my work. It was a small act, a tiny one, not really geared to reattach life to—well, to what, really? It was a splendid day.
>
> But after the laundry dried, after the lights began to come on in the stairwells of the facing building, I sat on this apartment's small balcony to watch the night fall. Chimney swifts chattered overhead, the jet planes roared from distance to distance, and at last a woman across the way came out to read the evening paper before the daylight disappeared. All around, the life of the comfortable city continued its background noise, and farther away, the more desperate lives in East St. Louis continued well out of sight and hearing.

Dodd evokes place by calling upon what she sees and what she reacts to in her new surroundings. At Cahokia her activities exploring the mounds lead her to reflect on her position in both time and place.

To stand atop this earthen structure today is still an exhilarating event although not a terrifying one. For people living in the Mississippi area almost 1,000 years ago, it might have been both. Tallgrasses—mostly switchgrass—riffle in the wind, and the sounds of traffic on the interstate to the north and the state route to the south both shift in tone, a sort of slow, subtle Doppler effect as one rises from the floodplain.

On a clear, warm day, breathing deeply from the 154-step climb, I'm alone on the artificial, nearly level summit. Distance becomes enticing, interesting in its new perspective. To the west, the tall buildings and Gateway Arch of downtown St. Louis look like a model city, the architect's miniature on display. Nearer, the clusters of mounds rise from the flat prairie in a seemingly scattered pattern. Of the original 120 mounds, 68 remain, nestled amid homes and highways—and recent, failed symbols of twentieth-century life. One mound was demolished in the 1950s in order to erect a drive-in theater. In Collinsville the drive-in has fared no better than it has elsewhere.

What she sees influences what she reflects upon; she doesn't have layers of personal prehistory in this place to draw on or to divert her attention from physical details.

The drive to Cahokia, across the Mississippi from St. Louis, takes her through the poverty and decay of East St. Louis, and when she considers the population density and cruel social customs of the ancient mound dwellers—their rulers were buried with slaves, and mass graves reveal brutal atrocities—she finds comparisons with the degradations of modern American urban life unavoidable. The contrast between the prehistoric world and the modern world may be there for any visitor to see, but not every writer would make those associations. But the essay isn't only pointing out inequality and injustice across millennia; the author also hints at similar, more intimate versions of these issues in her own crumbling marriage. This is the way that writing about place uncovers intersections of social and personal and natural history across time and confronts the writer not only with what she observes but also with who she is.

An interloper writing nonfiction about a place is as obligated as an inhabitant to write honestly about whatever he or she observes, but unlike the dweller, the transient makes no claim that the views presented weren't collected in passing. The reader is obligated to accept those conditions for considering place—

all of us, whether we write or we don't, experience place both as inhabitants and as interlopers and can acknowledge the credibility and vitality of either perspective.

If the poles of perspective for the nonfiction of place are occupied at one extreme by denizens and at the other by drifters, it's obvious that there are a multitude of sites in between, innumerable intersections of longitude and latitude where others situate themselves—those who stay in a place long enough to become acclimated beyond the casual but not long enough to feel thoroughly intimate. No one writer necessarily occupies just one site throughout his or her career. Thoreau, the über-inhabitant of Walden Pond, was an interloper in his writings published posthumously as *The Maine Woods, Cape Cod*, and *A Yankee in Canada*. E. B. White also often took on the role of interloper—or visitor or outsider—in his essays; in one titled "Walden" he visits Concord, reports on what he sees and does, and reflects on what he feels and how he responds, but doesn't pretend to an insider's perspective. This is in direct contrast to his presence in the great essay "Once More to the Lake," in which he is so steeped in the setting of Great Pond that memory continually supplies him with a context against which to measure his immediate experience; he is virtually unable to avoid an inhabitant's point of view.

Perhaps some of this shift in perspective simply is unavoidable. If we write about a place we know we almost can't help conjuring contexts that affect how we perceive the location; if we write about a place we are encountering for the first time, we almost can't help dwelling on direct observations and the associations and reactions they produce. Our longitude and latitude may be determined by our relative distance from each of the two poles of perspective.

However, on many of the intersections are transients traveling while immersed in texts written by earlier inhabitants and interlopers. They not only see place directly, as the other writers do, but simultaneously view it through an additional lens, a textual prism. If we write about a place familiar to us from our reading, our vision is refracted by the earlier writing; we see the place principally in terms of how it compares in reality—how it appears to us at the moment we encounter it—to the way it appears in another writer's text. This is not an uncommon approach to the nonfiction of place; witness the number of books retracing the routes of Lewis and Clark in the American West or of Johnson and Boswell through Scotland to the Hebrides. Witness Richard Holmes (in *Footsteps*) on the trail of Stevenson traveling without a donkey through the Cévennes or John McPhee (in *Pieces of the Frame*) making his reading of *Macbeth* concrete by walking with his family from Birnam wood to Dunsinane or Christine Jerome (in *An Adirondack Passage*) retracing the canoe travels of George Washington Sears ("Nessmuk"). Such an approach presents a portrait of place through a translucent scrim that changes, with the intensity of the lighting, from nearly invisible and transparent to wholly visible and solid, like those two-way mirrors that, with a twist of a dial, superimpose the image of your face onto the face of the person on the other side of the glass. We seem to occupy two (or more) different compass points at once.

Even works that don't expressly follow in another writer's footsteps display echoes and reflections of earlier writing, other investigations, literary influences, and factual resources. These ingredients give essays of place distinctive flavors, according to how they're mixed. Some are more lyrical or more narrative or more expository because of the mix; some border on poetry, some on science; some are such a jumble of motives and modes and intentions and conventions that only vague terms like *creative nonfiction* and *the nonfiction of place* are sufficiently encompassing. As Deborah Tall observes in her commentary on place, "books about places are . . . often adventurous hybrids in which physical description, character portraits, statistics, analysis, personal narrative, dramatic event, argument, meditation, and flights of fancy can happily coexist. Books of place are geographical, ethnographic, environmental, political, spiritual." This truth about the nonfiction of place helps explain why its titles are shelved and scattered throughout bookstores and libraries rather than handily grouped in one location.

The nonfictionists who contributed commentary and essays for this collection suggest how various the nonfiction of place can be. The landscapes in which their essays place them as figures range from Kyrgyzstan and Krakow to Mexico, from the Sea of Cortés to the North Atlantic and around the United States. The terrains vary as well—beaches and deserts, islands and forests, plains and mountains, towns and cities, caves and canyons and marshes. Some of the writers stay close to home, walking familiar ground; others locate a distant terra incognita and embark on voyages of discovery. In the course of exploring place, the writers here draw on a host of disciplines—archaeology, anthropology, botany, ecology, geography, geology, ornithology, literary criticism, history, zoology, speleology, theology, and philosophy. As the nonfiction of place may be found in subgenres across the spectrum of nonfiction, so these writers compose in a variety of forms—personal essay, memoir, travel narrative, nature narrative, cultural criticism, literary reportage. Kim Barnes reacts to moving to the mountains after years living in the Clearwater Canyon of Idaho; Alison Deming ranges from Isla Tiburón in the Sea of Cortés to Seal Island in the Bay of Fundy, places she identifies as part of "the territory of birds"; Elizabeth Dodd explores the natural and cultural history behind the Picket Wire Canyonlands in southeastern Colorado, where dinosaur trackways may still be seen; David Gessner connects the impact of terrain, particularly Cape Cod, on his identity as a nature writer; Barbara Hurd examines her experience exploring the underworld of caves in Virginia and New England at a time when she must also face the loss of people she loves; Lisa Knopp reclaims an inland salt marsh near where she lives in Nebraska; John Hanson Mitchell shares a moment in his experiment in Thoreauvian living on Scratch Flat, not far from Walden Pond; Simone Poirier-Bures reports on her travels among the Kyrgyz of Eastern Europe; Robert Root investigates his fascination with the Anasazi cliff dwellers and pueblo builders of the Four Corners area; Scott Russell Sanders returns to familiar ground in Ohio, where he grew up, to consider change; Reg Saner wanders the mesa near his Colorado home and follows threads of connection to other places and the meaning of home; Natalia Rachel Singer recalls her experiences as an expatriate in Mexico; and Deborah Tall visits Krakow, Poland, to discover what an ancestral site might mean to someone who has never been there but knows well its true history.

In addition to the essays collected here, these writers have contributed commentaries exploring the perspectives they bring to place in their writing, the influences on those perspectives, the processes by which they discover what makes particular places resonate so strongly within them. Most would agree with Simone Poirier-Bures's remark, "The act of writing . . . is always a clarifying. You don't always see things until you write about them." The writing comes not only out of an act of exploration, in terms of place, but also out of an act of discovery, in terms of the writer's connection to place. As David Gessner observes, "The truth is that if you develop a deep relationship with a specific place, you almost can't help conjuring up strange, deep, and, yes, nearly mystical emotions." Understanding what underlies those emotions is what makes the writing essential.

In a sense this book invites several different approaches to reading. One way to read it is simply as an anthology of the nonfiction of place, a collection of essays, memoirs, and travel writing that ranges widely across the country and the world; separately these are companion pieces for the reader's own explorations of place, and collectively they are a prose collage representing the nonfiction of place. Another way to read it is as a book *on* or *about* writing, a collection of commentaries by writers on the ways they compose their nonfictions of place; here the invitation to the reader is to find a place of his or her own, daybook or journal in hand, and spend time discovering and reflecting upon what impact that place generates upon its visitor. The most thorough and complete way to read the book is to read an author's commentary first and then read the writing sample that follows it, and so continue throughout the book as if it were a sequential conversation on the nonfiction of place that you've been invited to overhear. (That the authors are speaking by last name in alphabetical order you may either ignore or pretend is merely coincidental and irrelevant.) For writers who read the book I hope they will want to continue the conversation in their own writing; for readers I hope they will continue it by reading further in the wonderful work these writers have published and considering, as they read beyond these authors, how many other writers might have been included.

In the end this is the way I hope to define the nonfiction of place—by the examples drawn from the writing and by the commentary of the writers themselves. Ah, so this, you may say to yourself after reading a selection, is the nonfiction of place. Ultimately, this is the way I hope you come to recognize it. It may be less concise and concentrated than a dictionary definition, more sprawling and intuitive, but it will ultimately be more encompassing, more suggestive, more accurate, more true.

KIM BARNES

Kim Barnes sets her work in Idaho. She is the author of two memoirs, *In the Wilderness: Coming of Age in an Unknown Country* (1996), which won a PEN/Jerard Award in Nonfiction and was a finalist for both the Pulitzer Prize and the PEN Martha Albrand Award for First Nonfiction, and *Hungry for the World: A Memoir* (2000). She has also authored a novel, *Finding Caruso* (2003). She coedited, with Mary Clearman Blew, *Circle of Women: An Anthology of Contemporary Western Women's Writing* (1994) and, with Claire Davis, *Kiss Tomorrow Hello: Notes from the Midlife Underground by Twenty-five Women over Forty* (2006). She teaches creative writing at the University of Idaho and was appointed to a three-year term as Idaho Writer-in-Residence in 2004. Her work has appeared in such journals as *Shenandoah* and the *Georgia Review,* and her essay "The Ashes of August" won a 2001 Pushcart Prize. Her essay "The Clearwater" appeared in the premiere issue of the nonfiction journal *River Teeth*; "Almost Paradise" originally appeared in *High Desert Journal.*

On Place

My writing is so tied to place that I have a difficult time separating the story from its setting, just as I find it nearly impossible to separate myself from the land around me. For the most part, I've had little desire to explore settings outside the western landscape, yet I believe absolutely in an artist's ability to imagine any landscape, foreign or familiar. Maybe this is because I'm deeply invested in the idea of myth and archetype. I believe that everything I need to know and write about exists vertically rather than horizontally—that is, I believe in the symbolic resonance of human experience in any given landscape. And even though I believe it is sometimes a good idea to "write what you know," I believe you can "know" things in ways that are not always experiential. Why are some of us innately drawn to cities or mountains or rivers or Parisian cafés? Why do we sometimes feel like strangers in a strange land—the land being the very place we were born into? Our connection to place isn't always defined by the physical and literal; sometimes the place we know best and feel the greatest affinity for is a place we have never been.

For me, I feel the greatest affinity for the defined landscape of the West, especially mountain rivers and canyons—the type of land in which I was raised. Yet I feel that my connection to wild open spaces has less to do with having been born and raised here and much more to do with having been lucky enough to find a place that I feel intimately connected to at some deep, perhaps genetic level. It is the landscape that I find most comforting, even when it proves itself most hostile. As an adult, I have often been given the opportunity to choose the place I wish to live, and, always, I have chosen the inner-mountain West.

In her essay "The Erotics of Open Spaces" Paisley Rekdal notes that she moved from the city to Wyoming, in part, she says, because she "wanted to experience how a landscape might dominate me." People, Rekdal observes, "fall in love with the geography they've adopted and, in turn, let this geography's mythos, its physicalities, define them, release or explain something deep within them." She goes on to say that "this is what happened to me: I fell in love with difficulty."

Everything about the West, Rekdal asserts, "dominates, proves you vulnerable." Finally, she came to believe that she "responded to the place with the same passion some women have to a rape fantasy: Wyoming was the partner that would overtake me completely, rule me body and heart, make me fulfill desire that I could only long for in secret." The land is like a lover, she says, and we need "different bodies and loves at different times." She ends her essay with the question: "Do any of us really understand the bodies of our lovers, the landscape of our desires?"

Unlike Rekdal, I always felt in balance with the western landscape, maybe because, as an intimate, as someone who came to an awareness of herself in the isolation of backwoods logging camps and was allowed to disappear for hours into the wilderness without raising parental alarm, I recognize and understand the nature of this landscape's demands. Rather than finding the West dominating and threatening, I most often find in it a sure comfort and familiarity. Recognition. A stable and monogamous marriage of need, expectation, and fulfillment.

Because I'm primarily a memoirist and writer of personal essays, this kind of intimacy is very important to me. Writing as an outsider doesn't appeal to me, unless there is a defined transition that takes place so that "outsider" becomes "insider." I do use the idea of "outsider" to define alienation, unfamiliarity, chaos, loss of narrative. In my memoirs I intentionally set up a kind of delineation between the wilderness and the "city"—civilization. Very Romantic. There are a number of scenes in which I describe the construction of the dam on the North Fork of the Clearwater—halfway between the wilderness and the city—as that point separating me from my childhood happiness. The scenes detail my journey toward my "new" life, which will be defined by loss of innocence, disaffection, and dislocation. I describe the pulp and paper mill at the city's edge in terms reminiscent of the Romantics' description of the Industrial Revolution: smoke, darkness, mechanical and monstrous. Hell. I am lost, an outsider, and must find my way back to some sense of who I am in this foreign place.

Here's the problem I have sometimes faced as an "insider" trying to write about place: I know it *too* intimately. I've taken it in, internalized it. There are times when I cannot separate myself in order to *see* it. I remember Mary Clearman Blew reading an early draft of *In the Wilderness*, my memoir about growing up in the logging camps and small towns of the Clearwater National Forest. One of the things she said to me was that I needed to step back and *look* at the landscape as an outsider might. In memory all I could see was very close-in: the shack we lived in, the nearby trees. Nothing more. Not the mountaintops or the lay of the land. I had to look at photographs and maps. Same with the flora and fauna. I grew up calling every bush "buck brush." I never knew the name of the many birds that flitted through the forest nor the specific names of the trees themselves. Everything was as common and un-notable as my own skin.

When I begin to write memoir, I detail the setting from a perspective that is more emotional than mental, I think. How I *feel* the place. Later I go back and find the correct and appropriate terminology, and I check my facts. I don't want to have chokecherry blooming in July if it really blooms in April or May, no matter what my memory tells me, and so I've surrounded myself with reference books: Peterson's field guides, geology texts, *Idaho Place Names*. I had to *learn* the land I'd known since birth.

Writing is about art and inspiration, and it is about craft and hard work. Writing about the land also involves each of these things. Lyrical language—the putting together of beautiful words such as *chalcedony* and *Barrow's gold-eneye*—feels like inspiration. The finding of these words and the researching of their definitions and appropriateness to my story is *work*. No matter what you choose to include about your physical surroundings, it must inform and complete the narrative—it must serve to characterize both the people and the place as well as to further inform the thematic arc of the story.

In his essay "No Step" Nicholson Baker obsessively details the writing he observes printed on the wings of various airplanes. I love how he creates such intimacy with the place he temporarily but often inhabits: the inside of a jet. It's this kind of authoritative knowledge and detailed observation, whether about commuting or shoeing horses, that draws me into a narrative. The setting can be a penthouse bedroom or Hells Canyon; it can be about the landscape of a lover's body or the craters of the moon. What I want is intimacy, either comfortable or uncomfortable. And I want that intimacy mixed with vulnerability, which is what may appeal to me about "risky" settings: airplanes, whitewater rivers, open fields in winter. Large cities. Perhaps Paisley Rekdal recognized how the act of immersing herself in an unfamiliar and threatening landscape might provide the kind of atmospheric conflict and vulnerability that often gives rise to art.

To me the story I want to tell exists in the conflict of memory. It's not *what* happened that's most important to me but *why* I remember it the way I do. If an image or detail has remained with me in memory and seems pertinent to the story at hand, I put it down. I've found that journals and diaries disrupt this process, but everyone is different in his or her methodology. Use what works. Just remember that, although we may know the factual details, we do not always know the "why" of our story. This is the journey of self-discovery that so many memoirists embark upon. "Who am I, and why?" I cannot answer this without looking to the land. At one point in my first memoir I say that the wilderness was where "my parents had first found their salvation, and where I would once again find mine." Because my father, especially, looked to the land for answers and solace, I grew up deeply ingrained with similar views. I cannot separate my story from the land any more than I can separate my story from the story of my parents' quest for a new life.

I noted before that I don't necessarily feel like I need physical or temporal distance from a place or event to write about it, but I do feel like I need enough narrative distance to see the story's archetypal rhythms and shape. When I can observe this thematic focus, I can determine what details and descriptions are important to more fully realizing the larger story. My approach is to write the story (what happened—the action) straight and simple the first time through—to just tell the story, as Bill Kittredge says. Then I try to separate myself from it, become reader rather than writer, see it as separate from my own experience, see it as an object of art. This is the point at which I start bringing in details of the land that harmonize with the story's themes. I can do this while surrounded by the very setting I'm describing, or I can do it while flying over Michigan. At this point the details are my palette of colors. I can mix, blend, define, by intentionally describing certain characteristics of the river or the deer I'm hunting or the incoming weather or last summer's wildfire. I can paint the picture, make the dream visually materialize.

For example, a piece that I wrote several years ago while living above the Clearwater River is an essay that came out of an "assignment" I was given by Mary Clearman Blew, who was editing an anthology of river essays. I knew immediately that I would write about the Clearwater—the river that I had known all my life and the geological presence around which all of my books have been centered. What I didn't know was what the essay would be "about" other than the river itself. You can write well about anything—or anyone—using lyrical language and heightened imagery, but, finally, the essay has to have some larger thematic arc: it has to be about something larger than itself, just as your story has to be about something greater than your individual experience.

So, here's what I did: I thought of five or six memory scenes involving the river, some from the distant past, others more recent. (This is the easy part.) Now I needed the "idea" or "theme" that would hold the scenes together—that would serve to develop my "thesis." I always tell my students: it's like fish on a stringer. The stringer is the idea on which you "hang" your scenes, the thread that holds the essay together. If you can discern this idea, which you often cannot determine until you've actually written the scenes and allowed them to show you what they're about, you're almost home.

One of the challenging parts of this process is determining which scenes to *leave out*. Just because the events occurred and happen to have involved the river doesn't mean they must be included. Again, what images, details, and emotions in the scenes connect and unify them thematically? What shared ideas might they contain? How do they resonate, harmonize, build on one another?

As I contemplated and started drafting the scenes I might include (at this point in the process, I really luxuriate in description and vivid detail, most often composing in present tense to gain immediacy), I asked myself, "Why am I telling them this?" and by *them* I mean my readers. Always, I ask, "Why is this important to know? What do the readers learn, not just about me, but about the 'big picture,'" which is more about the human condition than it is about any one of us? Remember that any single event can be about any number of things, but our task is to impose, for a time, at least, a single narrative of meaning—to look through one window of the house and describe what we see framed there.

When I'd written a few of these scenes, remembering that scenes are like five-by-seven-inch story cards and can be moved around, in and out of chronological order, into backstory or contemplation, I saw that they were being informed by a sense of loss and anger. And I have to stop here and say that we seldom write anything that isn't informed by a current emotion. Write about the river or the moon or the cityscape on any given night, and your emotional state at the time will tint your word choice, color your description, direct the details you choose, and set the tone of the piece. This is often a subconscious involvement, but it's the writer's job to observe what the subconscious is conveying and make the choice to either work with or against that impulse.

During the time I was writing this essay, our close circle of friends had been thrown into upheaval by a certain kind of dishonesty and betrayal, and our connections to one another had been shattered. As I composed the essay, I began observing elements in the scenes not only of loss but also of weakness and strength, appearance and reality, and the physical vulnerability I sometimes feel as a woman, wife, and mother. One scene described my taking my young children to the river because, in the face of so much fragmentation, I needed to feel connection to the land that had always sustained me. But on this particular trip I made some poor logistical decisions, probably because of the kind of desperation I was feeling, and I ended up marooning myself and my children in a ravine close to the water. Instead of a trip that might bring comfort, the journey had taken me deeper into danger, both physically and emotionally. And perhaps what I was feeling, in Rekdal's words, was a need to be confronted by something larger than myself, to feel a kind of absolute dominance in the face of the fragility of human relationships.

I then saw how I could connect this scene to the sense of loss I still feel over the damming of the Clearwater when I was a girl and how, in a certain way, I feel as though the river has betrayed me, that its current was no longer true, its life no more certain than my own. (Rekdal writes that people sometimes need a variation of landscape just as they need "different bodies and loves at different times," but I have always felt jealous and proprietary of the landscape I have chosen to call my own.)

Then came the hardest part of all: providing the "glue" to hold it all together, actually articulating the substance of that thematic fish stringer. There are times when a series of scenes can stand alone as an essay, times when the images, as is the case with some poems, can carry the meaning as a kind of "collage" composition. More often, however, we must attempt to contemplate and explore the very scenes we have created. Someone—was it John Gardner?—once said that all stories are made up of action and thought. In composing this essay, I now had my scenes of action but was missing the authorial exposition that would help bring those scenes around and make the essay more fully realized.

This glue is often made up of "vertical movement" in the essay, and by this I mean movement that delves deeper rather than moves forward. Vertical movement is usually made up of contemplation, but it can also be seen in moments of associative memory, figures of speech, lyrical description, or direct questioning of meaning ("Is this why I have come here? To test myself, the river? To see if one of us remains true?"). It is this movement that can sometimes take the essay to a more complex level of emotion and self-inquiry.

Then came the challenge of the ending, of course, which always feels like *resolution* to me, even if the "true" story itself really doesn't have resolution. At the level of craft resolution means that the images and thematic progression come together and, if you're lucky, transcend the individual parts of the essay's structure. I have a tendency to rely on bittersweet, almost paradoxical endings, as is the case with "The Clearwater": the river brings both comfort and danger; it sustains and destroys; it gives me all that I want and takes away all that I need.

The river has always provided me with these metaphors, easily observable, accessible, and true. Recently, I have had to face a loss of narrative meaning, a loss of a large part of my story. Four years ago (has it been that long?) my family and I left the river and moved an hour north to Moscow, where my husband and I now teach at the University of Idaho. It's a beautiful setting: we live on a mountain surrounded by trees, and the Palouse Prairie spreads out across the foothills. But there is no water. Not even a small stream. The river that was so central to my life is no longer part of the landscape in which I live and write. The essay included here, "Almost Paradise," is about moving to new terrain and striving to develop a fresh connection to the land: a western landscape, yes, but foreign to me nonetheless. What I struggle to understand during the course of the essay is why I cannot escape the grief of separation. As I detail the move and attempt to observe the emotional upheaval I experience, what I come to see is that my connection is made up of much more than physical and aesthetic engagement: what I'm grieving is the loss of time and the nostalgia of memories associated with place. Our move corresponded with my children's move toward independence. The river will always be the land of their "lost" childhood, just as it was the land of my own.

Bringing the intellect to bear on the stories of our lives through craft, contemplation, and context; attempting the sometimes liberating, sometimes terrifying journey toward the "why" of our lives—I believe that these are the greatest challenges for the writer of personal nonfiction. But it all begins with the most basic elements of story—the creation of the "uninterrupted dream" that John Gardner spoke of through the use of detailed description to transport us into a specific time and definitive place. And isn't that like memory?

I believe that writing well involves a certain kind of submission—to impulse, to hard work, sometimes to the truth of difficult memory, sometimes to the acceptance of memory's failure to sustain the truth we have always believed. Perhaps I will have to bow my head and let go of the river; perhaps its memory will always sustain me. Perhaps I have had it wrong all along and have, as Rekdal asserts, been drawn to the rough canyon landscape because of its hold over me; perhaps the river was "that first, fierce, liberating lover to whom I could never commit because I would be his subject," but I doubt it. More likely, it is I who have attempted to own the river and now must let go.

Almost Paradise

Four years. That's how long it's been since I "left the river." I don't say since I "moved to *here* from *there*" or "since I began living on *the mountain*." I say "left the river," as though I were saying "left the church" or "left my husband" or "left the country of my birth."

I left late-autumn mornings with the windows open, when I woke to the cool mineral smell of silt. Afternoon picnics along the sandy shores, my children sifting the shallows for tadpoles, water skippers, mussel shells. Evenings fly-fishing the V of current for rainbow, steelhead, salmon, then watching the moon rise over Angel Ridge, its silvery wedge of light illuminating the bridge below our house so that the ribbed structure itself seemed to levitate above the water.

The "lasting place." That's what we called it because we believed we would stay there for the rest of our lives, and we didn't.

We knew it was a move we had to make. My husband and I had taken positions seventy-five miles north, at the University of Idaho, and the hour-and-a-half commute each way was impractical and sometimes treacherous; our children would soon be of driving age, and we dreaded the thought of the deadly Highway 12 being their proving ground; they needed more opportunities than our small settlement could provide teenagers not raising 4-H steers. And so, after a decade of living on the Clearwater, we moved from our home on the river to our home in the woods—three long August days of manic runs up and down the canyon, back and forth across the prairie, the largest U-Haul we could rent stuffed full, potted plants and grubbed up herbs wilting behind the cab's hothouse windows.

By the time we made our last trip, I had been saying good-bye to the river for weeks: each morning I would stand on our deck, soaking up the canyon's warmth as though I might hold it in reserve for the long winter I knew was coming. Twenty-five hundred feet higher in elevation, our new home wouldn't give me the early springs and long autumns I'd come to love. No more garden tomatoes lasting past Halloween. No more basil plants lush enough to provide us with a year's supply of pesto.

But, then, the bright side: no more wrist-thick rattlesnakes *mating* in the basil. No more star thistle so dense and vicious we couldn't find our way to the river except on paths worn through by deer. No wasps nesting in the eaves by the thousands, a hundred ticks carried in on the bellies of our dogs and cats, set loose in our beds to find the warm nests of our armpits. We could go to a movie on the spur of the moment, have dinner in town. And even though there would be no river—not even a spring moistening the granite and clay embankment outside my kitchen window—there would be the woods.

I knew how much I'd miss the river. Or I thought I did. But I also knew I was going back into the dream of my childhood—back into the forest I'd left at the age of twelve and believed I'd never regain.

My parents had come to Idaho from Oklahoma in 1956, leaving behind lives defined by poverty and alcoholism. My mother was sixteen, my father eighteen, when they were married in the small logging town of Pierce by a Pentecostal minister. My mother set up housekeeping in an eight-by-twenty-foot shack—one of several circled in the logging camp along the North Fork of the Clearwater River. No electricity or tapped-in water but enough isolation to make my mother long for her red-dirt home. She missed the open midwestern horizon, the way you could see a visitor coming for miles because of the rooster tail of dust along the flatland road. But not my father. He had found his paradise in that circle of trees that shut out the sky and kept the world at bay. My mother and father both found their salvation in that little Pentecostal church. They set about making a new life for themselves free of their inherited sins: no drinking, no gambling, no dancing. My mother threw away her makeup and swimsuits; my father gave up his love for Willie and Waylon. They purified themselves in the snowmelt of May, both baptized in the same watershed we drank from, from which we took enough trout to hold us through the longest winters.

I came to an awareness of myself as a young woman in that time of national turmoil that hardly touched us at all. Even though it was 1969, the war that raged overseas came to us muted and late, if at all. No television, no radio or newspaper, to distract us from our daily attention to doctrine. No teenage fashion magazines for me to moon over. As a member of the Holiness sect, I could not wear earrings, cut my hair, listen to worldly music, or join the cheerleading squad. As a daughter of Eve, I was a temptation to myself and those around me, and, like my mother, I must remain silent and invisible. Surrounded by the women and girls of the church, physically isolated from the world around me, I had no sense of what I might be missing, of how different I might be. I was *saved*, and my family was saved, and we lived, I was told, in the palm of God's hand.

I remember warm summer days playing in the mica-laden creeks, my mother—so young!—sunbathing on the pebbled banks. I remember cold fried chicken and watermelon laid out beneath old-growth cedar, my father fishing the still free-flowing river while my younger brother napped in my mother's lap. I remember my own baptism, how the preacher bent me back until my face submerged and the world warbled in my ears. I remember little other than contentment. I remember a pure happiness. What I feel is nostalgia for my own innocence, of course, but it's more than that: I remember my parents' laughter. I remember *their* youthful pleasure. I feel how close they came to Paradise.

It was a crisis of faith that took us from that place. The summer before my thirteenth birthday my father believed he heard the voice of God telling us we must leave the land that had nurtured us, given us our living, held us together as family. Perhaps he believed that he loved it too much. That he had forgotten that Paradise could never be found on Earth but only in Heaven. Within twenty-four hours we were packed and gone, leaving our shotgun-shack behind. We followed the river to the small city of Lewiston ninety miles southwest, to where the Clearwater joined the Snake and continued on its way to the Pacific.

Could my father have foreseen how that journey would break us all? How he would spend his nights driving a truck loaded with wood chips from mill to mill rather than sitting on the step of his shack, watching the moose dip its great head into the nearby pond? How my mother would have her own crisis of faith and begin to question her subservience? How his daughter, lost to herself, would find company with others existing on the fringes, marginalized by appearance or circumstance?

I rebelled, ran away from home, was found and brought back. I graduated from high school and left my father's house that night. I worked at fast-food drive-ins and mill town bars, stayed with men and left them, or they left me. Always, it seemed, I was searching, questing for that place left behind. Days off, I would follow the river back into the woods, alone or with a boyfriend, to hunt, fish, lie in the high meadows. I believed that there was something I might still find there, along the feeding streams of the North Fork. Cold mountain water surrounded by ponderosa, hemlock, larch, white fir: it remains my slice of Heaven.

In the summer of 1990, after several years of living in Lewiston, my husband and I discovered the house for sale in the Clearwater River canyon, halfway between my childhood home and the city. I remember us standing on the deck, looking directly into the eye of an osprey hovering for fish. I remember my husband saying that it made his soul sing. And even though the land was visibly barren—steep hills of thistle, sage, and cactus giving way to ravined basalt—I could stand in the kiln of high summer heat, look out over the river, and sense the cool promise of deeply running water.

Only one thing was missing: trees. But some happiness *can* be bought. I made forays into town, brought back expensively bundled saplings from garden stores, cleaned out the bare-rooted dregs at Wal-Mart. Ten Christmases running, I hunted down and purchased live evergreens that we painstakingly acclimated into—and back out of—our too-warm house (sap rising, falling again) before pickaxing holes into the still-frozen soil for planting.

Still, it would be decades before our slips of green became a forest. Every summer, when the temperature on our deck hit 120 and the only mature pine cast its thin line of shade, we loaded up and headed out for our friend's high-country cabin, abandoning our river for the forested cool of mountain evenings. Our "pet cemetery" was crowded with chickens and rabbits that had expired in the heat, often because we had left them to a climate we ourselves could not bear.

I thought, then, that I might welcome the moderate summers on Moscow

Mountain, our deck shaded by a tight stand of bull pine. In an area known for its peas and lentils and wheat, I have my trees—an island of wooded wilderness afloat on an ocean of loam. From where I sit, sheltered by the massive trunks and elongated boughs of conifers, I can see the land stretched out before me, undulant, as though sculpted by the movement of water, like an undersea bed of mounded sand.

But the water, if ever here, has gone. There is no lake, no river, no stream, that I can see, only dry-land farming, marginal wells, and seeps that sometimes feed the smallest of ponds. Our first spring on the mountain, before the snow had melted from the roof, I badgered my husband into driving north with me to the nearest creek, where I waded into the icy melt and dropped a nymph into an eddy. The fry I caught and cast back was a tiny pleasure, but the feel of the frigid water around my knees, the smell so crystalline I could taste its sharp edges—I breathed it in, let it drill to my bones, and believed it was enough to sustain me a while longer.

Still, I grieved. Give it a year, a friend said. Moving is hard. But I was happy to be in our new home, our new town, among people I respected and friends I cherished. I know, I told them—I know!—how lucky I am to be in this idyllic place we have chosen to live, blessed by family and a profession I value. I argued with myself, scolded. I understood that I could not have it all. Why, then, did my heart feel as though it were breaking? I felt true grief, as though I had lost a lover. When my husband asked, "What do you need to feel better?" I knew the answer without hesitation: water. I want, I need, I desire. *Water.*

In his memoir, *Memories, Dreams, Reflections,* psychologist and philosopher Carl Jung tells of one of his first memories: a childhood visit to Lake Constance. He remembers how his mother could not drag him away from the water. "The waves from the steamer washed up to the shore, the sun glistened on the water, and the sand under the water had been curled into little ridges by the waves. The lake stretched away and away into the distance. This expanse of water was an inconceivable pleasure to me, an incomparable splendor. At that time the idea became fixed in my mind that I must live near a lake; without water, I thought, nobody could live at all."

Jung's words are literal and absolute—no living thing can survive without water—but his words are also figurative and limited: not all of us need water to remain spiritually alive, but for some it is the element that metaphorically nurtures the soul.

For Ed Abbey it was the arid desert of the Southwest; for my cousin Terry it is the streaming populace of New York City; for my daughter the intimate sidewalk cafés of Paris. We are not all born to love rivers. But, for me, the river is more than water and canyon. It is my history, my past, my inheritance. It is the story of my parents' quest for the perfect home in the logging camps of the Clearwater; my coming to awareness of myself along the banks of Reeds Creek; the way my life is divided by the building of Dworshak Dam; how the death of the upper North Fork mirrored the demise of my child's sense of happiness, contentment, and shelter. And then, in the canyon of the Clearwater, my husband and I at the beginning of our life together, our daughter and son still young and in need of me.

If, by some true miracle, I were to be granted my river, have it carved out at the base of this mountain and filled in a thunderous moment of granite-shatter, would that erase my grief, grant me my sense of "home," give me my remembered Paradise?

That first fishing season after our move from the Clearwater to Moscow, we loaded our daughter and son, fishing gear, tent, and coolers into the car and headed north for the upper reaches of the St. Joe River, only a watershed away from my childhood home on the North Fork. The closer we got, the more vibrant I felt, as though I were passing backward through time, regaining lost years. I rolled down the window, breathed in, hung out my head like a dog, grinning foolishly, my eyes closed against the sting of wind.

I didn't wait to help unload, and no one asked me to. I nosed straight for the water and waded in. It was like eating pie after a long fast: I was faint with happiness, adrenalized with a sugary pleasure that I couldn't get enough of. I stood in the river for hours, casting my line, reminding myself to *look*, to *feel*, because I knew that soon it would be gone from me. And two days later, when it *was* time to go—after we had taken down the tent and stowed the coolers and everyone was belted in—I stalled. "Just one more minute," I said. "I'll be right back."

I ran to the river, bent down and filled my hands, rinsed my face, the back of my neck, my shoulders. I knelt on the hard rocks and began to cry and couldn't stop, not even with the cold water against my eyes and my husband coming to check on me. Not just tears but gulping sobs. I felt as though I might die—as though some part of me might not survive—if I left that water again.

My family was very gentle with me, and more than a little frightened, I think. My children had never seen me like this, and my son worried that I was having *a nervous breakdown.* By the time my husband got me into the car, I was nearly immobile. Having left the river, I found myself lost, as though the story I had told myself of who I was had somehow disappeared, fell from my hands like a wind-torn map. All the long miles back, I remained rigid, unable to converse, as though caught in a limbo between two worlds, paralyzed by my inability to exist in either.

When she moved to Idaho, had my mother grieved for her Oklahoma farm as though she were burying her own mother? Had my father felt this same loss of direction when he left the wilderness he most loved? If so, how had they gone on to make sense of their lives? How had they resolved themselves to such grief? These were stories I had never heard, and without that map to take the place of the one I had lost, I felt as though I were in exile, a wanderer of dry lands, no compass, no crumbs to find my way back home.

I think of Joseph Campbell's examination of myth and the adventurer's journey toward rebirth. "There can be no question," Campbell writes, "[that] the psychological dangers through which earlier generations were guided by the symbols and spiritual exercises of their mythological and religious inheritance, we today . . . must face alone."

If we lose our stories, our myths of shared journeys, what are we missing? If paradise is not simply a place on the land but that place we must continually travel toward, meeting our demons and rescuers along the way, who or what, if not our gods and our ancestors and the stories of the land itself, do we expect to guide us? "In the multitude of myths and legends that have been preserved for us," Campbell says, "we may yet see delineated something of our still human course. To hear and profit, however, one may have to submit somehow to purgation and surrender."

Purgation and surrender. Words I know well from my Pentecostal upbringing. Words I know not simply as concepts but as experiences, having taken myself to the altar of penance and into the icy waters of Reeds Creek for baptism; having given myself to love and to the bearing of children and to the possible loss of both. I understand that purgation and surrender are about nothing so much as letting go: of control, of dread, of desire.

I think sometimes that what we long for—what we desire—is the very life we are living but can't yet recognize. Like the major in Hemingway's story who has lost his wife and cannot reconcile himself to her death, my grief for the past often causes me to separate myself from the present. I mourn that "other country" I am no longer a resident of. The future is a narrative that does not yet belong to me, and so I fill that void with what I have known, cannot let go of, and fear I may never regain. "There are periods of decline," the author Ernst Jünger writes, "when the pattern fades to which our inmost life must conform. When we enter upon them we sway and lose our balance. From hollow joy we sink to leaden sorrow, and past and future acquire a new charm from our sense of loss. So we wander aimlessly in the irretrievable past or in distant Utopias; but the fleeting moment we cannot grasp."

You see, it is not simply the place that I miss but the recognizable stories it contains. I miss the river because we took our children there to learn to fish and to find the shells called angel wings and to swim carefully at the edges of eddies. Because it was there that our daughter buried her precious stuffed bunny in the sand, where she believed he'd be safe and warm, and no one knew until it was too late, until the water had risen and carried him under. Because her little brother wanted to go back and find it for her, even in the fearsome dark. Because that is where our black Lab Violet, now dead, swam out to fetch sticks and returned them to us, again and again, until dusk made it impossible for us to see her and we feared she'd been swept away. Because my husband and I found solace and inspiration there, alone or together. Because, at night, we spread blankets on the deck and watched for shooting stars, and when the children had fallen asleep between us, we talked quietly about our lives in that place—how blessed we were to be there, the moonlight off the river a silvery reflection.

If we had waited another year, or even two, would my enchantment have lessened? The children would no longer be satisfied with hours playing in sand, and our time spent driving the dangerous river road would have increased with each new activity: music lessons, sporting events, girlfriends to proms, boyfriends insisting they will drive out and pick up. Perhaps I would have found myself sitting on the deck alone, waiting for the stories to continue when their endings had already been written, even as the river below me flowed on.

What I know is that the stories that take place in a particular landscape are what give us a strong sense of belonging, of attachment. They give us a sense of shared history, a narratival investment. In an interview Barry Lopez once said, "For me to know a man, I must have him walk me out into his land and tell me the stories of that place he has *chosen* to live."

How can we separate ourselves from the land that holds our stories? As mobile and transient as many of us are, how do we maintain a stable identity and not lose some sense of our place in the world? What do we *miss* when we can no longer say, "*There* my mother made us a pallet beneath stars. *There* my father lifted me into the branches of the elderberry. *There* we buried my grandmother. *There*, where my son and daughter built cities in the sand, I myself once played, and the water that washes their feet once washed mine"?

"When in Kyoto, I long for Kyoto," wrote the Japanese poet Basho. What I long for are the hours of my life both forward and back to be with me always. I want the river *and* the trees, my youth and my old age, my virgin state and my lover and the children I've borne. I want my story to contain all that I want. And in that wanting is my life going on without me.

What I *need* are the stories that will keep me moving forward in a narrative I recognize and understand. The stories of travel, travail, and transformation that my people have created for me, and the stories that I must now listen for and relearn so that I might pass them into the ears and mouths of my own children.

In his memoir *Hole in the Sky* Bill Kittredge writes: "knowing the story of your people in gossipy detail means you're nearer to placing yourself in relationship to what is called the blood of things. I tell my own stories, and I move a little closer toward feeling at home in the incessant world, but I can't imagine where I would want my ashes scattered, not yet." Kittredge goes on to say that "if we want to be happy at all . . . we have to acknowledge that . . . we are part of what is sacred. That is our main defense against craziness, our solace, the source of our best politics, and our only chance at paradise."

I sit on our deck on Moscow Mountain, breathe in the incense of yarrow and fennel, hear the California quail calling "*Chi-CA-go, Chi-CA-go.*" My children have found their footing in this new place, ventured out into the world to set the course of their own lives. Just as I feel the loss of my own childhood, I grieve the loss of theirs.

I miss them like I miss the river.

Even now, the river's echoing thrum follows me into sleep. Often, my dreams are made of nothing more or less than the simple and singular event of standing in moving water. What I know is this: I am on a journey, being carried along by the swiftly moving waters of my own life.

There is the tangerine slant of sun and the elongating shadows purpling the hills. There is the promise of mild September nights, a bottle of wine, and baseball on the radio. There is my husband beside me, making plans for the woodshed he'll build next spring.

When he goes inside, I'll stay a little while longer, try to *feel* this place that I have come to, wait with a certain kind of faith for that part of my story I cannot yet know. If I listen, I'll hear it: the wind sifting the trees. It is a sound particular to yellow pine forests—a gentle shushing through the long-needled branches. A rushing current of air.

▄◖ ALISON HAWTHORNE DEMING

Alison Hawthorne Deming's nonfiction includes *Temporary Homelands: Essays on Nature, Spirit, and Place* (1994), *The Edges of the Civilized World: A Journey into Nature and Culture* (1998), and *Writing the Sacred into the Real* (2001), as well as three books of poetry, *Science and Other Poems* (1994), *The Monarchs: A Poem Sequence* (1997), and *Genius Loci* (2005). She is the editor of *Poetry of the American West* (1996) and coeditor, with Lauret Savoy, of *The Colors of Nature: Culture, Identity, and the Natural World* (2002). Her nonfiction has won both a Pushcart Prize and the first Bayer Creative Nonfiction Science Writing Award; her poetry won the Walt Whitman Award of the Academy of American Poets. She teaches creative writing at the University of Arizona and is the former director of the University of Arizona Poetry Center in Tucson. "In the Territory of the Birds" is collected in *The Edges of the Civilized World*.

Where Time and Place Are Lost

The secrets of the hoary deep, a dark
Illimitable ocean without bound,
Without dimension, where length, breadth, and highth,
And time and place are lost; where eldest *Night*
And *Chaos*, ancestors of Nature, hold
Eternal Anarchy, amidst the noise
Of endless wars, and by confusion stand.

—John Milton, *Paradise Lost*

I worship places, like the crook in the mountains where the Santa Catalinas meet Aqua Caliente Hill outside the northeast corner of Tucson. There is a swale between the two geologic forms, the mountains running west to east, and the hill running south to north, so that where they meet forms a shelter from whatever lies beyond the mountain heights. That meeting place looks like a swale from a distance, but approaching it, entering it, reveals a canyon where sheer cliffs tower over several bottomless pools of black water contained by the unyielding stone. I live in the shelter of that corner of the Sonoran Desert. Driving home on nights when the moon is full, I see the lunar high-beam burst out of the night sky, and it seems the place I live in is heading for me, instead of the other way round, and I open my heart to its beauty as I suspect a mystic opens his heart to the cosmos or a nun opens hers to Jesus. I worship places where the earth lets its knobby backbone show, where its thin and living skin is made to shine from moonlight, where the night-stalking coyotes and bobcats turn their heads to look dismissively over their shoulders at me as they pass on their evening errands.

I worship human-made places too, like the house where my relatives gather for holidays, weddings, and funerals, the farmhouse on Wayside Lane in West Redding, Connecticut, with its oak meadow and snapping turtle pond, with its fireplace so big a child could walk inside it and perhaps enter another story lying beyond its sooty back wall. In the dining room a circular wrought iron candle sconce hangs over the long rustic table, and the walls have been papered with African animals grazing on pale savannah—gazelle, lion, zebra, and giraffe lazily feeding beside us where we have gathered together to share food and stories for the near-sixty years I've been alive. I worship that gathering place, that belonging in stories occasioned by the place. How Aunt Gwen and Aunt Hildegarde, great aunts on my father's side of the family, once argued about who could walk the farthest until they burst from the table to prove the point, walking all day through woods and down village lanes, until Gwen won by hiking all the way to Massachusetts. And how Imogen, their sister and my grandmother, once pleaded with Hal, then a boy, to let go the heron he had caught on his fishing lure and kept locked in the barn and how she had civilized him on that day into caring as she cared for the freedom of wild things. I worship this place in which my ancestors are turned into myth and from which all our journeys have set forth. It is the place that has bound us as a family in belonging.

I worship cities too, like Manhattan, which I visit to see paintings in the museums that will mystify and arouse me; the Chrysler Building that is not a building but a work of art making the whole city a museum; Christmas lights on Park Avenue and the winter blur of exhaust rising from yellow cabs; the small uptown committees of dogs, some wearing plaid or fleece jackets, being taken to Central Park by professional dog walkers; throngs of people moving with purpose and direction day and night, the fragments of their conversations a concatenation of longing and complaint and business that drives the planet on its joyride through space. I was sixteen when the city first called me up to tell me that people are the authors of their own lives, more complete and true to themselves than to families or places or states. This city has shaped me without my belonging in or to it, because it lives in my mind like a god—the hustle, the glory, the arty soot of its inspiration.

Place is connectivity. Everything that has occurred in a place—from the slippage of its tectonic underworld, to the human and animal blood spilled on its ground, to the germination and degradation of plants, to the tunneling and cone building and fungus farming of ants, to the café lingering and banquet feasting and hunger on the streets—gives place its soul. Place links events and entities, writes Edward S. Casey, and allays the metaphysical anxiety of being adrift in changelessness. Aristotle says that to be in a place is like being in a vessel. To be in a place is to be held, contained, surrounded, by a defining presence. Everything that is, is in a place. Everything that happens, takes place. Luce Irigaray considers even the body a place, and the female body a place that is always slightly open, slightly moving, slightly wet. What would it be to live in a state of placelessness?

A man I know once experienced a sexually induced amnesia in which he lost memory of place. He had taken a walk into the woods with his companion. This was a sunny June afternoon, and the man and woman wandered down an abandoned forest lane, the wheel ruts of a hundred years past visible as impressions on the leaf-thick ground, an area once farmland now grown to deciduous forest where ghost tracks of stone foundations and pasture fences ran for miles, the old hand-hewn grid where sounds of sheep, chicken, horses, and children had mingled with those of the songbirds the man and woman heard on this bright green day. The man had felt amorous all morning, and when the mood returned he suggested they explore the sunny patch of woods on a hillside off the trail.

"You've been walking in the woods alone for too many years," he teased. "There are some things in nature you've been missing."

What could be sweeter than two old fools making love in the woods, canopy of sunlight and young oak leaves over their graying heads?

"This isn't being *in* nature—this *is* nature," he said, falling into a passion that made him let go more exuberantly than he usually did. Then as they sat up, joking and brushing the forest duff off one another, he began quietly to study the leaf impressions on her bare back.

"I was going to tell you," he said, "I had a dream about us making love in the woods."

"What was the dream?" she asked.

Then they sat and he was quiet, remote.

"Did we just make love?"

"Yes."

"Did we finish?"

"Yes."

"Are you sure?"

Quiet. He nodded at her confirmation. He looked around him, smiling, happy, curious.

"Where are we?"

"In the woods."

"Yes, I know that, but where are we?"

"Up the dirt road behind my mother's house."

Quiet.

"Where does your mother live?"

"Connecticut."

Quiet. He looked around.

"Where's your mother?"

"In her house?"

"Where is your mother's house? How did we get here?"

"Her house is down the road in the woods, and we walked up here. Remember, we stopped at the new house and admired the stone work?"

Nothing. Quiet.

"Where do *I* live?"

"In Arizona, in the wash. You don't remember *that*?" This was a man, she knew, whose homeplace meant a real sense of belonging, the handmade adobe beside a dry streambed tracked by coyotes, javelinas, and crowds of peaceable doves.

"It's all right." He patted her arm in reassurance. "I know who I am, and I know who you are. But what am I doing here?"

"You flew in yesterday for my family's summer solstice party."

"What family party?"

"You know, at my cousin Rosy's."

"Who's Rosy?"

"You know, my cousin with white hair who sits quietly and watches everyone. You don't remember that?"

"No, I don't. I don't know anyone named Rosy with white hair."

Quiet.

"What does her house look like?"

She described the farmhouse set in the oak forest and how they'd sat in the shade beside the pond where the little twins Will and James had caught tadpoles in the shallows, and then they had joined her on the dock to soak their feet in the cool black pond water, and how his favorite person had been Olcott, the family elder, a retired statesman, who had come up from DC for the party, with whom the man had sat and talked in the summerhouse, later commenting with affection about his scruffy fifty-year-old Oxfords. She hoped that by describing things he had connected with, he would remember.

Nothing.

"Don't you remember my daughter and the boys coming and that they just left an hour ago with little Ray at his happiest hanging out the car window shouting, 'Goodbye, Goodbye, Goodbye,' as their car rolled off down the dirt road?"

Nothing.

"And where are we now?"

"Are you kidding, do you really not know?"

"I know I'm scaring you, but it's all right. I just don't know where we are."

The man showed no anxiety and no clouding of consciousness, only disorientation about time and place. On the walk from the woods back to the house, he continued to ask where they were, though otherwise remained trusting and happy.

"This isn't the way we walked up here. This isn't the mud we tried to walk around."

"Yes, it is," she reminded him. "Here are those odd lines in the mud you commented on."

He spoke calmly about getting ready to drive to the airport. He was scheduled to fly out that afternoon for a teaching engagement in the Midwest. The woman told him he couldn't go, that even if he felt all right about not knowing where he was or how he had gotten there, it really wasn't all right, and that these were things people usually did know.

"I just read an article," he told her, "that said after an ischemic event it's important to get medical attention within a few hours." There was not a hint of alarm in his voice. As they drove to the hospital, the reality had settled for both of them that something unusual had happened in his brain, and he spoke about his family's medical history, concerned that she had not counted on this when she fell in love with him. They wept together in grief and potential loss, bound in togetherness, knowing the shortness of life and the comedy of the presenting symptoms.

"What happened to you?" asked the young woman who wheeled his gurney to the CAT scan.

"Well, we took a walk in the woods, and as things went we decided to make love and then . . ."

The young woman laughed and said, "Well, the love sure must have been good."

To calm himself as he slid into the scanning tube, the man pictured the green sun-dappled leaves overhead, as he had seen them just before becoming disoriented.

Place had become for the lovers not merely a setting but an emotional and spiritual matter. They wondered, had the old ghosts of the place reached up through the soil to try to grab him? They thought of asking their Navajo friend if there were any Native stories about men losing their memories. What would the medicine men say? The man had been reading a novel about a spy who suffers amnesia, and he had been fascinated with this case and wondered what it would be like, and he speculated that he had somehow unconsciously talked himself into experiencing that. The medical explanation was clear: the man had experienced an episode of Transient Global Amnesia. Well documented since the 1950s, it affects about thirty out of one hundred thousand people over age fifty. The amnesia occurs when blood flow is disrupted to the region of the brain associated with forming new memories. Long-term memory and meta-memory (awareness of things one should know) are preserved. But the ability to form new memories, particularly those having to do with time and place, is lost during the episode. "Where am I?" the afflicted one asks again and again. The diagnosis can only be confirmed if the episode is witnessed by an observer, as the patient will have no memory of his questioning once the experience has passed. The condition is "prognostically benign," meaning that it rarely recurs, indicates no increased medical risks, and memory-making ability returns in a few hours.

On a few random mornings I have woken up in a state of alarm that I did not know where I was in time and place. "Where am I?" I have asked myself, making a heated assessment of the data at hand—red digital numbers on the morning's screen and out the window six pastured Morgan horses leaning into soggy winter hay—aha. And the day settled into normalcy. But what if the data yielded no eureka moment and minutes later the question returned? I imagine that would mean panic for me, not that calm reflectivity of the man who lost his mind in the forest. What then is place in the mind? Not identity, which plays itself out as nationalism; not destiny, which plays itself out as the hero's calling. Place in the mind is a place in the brain. And when that place is disturbed, it leaves a person stuck in the loop of a single question and unable to move forward.

Place can also become the vessel for politics, the contested meanings of a place boiling into battles fought with weapons, words, and laws. No more poignant and ironic human emblem of this territoriality exists in our time than Yasser Arafat. Born in Cairo, he became the master guerrilla, master terrorist, of the Middle East, waging what he called "the battle for peace," which really was the battle for a place for Palestinians to live among the Jews. He once famously spoke to the United Nations wearing an empty gun holster and waving an olive branch, an image of perfect contradiction, which is what his life measured up to in the end, neither war nor peace completed after nearly fifty years of fighting, when he died in Paris of mysterious causes. Where to bury such a man? Where finally was his home? His dreams had shrunken to the size of a besieged compound in Ramallah, and that place became his grave.

My longings for place have mostly to do with the desire to connect with the beauty of the world on which, as Thomas Berry writes, our minds depend. And so on a winter's day I find myself visiting a farm in Maine where in the gray afternoon light with the desiccated sunflower heads leaning from their drooping stalks and a heron loping across the sky, I watch two cows labor to cross the muddy snow-edged stream and climb the crusted slope to meet the man spreading sheaves of baled hay along the hillside. Have I come to love simple beauty because the world is too cruel to bear? Yes, there is still this balm of the pastoral, but it is not simple. Two men have lived together here as companions for twelve years, one rebuilding grand pianos in the barn, the other driving twenty miles of redneck country road to work for a company that builds battleships and destroyers. The cottage where I sleep was once a corncrib, the old beams hand-hewn, screed of bark beetles readable on its surface, joints pegged together. This place then is joined by invisible threads (the poet's string theory?) to a forest two hundred years gone and to the war going on presently in Iraq and to the glorious history in Europe of piano building, musical composition, and performance. Place is the lens through which the world passes. Place is the hub of history's axle. Place is a nest for contradiction to dwell. Place is the eye through which I see.

Of course the eye through which I see is human, and there are days when I wish that were not so, when I wish I could see through eyes not milked over with moral dilemma and political urgency, when I could see all things with transcendent intensity. Aristotle said that places were unchangeable and that no matter who or what was in a place, the place would remain the same. That is no longer true. Even the continents, we now know, have endured profound change in their shape and location over the millennia of their tectonic drifting. And local places change so rapidly under the current regime of commercial velocity that their spirit becomes smothered. When I was working on *The Edges of the Civilized World*, I got fed up with writing about places that were enduring these changes (mostly with negative consequences to nature and culture), fearing that if I could not crack the imprisoning shell of my human-centered perspective on the world, I could never appreciate how sublime the world is, even in its wounded condition. Writing the essay "In the Territory of Birds" became the exercise of attending to how birds appeared to be experiencing place—not all birds and not superstar birds like the eagle or the dodo, but the birds that came into my experience and made an impression on me during the period of time I was writing.

Birds live in a world where time and place are lost—at least as time and place have been defined by human beings. Birds live by the light and the dark, not the numbers of a clock. Birds declare their territory by imperatives shaped by millions of years of relationship with place, as when hummingbirds follow the efflorescence of spring from Argentina to Alaska, pacing their journey on the opening of flowers, not of maps. Some birds stay in the same neighborhood all year long, like the curve-billed thrashers that nest in the cholla in my backyard. Some birds make a global journey each year that defines their place, like the arctic tern that breeds on islands in the northern Atlantic, then flies over to the west coast of Africa, then down to the Antarctic shore, and then heads back north to settle down and raise some nestlings before setting off again on its grand tour of the uncivilized world. The magnificence of such lives remains invisible and insignificant in the story of human affairs, and the task of the writer always has been to call attention to significance and give it a place on the page in the unfolding story.

In the Territory of Birds

Punta Chueca is a dry and hungry village, a clutter of cement block houses, ocotillo rib fences, hairless black dogs and mangy chickens, and a few hundred Seri Indians who have made a more or less permanent encampment on a bleached little crook of sand protruding from the infernal southern reaches of the Sonoran Desert into the Sea of Cortés. Nomadic people accustomed for centuries to moving when water grew scarce, the Seris are pretty new to the idea of staying put. Their parched homeground led them never to camp for more than a month or two in one place. As recently as the 1950s, their homes were built of brush and sea turtle bones, their weight on the land slight and brief. But now they have the heavy goods of civilization: cement, electricity, convenience store, and satellite dish.

I went there to meet a friend who had been visiting the village for twenty-five years. His friendships among the Seris helped to soften the feeling that my presence was something hard. He had arranged for us to camp on Isla Tiburón with a local guide and a small group of American students interested in learning how the loss of native language was eroding the Seris' natural history knowledge about indigenous plants and animals. What is this animal's name? Where does it live? What does it use to build its nest? What does it eat? Does it lay eggs? When? How many? What stories do you know about this animal? When is this plant harvested? Is it used for food or medicine? They asked the children in Spanish, the elders in the Seri language. Every animal, some plants, used to have a song. They taught us a few. One about the horned lizard who had gone out to gather firewood, loading it on his back as he climbed into the ironwood tree. Come here, come here, the people in the village called, bring us that firewood. But ants had begun to crawl up his legs and bite him. With all that wood on his back, he could not get them off, lost his balance, and fell out of the tree. Every time someone sang this, the Seris lit up, shaking their heads and muttering with affection, "*Pobrecito, pobrecito.*" Poor little one. The lizard, it seemed, carried their burdens along with his own. He shared humanity with them; they shared animality with the lizard.

A woman told us about a mushroom that looks like a penis but refused to say more, explaining, "I am a Christian." Then an older woman sang its song. The others laughed so loud we never caught the words, but the woman was too modest to sing it again. She would only say that it was very dirty.

It was in this place that I found myself an accidental tourist in the territory of birds. I did not plan for this to happen, nor did I regret it. We set out across the Infiernillo Channel for Isla Tiburón, five visitors in all, in the care of Ernesto Molino, our Seri guide. He ferried us in his panga over the gray chop to the island's long *bajada*, where we stepped onto twenty stark miles of *cardón*, mesquite, and creosote bush with the rosy Sierra Kunkaak rising along the island's spine, its shark fin summit cutting into the bare sky. We set up our tents and hung a blue plastic tarp over arched ocotillo ribs at an ancient encampment site on the beach. Clamshells and clay shards littered the mealy sand—some thick-walled fragments lipped at the top and some delicate eggshells from the large ollas made for carrying water from the mountain. We found a few discarded metates and manos made of black volcanic stone not native to the place, remnants of a time when eelgrass and mesquite seeds were milled into flour near the place they had been harvested.

Osprey and pelicans dove offshore for fish. A single curlew waded in the shallows, a gull and crow picking their way across the mudflats. Three of our group walked a mile up the beach and found the clean, meatless skeleton of a dolphin stranded above the tide line, its ribs like pairs of stylized doll arms embracing nothing. Three teeth lay bedded in their sockets. We loosened them, stroked the soft ivory, then slipped them into our pockets, one for each of us, to take home as talismans of our good fortune in discovery. It did not matter that our discovery was of death. Being human, we found joy in the new, even if the new was grotesque or played at the timbre of elemental fears.

Perhaps with those dead teeth in our pockets we felt we had stolen a little of death's power.

The Seris have lived in the region for over two thousand years, and Isla Tiburón has been significant to them for its clean mountain springs, wild game, and plants gathered for food, medicine, baskets, and dyes. They have thirteen names for mesquite, seven of which are for growth stages of the seedpod. The names for eelgrass, another important food plant, signify stages of its life cycle: when it first sprouts, when it grows above the surface of the water, when it detaches and floats up, when it piles into windrows on the beach. These are the last hunter-gatherers in Mexico and quite possibly the poorest people in the nation. There were once six groups speaking three dialects scattered around the region. According to Richard Felger, the prominent anthropologist of the culture, the remaining Seris are an amalgamation of survivors from these regions. Their longevity on the west coast of Sonora has been established by carbon dating of eelgrass found in an ancient burial site.

Ernesto wanted to take us to a spring in the mountains, a place where the Seris had gathered water for centuries. We hiked inland toward the crinkled heights, Ernesto marching purposefully through the scrub as if there were a path, his blue satin baseball jacket a beacon ahead while we picked our way, sweaty and leery of rattlesnakes, through the thorns and brush. I guess there was a path in his mind, for he never hesitated unless to explain how the creosote bush provided a decongestant and nerve tonic, the sap of the *torote blanco* served as a cure for cataracts, the roots of ratany were woven into baskets, and blue dye made from ground-up snails mixed with four or five of these plants. One of our group told him that he ought to become a biologist. "I already am a biologist," he answered.

As a community leader, Ernesto had received training in Mexico City in ecotourism. The government hopes that the industry will help to support poor indigenous communities that are less able to live by traditional means because of shrinking and degraded habitats. The Seris have a reputation for being opportunistic. When the Spanish settled in Mexico in the seventeenth century, the nomadic Seris made good use of new resources by raiding and rustling cattle to augment their hunting. In the twentieth century they expanded their subsistence fishing to serve the growing commercial market. But in the Sea of Cortés, as elsewhere, wild resources are strained. There is not much left to fish for except tourists. Ernesto was not naive about the impact of outsiders. He told us about a rich Mexican who had settled on Seri land and killed off plants by the thousands in order to build his enormous house.

"We got rid of him," Ernesto said, "even though the sky threatened to kill us if we did. We used to fight with guns. Now we fight with knowledge."

He was studying the Mexican Constitution, and though he had his reservations about the negative impact of tourists on Seri land and culture, the options being negligible, he was willing to give it a try.

As we walked farther into the heat of the day, our pace lagged and our eyes wandered to the ground at our feet with more longing than to the heights that still lay an hour ahead. We stopped to rest. Someone found a bleached deer rack. Ernesto said that before the Seris had guns, his grandfather had hunted with the whole head of a deer, wearing it on his head, hiding behind a bush, moving gradually closer to the herd. The deer thought the interloper was one of their kind and little by little would approach, until one got so close that the men could jump it. In his lifetime Ernesto had seen one guy do it, and he said that the movements were incredible. "It's dangerous," he cautioned. "If you screw up, the animals are right on top of you."

He said little about other aspects of his grandfather's history, except that the place where we were headed was called "the place where we go when the enemy chases us." We had read about the battles with the Mexican army fought on that ground, the slaughter of women and children who had run to a cave in the mountains to hide. At certain points along the way, Ernesto murmured under his breath, "*Pobrecito, pobrecito,*" and we sensed that he knew just what terrible thing had occurred in that spot. Even now the Mexican marines maintained a small base on the island, though a government decree had designated the place to be under Seri jurisdiction. Some of the people worried that what had happened in Chiapas last year—the official government slaughter of indigenous rebels—might happen here next. I wondered if leading groups of foreigners over ground hallowed by his ancestors' suffering might feel to Ernesto like a sacrilege. I knew that it must be so and also that for the Seris to survive on their homeground, such tours were one of their best bets.

There were six in our party, three men and three women. Perhaps the cause was the heat of high afternoon, perhaps the fact that several of us already had begun to suffer from an unfriendly intestinal colonization, perhaps the sadness and complexity of history had crept into our idle mood, but whatever the cause, after we had stopped in the shade to snack and sip from our canteens, the women decided we were too tired to go on. The men continued up the slope, hoping to reach the mountain spring. We lay in the sparse shade of paloverde and ocotillo to nap and talk about the troubles women save for one another's listening. Mostly it was the subject of men that occupied our conversation, wondering what makes it work or not work between a woman and a man. One told of meeting the man she loves during an outdoor leadership program. After a month in the wilderness they were covered with grime and the stink of their bodies. That's when they fell in love—it was pheromones, she said, I'm sure of it. Another told of her lingering break from a brilliant and charming man who refused during their last year together to touch her. I told of infidelities suffered and the attraction I could not resist for someone new, though I saw in the man the same tendencies that had wounded me before. We lounged in the sweet togetherness of women in which our hopes for love thrive.

While we talked cactus wrens trilled, a Gila woodpecker worked the *cardones* and high in the perfect sky a black vulture circled. Lying on our backs, we watched it absently, as we might have watched a small fair-weather cloud, never considering that its presence had anything to do with us. But while the other birds flitted in and out of our view, the vulture stayed directly overhead, circling and circling. I began to think it was homing on some rank thing that lay near us or on a creature close to dying that would make a fresh meal. I knew, or thought I knew, that the presence of a vulture means death.

I do not know what draws such a predator to its table, whether sight or smell or a synesthetic sense that humans will never know. The Seris have a story that explains the vulture's skill. They say that in the beginning of the world the fly invented fire. They say that now when a fly lands on a dead animal it makes fire by rubbing its front legs together and sends smoke signals telling the vulture where on the desert the carcass lies.

We heard the men coming a long while before they arrived, men we all loved in friendship, and we knew they would play a joke on us. The crunch of gravel slowed, then quieted. A set of antlers rose from behind a bush. We weren't surprised and did not pretend we were. Still everyone got a good laugh. One guy asked us if we had seen the vulture circling us. Yes, we answered. He joked that after camping out we smelled so bad the vulture thought he might have found something to eat. We all got another good laugh, except Ernesto, who looked sober and shook his head.

"No, no," he said to the other men, "that's not it at all. The vulture was guarding them, because they are beautiful." We were puzzled, the gap between our way of seeing and his filling up with awkward silence. Then he explained that if the men had gotten lost and not returned, anyone from the village a mile across the water would have seen the vulture and known where to find us. It was our turn to look sober, for what was black suddenly looked white, what was harbinger had become protector.

As we started back to camp, the quiet stayed with us, each holding fast to Ernesto's way of seeing. It was not our way, and we knew it. That's what made it stick in our imaginations like a puffy airborne seed lodged in thorns. The world looked both kinder and more dangerous than it had had before. We fanned out in search of dead wood for our campfire, hefting bleached gray branches and root burls onto our backs and shoulders.

I migrated to the Atlantic North in the summer to clamber about the bogs and forests I have known since childhood. I was not looking for much, the usual summer pleasures of freedom and peace. But it had become a summer when change impinged upon my sense of refuge. A film crew was headed to our quiet island, the locals hustling to make a buck or gawk at would-be stars who would soon swarm in to produce a celluloid gothic horror story in which molten corpses would crawl from their graves. The spectacle seemed to me nothing to get excited about, and so I chose each day to head out as far from the buzz as I could get. And what I found were birds.

Ox Head is a spit of heath overgrown with red-tasseled sorrel, water hemlock (the weed that finished Socrates, not the more familiar and benign coniferous tree), and sheep laurel. The landform does not look at all like an ox. Perhaps oxen once were pastured there and gave the remote promontory its name, as happened with the numerous islets that bear the name Sheep or Ram Island. Ox Head is only a ten-minute walk from Great Pond, where for years I have tempered the impatience induced by muggy July days with floating beneath the spectacle of flocked gulls that turn there in the sky like a daytime zodiac. But I had never set feet to the ground to see what lay beyond my idling nor noticed the promontory's name on an island map I thought I knew by heart. The sheep laurel was the first surprise, its magenta blossoms blaring from the scrub. I have found those bright little parachutes deep in the forest in August, and, knowing the propensity of plants to be specialists, I wondered if it could be the same species blooming in a wild pasture in June. But there was the unmistakable evidence—spokelike anthers rising from the flower's center, bending into pits on the perimeter, a stubborn little generalist not easily deterred from its existence.

Eiders coasted in the shallows, a crisp contrast of white-on-black gliding on the sloppy gray sea. No creatures are better than wild birds at fostering an enchantment with nature, that trance in which history becomes as evanescent as weather and what stays in mind is the perfectly balanced equation of a creature in its place. Birds are radical in their relationship with place, freely ignoring national boundaries, turning urban spaces into forage and nesting grounds, whitewashing entire islands with free-falling excrement, crossing every desert, ocean, mountain, and icefield on earth in adapting to seasonal or millennial change. Birds grow, wear, dance, and sing their sexual attractions without embarrassment or shame, enact their courtships with high elegance, and mate erotically without remorse. Their flight has inspired both poetry and jet propulsion. In their migration behaviors birds exhibit an intelligence for navigation without instruments far surpassing that of humans, instructing us in the complex geographic relationships a species can accomplish over time.

Birdsong can charm, enrage, or terrify. The water music of a hidden Swainson's thrush or canyon wren says that a love of pattern and beauty interweave the creaturely struggle for survival. The merciless nocturnal repetitions of a whippoorwill (John Burroughs recorded 1,088 consecutive choruses of its "purple-RIB" call) is template for an insomniac's theme song. When my mother remembers the whippoorwills that kept us awake at our Connecticut home, she speaks as if they were marauding locusts: "And every night they came closer and closer to the house." It seemed unnatural that we, in our secure and comfortable home, should be deprived of sleep by creatures we could never see. We hated them. And any student of Edgar Allan Poe can readily conjure the raven's one-word call as the soul-waking messenger of death.

The eiders drifted in the shoals, fitting so well in the place that I could not imagine the evolutionary legacy of strained relationship with climate, food, and predators in other places that must have led them to these northern shores. Birds do not do much to change the places they inhabit. If what they need is not there, they move on or die. People make a sorry comparison, finding few places on earth we can live without radically altering them. That is our evolutionary strength, of course, the ability to reshape nature to suit our needs. We have no choice but to transform the surface of the earth, since we are frail, thin-skinned, and vulnerable even to most weather. The average housecat, stranded without provisions in the wild, would stand a better chance of survival than the average civilized human being. But people don't get stranded in the wild today, unless they choose to for adventure, or their plane goes down, or they want to die like an animal. We live in a human-made world of protections and pleasures, drunk on our freedom to move where and when we wish, insulted by any hint of risk we ourselves have not invited, imagining that no condition of nature is so hostile we cannot find a method to gentle it. What we cannot seem to gentle is the hostility inherent in those methods. We make war with nature, nations, and ourselves in order to be at peace.

Elie Wiesel, speaking of the Nazi Holocaust, has said that winds of madness blow through history, times when blindness prevails and people become too morally sick to save others from suffering, humiliation, and death. He refers to employees of the regime who worked in the death camps, unable to see the evil in what they were doing. The human relationship with nature often looks like a form of madness that, taken to its megalomaniacal extreme, imagines we can live in an entirely human-made world—the ultimate civilization in space—as if we had no material or spiritual need for the other species on Earth, as if we had no obligation to protect them from suffering, humiliation, and death, as we would protect our own.

This madness is embedded in the language historically used to describe the moral enemies of civilization: *heathen, pagan,* and *savage.* Pulled up at their roots, the words are emblems of the nature-as-clay-for-our-hands view. Heathen, descended from the Old English version of *heath,* meaning "open uncultivated ground covered by heather or related plants," once was a timid descriptor meaning simply "inhabiting open country." *Pagan* derives from the Latin *pagus,* referring to a rural district or village; *savage* from the Latin word for forest, *silva.* The fact that all three words once described people who lived more rustically than urban dwellers and then came to signify idolaters is an artifact of a long historical period in which threats to civilization lay primarily outside of its urban centers. Those threats included the elements, predatory animals, and foreign invaders who were not "civilized," that is, not subject to *our* laws. From these dangers—the lawlessness of the wild—our ancestors found protection within the fortress, physical and moral, of the city, and these three words became their shields.

But the world is smaller now, and civilization is its own worst enemy. The barbarians have nearly all been murdered, a process that began three thousand years ago and will end in our lifetimes as the last of the original forms of humanity turn into capitalists. Everywhere on the planet a radical hybridization of cultures—of nationality and ethnicity, of rural and urban people, of tribal and corporate and even genetic structures—is taking place, and it is all held together by invisible electronic threads that beam up from our homes and offices to transmitters we have sent into orbit around the Earth. We do not have a language to describe this dizzying turn of the cultural axis, for as soon as we find a name it becomes obsolete. Once it seemed an impossible task to draw the curved face of Earth on a flat map. The new map of the world is too complex to imagine, for it must represent not only major landforms, bodies of water, and human habitation but also the whizzing transcultural movement of our marketing, entertainment, and communication technologies and the brown air they leave in their wakes; not only the nationalities and ethnicities but also habitats, natural resources, extinctions, and preserves. We have so many ways to view the world we can hardly stand to look at it. And if we would be honest and honorable to Earth's history as the metastory to human history, we would need to draw a map of the losses witnessed since our species arrived on the scene, to keep alive at least a mental presence of the Hun and Taino, the Pict and Pericue; and of the birds, which have paid for human wealth more dearly than any others—the long-lost dodo, passenger pigeon, dusky seaside sparrow, New Zealand laughing owl, Jamaican macaw, Samoan wood rail, Guadalupe flicker, the Ryuku kingfisher, the Lord Howe Island white-eye, the Hawaiian honeycreeper, koa-finch, akialoa, kakawahie, and ou.

Aldo Leopold proposed "the land ethic" as a possible and necessary new element in an expanding sense of human ethics. "Our first ethics," he wrote, "dealt with the relation between individuals. . . . Later accretions dealt with relations between the individual and society." Roderick Nash in *The Rights of Nature* has expanded the territory, tracking how the extension of ethics to the natural world has begun to take hold. "One of the most remarkable ideas of our time," he writes, "[is] the belief that ethical standing does not begin and end with human beings."

The emergence of this idea that the human-nature relationship should be treated as a moral issue conditioned and restrained by ethics is one of the most extraordinary developments in recent intellectual history. Some believe it holds the potential for fundamental and far-reaching change in both thought and behavior comparable to that which the ideal of human rights and justice held at the time of the democratic revolutions in the seventeenth and eighteenth centuries.

Most recent studies of biodiversity assume that between 50 and 90 percent of the world's current plant and animal species will disappear within the next hundred years as a result of human impact. According to biologist E. O. Wilson, we are in the midst of one of the great extinction spasms of geologic history. Even using the most cautious parameters, he estimates that the number of species doomed each year is 27,000; each day is 74, and each hour is 3. Birds are among the most vulnerable, the canaries in the coal mine that are first to show the signs of danger. Within the past four centuries 171 species and subspecies of bird have gone extinct. The more we learn about this hemorrhaging of life from the planet, the sicker we feel. When we watch a flock of birds pass by, we see our own wild innocence recede.

I left the eiders to pick my way along the shore, the fog closing in, chilling my bare arms and making me eager for home. Along the intertidal stones of low tide the salt grass glistened even in the fog's dulled light. Ahead a sudden flurry broke out, squawking balls of fuzz scattering in all directions to get out of my path. The mother—a mallard or black duck, dusky body and morpho blue wing patches—limped away with wings drooped, staggering, dragging her right wing on the ground. According to her plan, I stared, held still, then followed, wondering if she was really wounded. I had read about broken-wing display as an avian defense of the young, but I never had witnessed it. The strategy would not have done a bit of good if I had meant business with buckshot. Such a defense was invented for less successful predators than the aggressors of our species, but against a merely curious interloper it worked.

I forgot the ducklings, which must have reached deep cover in the scrub. I was fixed on the mother's deception as she scuttled low over the rocks, flapping pathetically along the sand, leading me farther and farther on. I was still not convinced that she was faking until, far down the beach, with a final glance in my direction, she hobbled into the water, floated a moment, rearranged her wings, and lifted with perfect ease to return to the nest.

There is not a single day of any year when I do not see or hear a bird, though I do not always notice that I am seeing and hearing them. But never before had birds insisted themselves upon me so emphatically. A few days later, feeling cramped in the house, I headed for the island's wooded backside. Not much there except beech trees, balsam, and hemlock, a trail hugging the edge of a cliff that drops hundreds of feet to the sea. One naturally formed breakwater holds a sheltered lagoon, where salmon pens float attached to a floating walkway and the red shack of the man who tends the smolts until ready for market. I have always wanted to ask him to run me out there in his dory and show me around. But more appealing than learning about the island's shaky industrial future is exploring its sylvan past, as if to walk far enough into the unpeopled woods were to find one's deeper origin.

I followed the scrappy trail along basalt cliffs, stopping at a lookout point to watch the work of fishermen a quarter-mile to the north. A row of dories had been hauled up on the stone beach; one was puttering out to the salmon pens but was so distant I could not hear its motor, only saw the bow rise as the throttle opened then settle back down as it closed. Whatever work was going on looked easy, something one man in one small boat could manage. I continued on far from anyone's work, the breeze rising from time to time, stirring tree scent into the air, acrid leaf mold and sweet gummy balsam. The fragrance spun up in gusts and eddies. Spruces near the cliff had been stunted by the wind, grown bare on the leeward side that winter had abused. The green sea far below had no sound, yet was so clear white stones were visible beneath the slough and heave. Miles across the channel lay a village, a distant speckle of buildings, small and quaint, folded into the lumpy blue mass of the land. It looked harmless posed against the broad scale of sea and land and sky. Somewhere underlying the intervening channel lay the imaginary line that separates Canada from the United States, a friendly border compared to most, one I have crossed yearly, almost as freely as a bird, in order to feed on these woods.

I walked farther than I ever had before into the tannin musk, into bunchberries littering the ground like white confetti thrown everywhere, into the apple green ferns, young, not yet filling the understory with the shoulder-high meadows they would become by midsummer. The deeper in I got, the more I gloated about my luck to know such a place—no tacky resort, no spandex high-tech wilderness jocks, no Saturday horde, no products and profits and hype. Just woods, piped with thrush and sparrow song and wind. Maybe it is a sorry state of affairs to have to leave human culture, if only for a day, in order to see the world go luminous again with significance, but so be it. In this place I can walk the misanthropy out of my system, the rancor at what people have ruined with their greed and blindness, the fear that I will lose my love and wonder for the world.

A rough sapling bridge crossed a stream at a place deerhunters and snow-mobilers use in fall and winter. In summer the logs grow mossy from lack of traffic. Those miles and hours of woods seem to own themselves, though I have heard that a wealthy Scandinavian has bought most of this land on speculation. People used to call it "the Queen's land," more out of respect for British royalty than for fact. The island was settled by runaway Loyalists who opposed the American Revolution. I do not care who owns it as long as I am free to wander there.

I was heading down into a sheltered draw, the trail overarched with dap-pled beech leaves, when a shriek shot out of the green. It sounded like a gull, though sharper and strong, one note repeated and repeated, *kaak, kaak, kaak.* I saw nothing but trees. Then a gray mass erupted from the foliage, diving low and fast straight for my face, big as an eagle. Its eyes were bullets aiming for mine. I dropped to my knees, wrapping my arms over my head. The muscu-lar gust of it Doppler-shifted over me. Then the woods went silent, though I could hear the creature's eyes on my back. Slowly I unfolded from my crouch, turned to see the bird perched and glaring on a high limb at the opposite end of the draw.

I watched it. It watched me. I spoke softly, though I do not know where the hope came from that my words might convince it of anything. It let me stand. For a moment.

Then came the shrill kaaking call, and the warrior decked me again. My courage was up, since I had survived the first kamikaze dive, so this time I tried to spot field marks—not an easy task when one is wondering just how close the lovely hooked beak and metal-sharp talons are going to come to one's eyes. I picked out some detail—soft gray plumage on the back, white breast with delicate tweedy bars. Black eye stripes, perhaps, though from this vantage I did not see much of a profile. Its face looked strangely owl-like. Af-ter knocking me to my knees three times, it figured I had been sufficiently humbled and let me pass, though, just in case, I twirled my walking stick over my head in order to make myself a more complicated target. The bird's eyes burned on my back.

Hours later, on my return, I had no choice but to take the same path home. The woods had grown tame by then, water music of the little birds bubbling up and sunlight dappling my arms. I wondered if I would recognize the place where the encounter had occurred, then wondered how the bird might be reading me as I got close. Big, noisy, smelly animal with clothes and stick. But a brain, even a bird or animal one, is not a machine. It reads not isolated sensory facts but the gestalt, the integrated totality, of a situation. Something of my thoughts and emotions must be attainable to any creature I encounter, some response both learned and immediate to the complexity that I am. This is why the common wisdom about dogs is that they can smell a person's fear or about street punks that you must not look them in the eye. This is why my housecats slink away from me when they have misbehaved and I catch them in the act. Just the aura of my scowl sends them running.

So what had been my gestalt at the time of the raptor's attack? I confess it, I had been gloating, spilling my joy all over the woods as if I owned them; haughty, feeling safe that there was no creature here—rattlesnake, grizzly, or cougar—that could harm me. Though I enjoyed the feeling of a risk-free wilderness, that view was not shared in the eyes that peered from trees and scrub. To them (in whatever manner they were capable of perceiving this—not as *idea*, surely, but as the bodily knowledge of startle or flinch) I was the dominant predator for miles around, not a quality that would draw creatures to my side. I began to feel the possibility of a more emphatic greeting from the fledged guardian of that darkened draw, and so as I got close to the place, I wrapped my sweater around my neck for armor and raised my walking stick for a scepter.

I am thoroughly a product of Western culture and happily so. I was raised in a house where classical music and Shakespearean plays spun on the family turntable. I studied the piano and flute, took modern dance classes, and secreted myself in the delicious privacy of my room to take Dostoevsky, Anne Frank, and Charles Dickens to bed with me. I read books as if I were possessed by them, my spirit occupied by their realities in a way that satisfied my hunger more than did the actualities of daily life. I learned very young to love the best of the human world, those creations that bring the inner world to light. But learning how to communicate with wild animals is not generally a component of even the best North American education. When we talk to animals, it is usually to our pets, whom we address in baby talk or commands. In earlier forms of human culture people spoke to animals as if they were elders, prayed to them, asked for their guidance, forbearance and forgiveness, read their behavior as we would a fine book. Animals played a significant role in people's inner world, as well as the outer one, and a kind of communication with them, such as Ernesto's reading of the black vulture in Seriland, was possible.

And so as I strode into the draw with my scepter in hand, feeling powerless and foolish and scared, I spoke to the memory of my attacker.

"Please forgive me for trespassing on your land. I am small and harmless, and I will soon be gone."

But there was no sign of the creature. Perhaps it was lodged deep in the foliage looking down in disdain. Perhaps it had gone off on a hunt. The beech trees at either end of the draw where it had earlier perched stood out among the others, having been dignified by the bird's presence. I was awake to the place as it might be when no humans are there, eager to pass through and let it be so.

Since birds kept insisting themselves upon me, I decided to take the upper hand and seek them out. I signed on to a charter leaving our island and heading for the bird island that lies a few hours to the south. Machias Seal Island is a fifteen-acre outcropping of granite and weeds a dozen miles from much of anything but ocean. Once feared by fogbound mariners of the North Atlantic, the hazardous area has been marked since 1832 with a light station maintained by the Canadian government. It became a sanctuary for nesting seabirds in 1944. A small team of technicians and researchers, along with the ceaseless din of their diesel-powered generator, live at the refuge. Most of the acreage is a tumble of boulders and rocky shore. The higher ground is covered with a lush green meadow, the consequence of birds, people, and domestic animals, all of whom have added to the seed lore of the island. Sedges, grasses, asters, parsley docks, and herbs have taken hold. And for a few months of the year Seal Island, as it is familiarly known to the locals, is populated by thousands of migrating birds.

"Last year I didn't know the difference between a puffin and a penguin," joked our guide, as we bobbed out past tubular plastic salmon pens in a fishing boat refitted with benches and canvas canopy for tourists. He was new to the job, but so is nearly everyone in a region where the beast of ecotourism is just beginning to wake. Still, he ably pointed out the common murres, gannets, black guillemots, and eiders we encountered riding the swells that rose and fell around us like breathing flesh. We crossed MacGregor's Shoals, a rough upwelling, then beyond to where the water flattened into a greasy sheen. We passed a raft of sea ducks, then a scattering of storm petrels that flitted and dipped low over the water like swallows.

"They're named after Saint Peter," the guide reported, "because they can walk on water just like he did." I was not sure about the accuracy of either the biblical or natural history, but I was glad to know the name of the small, dark travelers.

As we neared Seal Island, a few scattered puffins and razorbills floated by. Pelagic birds, they spend their lives far at sea, except during a few months of breeding and nurture when they nest on remote patches of land.

"And we think we have hard lives," quipped our guide like a stand-up comic. Like most places serving as sanctuaries for wild animals, Seal Island is increasingly a mecca for naturalists, birdwatchers, and photographers. As we approached the little bump on the horizon, we saw two tour boats already at anchor offshore. Our boatload joined the party, the dozen of us riding a dory in batches of four across the coastal chop to the rockweed-draped shore, our skipper standing astern at the tiller doing his own version of Saint Peter. Running down from the island's summit—all of fifty feet above sea level—the rusted tracks of an old tramway traversed a stained and eroded concrete ramp. The wildlife warden greeted us from the ramp. A ten-foot-wide chasm separated us, waves slurring over rocks far enough below to make us check our footing. He hefted a two-by-ten plank across the gorge, and we single-filed from the slippery rocks over a churning inlet to the battered concrete on shore.

The warden's Wildlife Service cap and jacket were streaked and smeared with the whitewash of his charges. While he stood at plank's end to help the new arrivals, he told those who had crossed to go the end of the ramp, pick up a stake we would find there, and wait. We followed the instructions, bemused but obedient, while the others teetered and joked about walking the plank. Herring stakes—three feet long and a half-inch square—have been used for the last century to string fish through the gills for hanging in the smokehouses. The islands in the region once prospered making smoked herring, but they now run only a few small operations. Most herring is shipped to the mainland, where it is factory-processed with "artificial smoke flavoring." The old blackened stakes turn up everywhere—excellent for building a pea fence or staking tomatoes and, I was about to learn, for deflecting the assaults of hyperactive arctic terns.

The air over Seal Island stormed with birds. They swarmed, dove, and curved in aerobatic flourishes, their tweaking calls fierce and shrill. Some flew past us with silver fry in their red bills, heading for nests in the grass. Others aimed their needle-nosed beaks at the tops of our heads and dove. When we had all assembled, the warden led us on, a little parade of marchers with fish-stake batons held over our heads, dozens of terns slamming toward us and screaming, cutting their dives just short of the tops of our stakes.

We gathered on the deck beside the lightkeeper's house for orientation. Regulations strictly controlled the nature of our visit: walk slowly, only on paths, do not linger in any place, give a wide berth to orange flags marking nests. We may stay on the island for three hours. We may cross the grass to the far shore where puffins and razorbills nest only on our way to and from a blind. We may remain in a blind for twenty-five minutes. Four people are allowed in the blind at one time. We must move quickly when we enter. The longer we are visible, the farther away from their young the parents will fly.

Some twenty-four hundred pairs of arctic terns nest on Seal Island (numbers may have been as high as thirty-five hundred pairs in the 1940s), along with two hundred pairs of common terns and a few roseates. In addition, about eleven hundred pairs of puffins, three hundred pairs of razor-billed auks, and fifty pairs each of common eiders and Leach's storm petrels nest on Seal Island. All of these seabirds come here for one reason, to breed, and they have established a community in which each species succeeds in that mission, each gaining some advantage from the presence of the others, or at least each finding no quarrel with another species so important as to upset the balance they have together established.

Most numerous are the arctic terns, which arrive at the end of May, laying their eggs in exposed nests, barely more than a matted area on top of the grass. Chicks hatch in late June, two to a nest, and need constant protection from preying gulls. Terns attack any potential enemy by diving toward it and letting out a rapid series of shrieks. The dive usually stops short of its target, but a solid strike is not unusual. I found this out when, wondering if our fish-stake defense was really necessary, I lowered my guard and learned in an instant the sharp insult of beak against scalp. By the end of July the young are on the wing above the island, practicing for long-distance flight. Juveniles and adults depart together in August to join other arctic terns that have nested in Iceland, Greenland, and other northern refuges. Their migration route is the most ambitious on Earth. They will fly across the North Atlantic, pass along the west coast of Europe and Africa, then southward to their winter home in the Antarctic Ocean. They will reach and likely circle the Antarctic ice pack, an annual migration pattern of twenty-five to thirty thousand miles, a distance greater than a trip around the world. Each year they will return to the north to breed, living and repeating this global dance for as long as twenty-five years.

In spite of the phenomenal migratory talent of the arctic tern, it is the puffin that draws most human visitors to Seal Island. A stout bird with a broad bill, emphatically banded with red and yellow, the Atlantic puffin is the bird of choice in this region for images on mugs, T-shirts, and posters. It is the creature that makes this place unique, stirring up immediate human affection with its attractive oddness and the apparently sad-eyed look of its facial markings. Nesting in sheltered burrows among the boulders, the puffin does not need such an aggressive defense policy as the tern. It tends to pose cooperatively for photographers, gawking at humans as curiously as humans gawk at it.

When my turn came to observe from the blind, I was lucky to wind up with a man leading a group of birdwatchers from Massachusetts. He, along with two of his charges and an excellent spotting scope, was already stationed in the darkened compartment, a few foot-tall plywood portals opened to the avian spectacle. The man was speaking in a hushed tone as I slipped into the blind and jockeyed past his tripod and students to take the last available window at the far wall. There was a beautifully human tenderness to their voices as each in turn took the scope and acquiesced to the newly seen. Watching the melee of birds that freckled the air, water, and rocks, they focused on the sulfur-yellow flesh lining the mouth of a razorbill in breeding plumage. The bird kept its distance, standoffish, unlike the puffins that perched on the boulders closest to the blind and watched us watching them through our portals. The birdman told us that the puffins are calm birds. Even after their chicks hatch, they show little aggression unless one goes into another's burrow. Cooperatively, one touched down on the nearest boulder with three fresh sardines drooping from its bill, stood idling before us to be photographed, then hopped between the rocks to deliver its catch. In addition to concealing the nests, the boulders serve as launching points. A puffin's small pointed wings are good for paddling underwater, but they make getting aloft a challenge.

The center of the puffin world is Iceland, where there may be as many as ten million of the birds. Seal Island, located at the lower end of the Bay of Fundy, is one of the most southerly colonies in their breeding range. Most successful mating takes place at sea, and according to one researcher, "a hoarse cry at the moment of pairing has been reported." Noisy billing is a part of courtship, one bird nuzzling and nibbling the other's bill, until they start repeatedly knocking their bills together broadside, other puffins rushing over to observe the displaying pair. The peak of the hatch is in mid- June. For a month or more both parents deliver small fish to the young. At the end of July they desert them for up to a week, during which time the juveniles learn to find their way from their burrows to the ocean surrounding the island. By August the adults and young depart for the open sea.

Because they are so placid, puffins suffer heavy predation by black-backed gulls. Their only other significant predator is people, who in the 1800s persecuted the birds for eggs, meat, feathers, and pure mean fun, wiping out the populations on some breeding islands. Black-backed gulls, which often breed in puffin colonies, will work in pairs to catch a puffin in flight and pull the living bird to pieces. After the kill they will eat the entrails and breast muscles, turn the skin inside out like a glove, pick the bones and skull clean. Sometimes a gull will swallow the head whole and regurgitate the undigestible parts. Gulls steal fish from puffins, eat their eggs and young.

Some of this behavior represents genetic learning and some bird culture— what's learned through fledgling experience and by watching conspecifics. Genetic learning is not fast, but by definition it has stood the test of time. How long did it take for puffins to learn that by nesting near terns they could remain pacifists and benefit from the aggressive defense tactics of their neighbors? How long did it take for terns to learn that by nesting near more vulnerable neighbors they could improve the odds for their own offspring? The breeding community on Seal Island has been shaped by each species' drive for survival. In some instances the drive is expressed as survival of the fittest, in some survival of the most cooperative.

Earth is a giant laboratory of learning, every living thing doing what it can to make its life work and meet the demands of changing circumstances. Some creatures depend mostly on the long-learning of their genetic history. The oldest bird, archaeopteryx, lived 140 million years ago. Six fossil specimens of it have been found in Bavarian limestone. This Jurassic early bird is no longer around, but some of its contemporaries are—frogs, squid, lobsters. Human beings are Quaternary latecomers—only one hundred thousand years old, unless one stretches the definition to claim our history begins one million years ago with the Pleistocene hominids. Even so, if duration of time on Earth were the measure of species worth, we would be pretty poor currency. Of course, we have made up for lost time with our impressive capacities for creating cultures and languages. These relatively fast methods of learning may be different from those of other species, but they are no better. The trouble for the other species is that we are moving so fast that they, stuck with their poky genes, cannot catch up.

The Massachusetts birdman nudged me over to the scope, pointing out the refinement of the thin white line running along the razorbill's covert, the sheen of its tuxedo black body. Two razorbills began courting, the male clicking his bill against the female's then mounting her, flapping to stay aloft, then both staggering into a crevice to their nest. More razorbills than puffins seemed to be standing around in pairs, and I wondered how the two species differ in pair-bonding habits. I wondered too what the idea of an individual means to species for which life is so collective.

The birdman was eager and knowledgeable, and he brightened when he saw me taking notes, leaned close to whisper and guide me into what he knew. I could not keep up the pace. A few land birds showed up, savannah sparrow and—was that tree swallow or barn swallow? That growling sound like a chain saw starting in the distance—was that the razorbill or puffin? The black bird with white eye ring—a murre or an auk? My head swam, but I no longer cared about the information. It was the hushed excitement of a man aroused by nature's complexity that owned me. I asked if he knew about the local raptors—yes, a bit—and I told him about how I had been strafed in the woods.

"Had to have been a goshawk. They can look pretty big when they're coming right at you."

I learned that goshawks live on forest edges near cliffs and swamps, where they have ample flight corridors for hunting. They hunt squirrels, grouse, and rabbits either in fast searching flights or by the perch-and-wait technique. In an all-out chase a goshawk will plunge through heavy cover in reckless pursuit for nearly a mile; its speed on impact can be fifty miles an hour. During breeding season it goes to great lengths to communicate its territorial prerogatives.

When our group of four left the blind and returned to the others waiting on the lightkeeper's deck, the birdman reported gleefully to his pals, "This lady got decked by a goshawk!" And we all felt wonderful that such a thing was possible.

Back home I fell into a two-hour nap, bobbing in and out of sleep, feeling the swells of the sea and seeing stout puffins, watchful, gliding by. My rest was so fitful I was uncertain if I was asleep or awake, until I saw puffins floating by in the air beside my bed and knew I was in a dream of their presence that made me feel awake.

I travel for the reasons people always have traveled—Delphi, Lourdes, Grand Tour, Walkabout, or Disneyland. I travel because a hunger leads me from place to place, a hunger that tells me I can be replenished by the world. It is something the birds have known all along, this knowledge making my head swim that the world in all its complexity is something we are born to devour, moving from place to place to satisfy the need that keeps us alive as long as it refuses to quit.

Once in the desert I watched a pair of Harris's hawks, magnificent in their chocolate and chestnut plumage, nurturing their young in the notch of a many-pronged saguaro. Two chicks perched and waited in the bramble of desiccated sticks and weeds that had been packed into a nest. They were too young to fly, scraggly in their adolescent plumage, mottled, awkward on long legs ruffled like Victorian pantaloons. At midday the parents stood panting, tongues pumping against the drying sun. At dusk they departed to hunt, and in the cool fading light the chicks pulled idly on strings of bloody flesh. Then they lay down, preened and rearranged themselves on the nest. It seemed peaceful, this family life of killing, eating, and growing up. Sunset flared across the western sky, turning the mountains red, the facing clouds in the east infected with that rosy light. All the voices of the desert birds grew active, flocking and calling in their last errands of the day.

◖◗ ELIZABETH DODD

Elizabeth Dodd is an essayist and poet. Her essays have been published in such journals as *Ascent*, *High Plains Literary Review*, *Massachusetts Review*, *Southwest Review*, and *Southern Review*. Her first essay collection, *Prospect: Journeys and Landscapes*, appeared in 2003 and was winner of the William Rockhill Nelson Award for nonfiction. She has published two collections of poems, *Like Memory, Caverns* (1992), winner of the Elmer Holmes Bobst Award for Emerging Writers, and *Archetypal Light* (2001). She teaches and directs the Creative Writing Program at the Kansas State University in Manhattan, Kansas, where she has twice won the William L. Stamey Award for Teaching Excellence. "Fragments," which appears here and also in the *Georgia Review*, is one of several new pieces that explore our relationships to landscapes—through history, ecology, aesthetics, and biography.

Call and Response

When I showed him a photograph of the pupils of the tiny country school, clustered outside the dull stucco building along Higbee Road sometime in the early 1930s, my father said, "Of course, I knew all those children." Yes, of course. He'd grown up in a little rural village in the shortgrass country of Oklahoma, during the same decade; his part of the universe then wasn't quite as dry and isolated as the little valley along the Purgatoire River in southeast Colorado, and he was just a few years younger than the dozen or so children who'd walked through dust or wind to reach their one-room schoolhouse, but in many ways it was the same world. He left and moved on to much, much wider horizons, figuratively speaking, and a life as an artist and intellectual, but he still knows deeply the literal wide horizons of the Great Plains, the flood and wash of sunlight over the vast horizontal of the earth.

It's a world I've also come to know very well in terms of landscape, having made my professional and personal home on the edge of the Plains, in eastern Kansas's tallgrass prairie, and having settled in as fully as I seem to know how, trying to learn plants, rocks, birds, the constituent vocabulary of the place where I live as it utters its ongoing articulation of being, here and now. I know how it feels to know these things, to be able to tell at a glance whether the grass on the hillside is big or little bluestem, and how interesting it is to see a juvenile redheaded woodpecker in a burr oak forest, only his neck a ruby red, with the young head still awkwardly gray. But the social world of those people, and the way their individual humanity struggled to put root in the particular soil of their home place—that's a world I don't know, can only try to infer by looking alongside natural history for human history. That's something I've been trying to work toward in my writing, as in this essay, "Fragments": to put the personal narrative of my individual life into a physical and intellectual habitat, if you will, of larger scope.

Science fiction writers often work with the concept of the space-time continuum, and for years I've been a great fan of the various *Star Trek* televised series, so the phrase often sounds in my mind through the voices of various actors from favorite episodes. But in that phrase and elsewhere space remains mostly an abstraction, whereas place is particular, gaining aesthetic or emotional or other value from its specificity. My travels, both by car and foot and on the page, are along a continuum of places-and-times, I like to think. In this, I'm another hominid in a long and varied lineage, moving across the landscape and the continents. That's an idea that keeps me company frequently these days, both at the desk and, ironically, on the trail. Places and times. Individual and environs. Specificity and scope.

What delighted me in visiting the dinosaur track site along the Purgatoire, and in writing the resultant essay over a period of many months, was how fully the personal, the historical, and the natural-historical all came together. Yet in writing the essay that emerged from the experience, I omitted a narrative that could have taken the piece in a very different direction. The day before the hike I describe here, my boyfriend and I took a guided tour, sponsored by the National Grasslands and the National Forest Service, in which four local residents led a caravan of visitors down a rough, four-wheel drive route to reach the tracks. Our approach was quite opposite to the one we'd take the following day: we came from the other direction, we came by car not foot, we came in a crowd, and our visit was shaped by narration rather than individual discovery. Our tour's leader was a friendly, beefy woman I'll call Beverly, whose family ranched in the area, and with walkie-talkies she directed us when to stop and get out to gaze at some significant site—rock art, a grinding basin, a nineteenth-century homesite. I recognized some of her information from the Park Service's management plan and from other publications. But when we reached the track site, she announced the approximate age of the tracks: "About a hundred and fifty million years, if you're an evolutionist; or about six thousand years, if you're a creationist."

I did not include this narrative in my essay for many reasons: it has seemed too easy to take potshots at our guide, and I didn't want the piece to become casually dismissive of what I still perceive as her willed ignorance. Then, too, for me, the real discovery took place in the experiential realm that didn't involve cars and crowds; the trip, and its revelations of loveliness and wonder both felt and actually was far more immediate—unmediated—during the sun-drenched day of our hike to the river. But that latter reason is the aesthetic pull of the world that draws me into the sustained concentration and investigation that eventually result in the writing. That's all about desire and what I frankly find the deeply sensual quality of the sensory world. It's what pulls me to any artistic encounter with the environment, whether essay or poetry or novel or painting or sculpture. The first reason, however, is more philosophical and is particularly significant for the writer of the kind of essays generally called "creative nonfiction"—that is, artistic, literary engagements with what Richard Rhodes calls "verity." And so ways of knowing the world, and the questions we ask about how we know what we know, seemed from the start important aspects of the essay. The art of epistemology.

The world is deeply complicated, fractal and fractured in its facticity. It demands much of us—awe, attention, diligent wonder. It can draw us up, out of our individual selves, and then can give us back to ourselves, enriched and enlivened by experiential imperatives. It can send us deep indoors, for study or research, and then lead us back out again, into visceral extremity—dawn or dusk, summer or winter. We answer it as best we can, through myth and art, through the bright and multicolored spectrum of our spirituality. Believing these things, as I do, and respecting the human endeavor to inhabit a universe that is meaningful rather than otherwise, I keep returning to think about Beverly and her easy translation of science into Christianity and her even-toned demeanor that could imply, liberally, all stories are equally valuable. But more likely, I think, it implies that the story is what really matters, the frame surrounding the scene before you. Richard Hugo declares, if you are a poet, you must believe one of two things: either that music conforms to truth or that truth conforms to music. He's talking about poetic form and the attitudes toward art's content that are implied by formal decisions. If you believe the latter, I fear, you can never train your eye clearly on the world that lies before you; you never fully experience perception but only apperception, echoes of the already glimpsed or previously defined. This is, I think, a form of fundamentalism.

Such distinctions are very fine for the creative author, who, despite allegiance to verity, need not attempt to efface herself from her own narrative, and the subjective lens is often the iris through which she gazes. A nonfiction writer maintains, however, a need—perhaps a responsibility—to cast attention outward as well as inward; for a writer whose subjects are specific places, the challenge is to explore the spiritual and aesthetic realms as they are housed in the greater horizons of the material world. That is, I believe that music must conform to truth and that language gestures outward as well as inward.

These are reasons why I love the genre of nonfiction, and particularly place-based essays, which call on us to bring the expressive and exploratory powers of language to the service of what I keep calling the world—things that are the case. As a reader, I learn things about the world and do so in the company of the personal voice; I enjoy the literary company, and generally in such work I trust the writer's command of details and facts. I feel cheered by such work. As a writer, I feel charged to extend beyond the limits of what I already know and to put myself in situations where I'll be surprised, or challenged, and finally in some way changed by experience. This means moving among various modes of exploration: the physical encounter with specific places, of course, while following different routes of scholarship, drawing on history, science, mythology, art.

Writing "Fragments" was personally rewarding because it allowed—indeed, at times I felt it demanded—just this kind of literary enterprise. I worked on this essay over the period of a year, with two actual visits to the Purgatoire Valley (once in October, another the following June) and much reading and wondering in between. From the Forest Service I received the management plan for the site, a thick spiral-bound document with a dry prose style and a marvelous fold-out map. I poked around in publications from the 1930s and read biographies of the early-twentieth-century "fossil hunters," all the while vaguely enjoying the fact that I was tracking these people and their actions from seventy years before, trying to find the languaged trail they'd left behind. I reread accounts of the dust storms of the 1930s, again studying maps to try to imagine the specific changes the Dust Bowl might have meant for that particular river valley. When I finally visited the Otero County Museum in June, I hoped to find photographs documenting the drought years, but when I didn't find any, it suddenly didn't seem to matter; there were the maps I'd spread across my study floor, my own memories of the sandy trail from a dry,

Fragments

By early afternoon, in Picket Wire Canyon in southeastern Colorado, on a mid-October day of brilliant air and sun, I am barefoot, in the river. I am wearing what has been a favorite pair of trousers, soft as chamois, rolled to the knee. This will be their last outing, since I ripped out the seat earlier in the trip, scrambling up a rock face. The day feels utterly golden and blue: bright sky, warm rock, dry grass, the hours rich and long and full, and filled with happy, languid company—we are two men and two women who have hiked down to the river to see dinosaur tracks. It is almost time to turn back, to retrace our way along the dusty trail, back through the canyon's mixed-grass prairie and occasional cottonwoods, up through the scrubby pine of the canyon wall, and rejoin the drought-beiged rim of the horizontal plains. It's still another five miles; we should get started soon. But for now, we are dawdling. Dorian sits on large limestone blocks, dangling her feet in the silty current. Dave and Roger prowl the level shelf along the bank, pointing out the shapes and peculiarities of the tracks and taking photographs. I'm wading in the gentle, subtle flow, searching the bottom until I find what I'm looking for: footprints in the riverbed. I step into them, walking upstream against the feeble current. Me and Heraclitus, I think, heading back.

For a moment I'm reminded of afternoons in college, in a sun-filled class-room on the second floor of Gordy Hall, where Prof. Wieman lectured on the pre-Socratics. It was a world of metaphor, of transformation, talk of accidents and essences, doctrines of opposites and of flux, the future opening out in its surprising complexity. "Other and other waters flow down on those who step into the same rivers," wrote Heraclitus. Some say this is different from the popular paraphrase, "You can't step in the same river twice." And of course, I can't read the original Greek, so whatever wordplay and poetry the prophet-philosopher first laid down are lost on me. It's Fragment 12 I'm talking about, which opens "*autoisi potamoisi,*" and I take it by eye and on authority that the onomatopoetic whisper of the river sounds in those first words.

Here are the footprints. "Trackways," they're called, clear lines of ancient footsteps heading roughly west, parallel patterns of animals who traveled together along some Mesozoic lakeshore, in the late Jurassic, some 150 million years ago. They're laid in limestone that has jointed and fractured into even blocks like some great paving stones, giving the impression of a road, or some old central plaza, a place rather than mere space, where the sauropods strolled together, heading somewhere.

Dave and I spent the night camped on the rim above nearby Vogel Canyon. When we pulled in, the other vehicles were a camper, whose occupants I never saw, and a van with two "semiretired" folks who came to our picnic table almost before we had finished dinner to pay a long, chatty visit in the gathering dark. The fellow, a sculptor and aficionado of antiquities, was full of bluster and statement. At one point he asked absurdly, "Where you live, do you have access to mammoth bones embedded with projectile flakes?" In the dry autumn air I grew chilly and impatient as the last light faded and seeped away, before Dave and I could stroll across the plateau and gaze down into the canyon, maybe hike the brief descent to a spring I saw marked on the map. The day was gone; the canyon waited in the dark, unchanged by any visit from us.

At last the couple left, and we crawled into the tent to sleep under clear, cold skies, in near proximity to birds, as the place-name (*vogel,* bird) would suggest—an owl in the night, early-morning bluebirds as we rose in the day's first light.

At nine we meet Roger and Dorian near the edge of the Comanche National Grasslands, park in a rugged juniper-and-pinyon-ringed spot five hundred feet above the river, and descend to Picket Wire Canyon. The name is a corruption of *Purgatoire*, a charmingly reshaped linguistic artifact from the age of Spanish explorers, who named the stream "El Rio de las Animas Perdidas en Purgatorio," the River of the Souls Lost in Purgatory. Some explanations trace the place-name to a grassfire that surrounded and consumed an exploration party or to an expedition bound from New Mexico to Florida that disappeared into the unmapped lands of the New World. But the landscape today is anything but desperate. Our gait along the dusty trail is an unhurried saunter, and we pause often, admiring the grasses, the rocks, some persimmon-sized gourds that sprawl in drying clusters of vine. Prickly pear cactus grows in aromatic, hirsute profusion here, and we stop frequently to pluck the plump fruit, wipe away the fine bristles, as if stroking a cloth along the nap, and peel back the rind. Inside, the fruit is rich and sweet, prune-sized clusters of flesh-and-mostly-seed. They are often delicious but labor intensive, requiring much seed spitting, and they stain our lips and fingers scarlet. Dave and Dorian discuss the seed-to-fruit ratio, and Dave says it's more like a pomegranate than a grape. "Persephone walked, spitting," I say, and we do. The seeds make a satisfying percussive sound as, like children, we spit whole mouthfuls out. Dave says he has eaten jelly made from the fruits and that it is delicious, and far more convenient.

In the bright sun we browse and amble, looking at everything. (We notice lots of seed-filled scat, scattered in the dust.) Along a bend in the trail, several yards above a similar bend in the channel, Dave and Dorian spot a gray fox and exclaim as it disappears into the brush. But Roger and I have missed the moment, talking of poetry and teaching, and by the time we look to where our companions are pointing, the animal is out of sight.

When we arrive at the river, just past noon, a sandy side-path takes us down to the water, past thickets of tamarisk that mimic native willows on the bank. Immediately, we find a large, three-toed allosaurus track on the near side of the river, which is easily recognizable from the photographs in our guide booklet. This is a large, deep print in fine-grained stone that feels silky to the touch. It reminds me of a turkey-foot petroglyph I once saw in New Mexico. Two less-well-formed ones are just behind the track, a record of the two steps taken before the larger, perfect print. A tiny pair of white tennis shoes, toddler sized, sits nearby, forgotten no doubt by earlier visitors. But within minutes they will remember them and come back; we'll see their owner's daddy jog back along the path and scoop them up.

The Morrison Formation, the geologic layer that contains the tracks, is deeply fossil-rich, known for the bones found throughout the late-nineteenth-century–skeletons of the brontosaurs that would be quarried, painstakingly packed out of their distant locations, and reassembled to loom tall in museums and the public imagination. Some of its deposits are lacustrine—set down in lakes—others are fluvial, deposited by rivers. Both words, I think, are lovely, holding liquids in their Latinate construction. While the Mesozoic era was marked by the central sea that covered the Plains states, limestone of the Purgatoire track site marks a lakeshore, not a marine environment. It is believed to have been a semiarid, savannah landscape, and has been compared to regions in contemporary East Africa; I like the comparison in part because we—people—at the earliest point in our species' being, lived and walked in such savannahs. Shales accompanying the limestone testify to the periodic flooding and evaporation of the ancient lake, with bits and traces of small fossils: algae, snails, seed shrimp and clam shrimp, tiny crustaceans that lived in quiet, shallow waters. Fossil ripple marks suggest it was a large lake, oxygen-rich and frequently an important source of drinking water for the Jurassic animals who lived along its shores.

The largest footprints follow one another at a gentle angle from the river, several in neat parallel lines that show it was a group of beasts who walked together here. These are the footprints of sauropods: great, gregarious vegetarians whose stride stretched from four to six feet as they swung thick legs from massive hips. The footprints themselves—ichnites, in the language of paleontology—are open basins in the rock, and I sit down beside one and put both my feet inside, as if I were about to pour warm water in to soak after the long hike. But in the drought the river is down, the footprints are dry, and only a little powdery dust swirls beneath my toes. In one large track prairie grass is growing, where some tough little seed must have lodged in another, wetter year of higher water. Though we stroll and linger along these most prominent prints—a half-dozen or so separate trackways—researchers have mapped more than one hundred other such individual trails, with at least thirteen hundred separate prints. We kneel to touch a smaller, three-toed track (some carnosaur, as near as I can tell from studying the guidebook) still holding unmistakable tracings from the scaly skin that pressed against the damp surface so many million years ago. Dorian and Dave take photographs, impressions I will later study, trying to match the specific shape with published pictures from what's called "the scientific literature," trying to put names and labels on the imagery we've carried home.

In the so-called Doctrine of Opposites, Heraclitus lays out the complementary constituents of the universe, and hints at their relation through change. Modes of being, cold and wet, combine to form Water; cold and dry form Earth. Neither is permanent, any more than their hot/wet/dry counterparts, Air and Fire. "Cold things grow warm," he says, "Warm grows cold, wet grows dry, and parched grows moist" (Fragment 126). Through these states the cosmos oscillates, each, it would seem, by turn. There is at the heart of things, he says, a "back-turning structure" (*palintropos harmonie*) "like that of the bow or the lyre." This is how things fit together, how pattern and order emerge from flux, how the tensile opposition of the arms of the bow create a thing of grace and power; how the lyre, similarly strung, strummed, renders, out of silence, music.

Because Heraclitus (known as "The Dark," "The Obscure") might have enjoyed these wandering associations and this wordplay, strolling along the Purgatory River and thinking of Time, I cast the imagery before us in terms of the Opposites. The cold, brisk air of sunrise, when Dave and I rose from our tent site on the canyon rim, has given way to midday heat. Dorian and I soak our Tshirts in the river and put them back on, shiveringly cool, though quickly they rewarm between the sun and our backs. Dave follows suit, annoyed that he is wearing black, a photon-sink, as he puts it. Then we wade across the diminutive ripples of the current, and I stop briefly to change back from sandals to hiking boots, while the others move a little farther on. We pause along a stretch of rumpled stone where once the wet lakeshore was churned by sauropods, as if, like cattle, they had gathered at the edge of the impounded water, milling about and roiling the ground beneath their feet. *Bioturbation* is the geologic term for such disturbances, and the guidebook puns that along the Purgatoire, the earth was marked by "dinoturbation." Again, I think of Heraclitus and the echoing shape of internal rhyme. Wet things grow dry. Soft things grow hard. Motion stills. We stand and scan the limestone surface for the trampled clams and plants left as fossils in the tousled limestone. Then, with a quick swig of tepid water from the packs, we move along.

In 1911 dinosaur hunter Charles Sternberg published a slender book of poems called *A Story of the Past; or, The Romance of Science.* Here he recounts, in broad strokes, the narrative of his search for bones from other ages, and he presents himself as a time traveler, an amazed visitor to the Permian and Cretaceous worlds. He is, indeed, the hero of adventure, telling his tale in verse heavily metered and rhymed, a romance of the stones. From the beloved hemlock forests of his childhood in New York state he heads west, on a God-inspired quest "To show to man His wondrous Work/Through all the scenes of time." In life his travels in search of fossil skeletons took him across the Plains—Kansas, Texas, Wyoming, and as far west as Oregon—but he never saw the tracks along the Purgatoire. I'm sure he would have liked to, and to have "read" the text of those ancient footprints. For to Sternberg geology held distinctly transcendental flavor: science lighted with the roseate flush of faith. "So God engraves in mouldering land/The works of his almighty hand," he wrote.

> Not Moses' tablets graved by God
> Seem more wondrous than the word
> He left recorded in the earth,
> When rocky strata had their birth.

In a long poem called "The Permian Beds of Texas" Sternberg declares, "I sail down on the Tide of Time,/My oar-beats keeping gentle rhyme." In his imagined "birch-bark boat" he "gently floats" back through millennia, describing all he sees—ancient lake and ocean, lush jungle and glades, combining unexpectedly convention's archaic syntax with precision's scientific diction. He wrote of erosion's uncovering power, "The rains of ages have laid bare/The ancient dead once buried there,/Far, far below in limestone vault." For Sternberg, as for some others in the late nineteenth and early twentieth centuries, tracks drew little notice. It was the bones, mostly, they wanted, and Sternberg found some fine specimens, including the concentric skeletons of two fish, one encased within the other's belly, an ancient record of footless predator and prey.

R. T. Bird, in the employ of the American Museum of Natural History's Barnum Brown, did pay a visit to the Purgatoire in 1938. It was something of a side trip, following a summer spent in Wyoming, when he came to Pueblo, Colorado, in early November, joined John Stuart MacClary, and made a car trip to the track site. He was puzzled by the prints and thought they showed a brontosaur walking on its front two feet, as if partially floating in the water. He took photographs, one of which is included in his posthumous memoir, showing huge, circular footprints in the jointed rock. The next day he headed farther south, and within weeks he'd found a large, accessible trackway along the Paluxy River, which would hold his attention as the Purgatoire had not.

It was left to MacClary to document the footprints. He'd been interested in the site for nearly two years; in 1937 he had organized a trip with some college friends, though, in his wheelchair, he could not reach the prints themselves. Even so, he drew a roughly sketched map of their route down Minnie Canyon, south of the Withers Canyon route my friends and I descended. MacClary went on to produce three small publications, which I track down in a couple of afternoons' library work. The first, from 1936, is a tiny note in *Life* magazine, a half-page spread of three photographs with a single accompanying paragraph by MacClary. One circular picture, cropped like a little spotlight falling on its subject, shows the allosaur print with a man's hat set beside it for scale. I find this source on a sunny afternoon on the fourth floor, where a nearly complete run of *Life* rests in crumbling bound volumes: this one is housed in a green preservation box, tied neatly with ribbons, since the broken spine sprawls pages that threaten to tear as I turn them. The next two must be recalled from the storage annex and are delivered the following day. From 1938 there is a full-page description in *Scientific American*, again with three photos. One shows a plaster cast of the allosaur track and a cement replica of the track itself, which, MacClary says, is "used as a bird-bath." (I briefly recall the cedar waxwings that come through my yard each autumn landing on the concrete lip, drinking and fluttering in a three-toed puddle of water.) MacClary describes a trackway we didn't see in our relaxed afternoon along the river. "One three-toed trail angles to follow that of the huge four-footed creature," he writes, "obviously indicating that the carnivorous biped pursued the huge vegetarian." He goes on to interpret the gait of the two beasts: the predator had a regular, forty-eight-inch stride that "gives the impression that the killer felt confident mastery of the situation." The other trail, he says, is spaced irregularly, which "may be regarded as evidence that the herbivorous dinosaur was aware of impending conflict, which it did not relish." I can find no other description of this particular confluence of prints, and when I study a detailed map of the tracks, painstakingly surveyed in the 1980s, none of the trails seem to illustrate his account of an ancient chase.

I wonder about this discrepancy. Was MacClary simply mistaken about what he saw? Did he "read into" the limestone annals some agonistic drama, with Jurassic players, that never did take place? Or have the movement of the river and the subsequent decades of weather removed all record of the pursuit? It's true: erosion has obliterated sections of the trackways, and the very blocks on which Dorian and I sat, soaking our Tshirts on that hot October day, are only pausing their slow tumble into the current. There is an archive of destruction here at hand: it is the very width of Picket Wire Canyon, where the river has washed and wandered across its floodplain, a shallow, fluid Shiva of creation and destruction. A Forest Service publication suggests that "the majority of the main footprint bearing bed" has been destroyed by periodic erosion and cites a catastrophic flood in 1904 and more recently another in 1965. Indeed, throughout their management plan runs a persistent theme of loss: erosion of the tracks, degradation of the riparian habitat, deterioration of prehistoric rock art along the canyon walls, "deliberate vandalism" of prehistoric and historic ruin sites. One of the primary resolutions in that decade-old plan is to arrest the river's erosion of the prints while maintaining its wild and scenic character.

I write to Martin Lockley, the lead researcher of the 1980s, and he doesn't know what to make of MacClary's description either. But real or imagined, the account lodges somewhere in my subconscious. One night I dream of driving, in a small SUV that suddenly becomes an open buggy, vulnerable like an old-fashioned sleigh, along a winding canyon road just above a riverbank. Of course, this being an anxiety dream, I'm in the dark. Headlights flash on the river as I make a hairpin turn, and I see a huge crocodile rising from the water, with amazing speed, and its gaze meets mine as it begins pursuit. In a later sequence some ungulate, neck rising from raised shoulders like a small giraffe, crosses the road. I see, in shock, that it has no head but is still moving, making a stumbling escape. A lion crouches beside the road, haunches turned toward me, but I can still see it tearing at the head it holds between its paws.

In his third published note, a 1939 letter to *Natural History*, MacClary reports that the three-toed tracks (represented by two of the previously published photos) are "undoubtedly new to science" and wonders what species could have made them. He confides that he'd long wondered about the tracks but had been unable to visit them until the previous year, "because of physical incapacity"—evidently he was an invalid, a housebound enthusiast of paleontology. He says he "had not dared hope it would ever be possible to see them." Of course, this means he probably couldn't go back again, to reexamine—reconsider—what he'd found. Back at my desk, I wonder whether it is now too late to ever see the trail of predator and prey MacClary studied over half a century ago.

And today I wonder whether the residents along the Purgatoire River ever felt themselves living at the end of the world, in the years of the Great Depression and the Dust Bowl. Picket Wire Canyon lies at the very western edge of the Dust Bowl, along the border between Las Animas and Otero counties. To the east and south is Baca County, one of the hardest hit places in the 1930s' droughts, along with southwestern Kansas and the Oklahoma Panhandle. While Picket Wire Canyon hit its peak of settled inhabitants in the 1880s— about four hundred people lived and farmed there at that time—the Depression and drought later drove many from the land.

MacClary's first trip took place in April of the single worst year for dust storms, if one counts the number of times visibility was less than a mile or the number of hours people in the region were besieged by dust in the air. While, unlike Baca County, Picket Wire Canyon had not been largely plowed up for wheat production, these must have been dark, despairing times. In the southern plains spring during these years was marked by black blizzards, when sudden cold air masses drove down from the north and lifted the loose, dry earth in great rolling clouds, sometimes extending as high as eight thousand feet. More frequently, the nearly incessant wind resulted in sand blows, where plants were buried and choked in the moving drifts. I think of the dry, sandy trails we walked along and imagine the canyon pocked and pitted by destructive drifts.

By other standards of measurement the worst year may have been 1935. In March and April the black blizzards descended repeatedly on the southern plains, in stunning storms that could last for hours. Historian Donald Worster details how fully these storms invaded the landscape of the former grasslands; by 24 March in that year, twelve consecutive days of storms had gripped the regions of southeastern Colorado and southwestern Kansas. He notes that the wind "carried away from the plains twice as much earth as men and machines had scooped out to make the Panama Canal." Then, on 14 April an even greater storm swept south- and eastward from the Colorado border, in what would be called "Black Sunday," a terrifying visitation of particulate darkness that lasted more than four hours, killing livestock and people who were caught out of doors.

Many of the National Grasslands in the west date back to the Roosevelt administration's efforts to remove what were called submarginal lands from agricultural production, an effort whose roots lie in the 1920s, before the dust storms arrived. Between 1933 and 1943, however, the theoretical interests of social scientists received practical policy enactment, through the Federal Emergency Relief Administration's program of buying up distressed land, later continued under the Resettlement Administration and the Soil Conservation Service. The 1934 Taylor Grazing Act closed the west—and there were then eighty million acres of unclaimed land—to any further homesteading.

Picket Wire Canyon, in the Comanche National Grassland, however, doesn't trace its public lands lineage to these Dust Bowl–era programs. When the Rourke family, who had ranched the area for three generations, sold their holdings—the Wineglass Ranch—in 1971, the eventual buyer was the Department of Defense. The land along the Purgatoire River became the Pinon Canyon Maneuver Site, and for twenty years the Army conducted training along the riparian grassland and the caprock rims. The track site, in one Army document, was referred to as one of the canyon's "uneconomic remnants," while citizens' groups called for the protection of the prints through transferring their management from the Army to the Forest Service. In 1990 Public Law 101-510, Section 2825, effected this transfer, and 16,700 acres of the larger military reserve unit were removed from the Army's purview and established as the Comanche National Grassland's Picket Wire Canyonlands. A few weathered poles and phone wires still string their way across the landscape, remnants of those years the army conducted maneuvers in the canyon. I can hardly believe they are less than thirty years old: gray and slack and tiny in the wide, light-filled landscape, they seem far distant and diminutive, dwarfed by the stretch of open grass, the upward reach of the canyon's cliff wall, and the sere, hot sun. I think of Emily Dickinson and how in many poems she speaks of Noon, markedly capitalized as starkly metaphysical, a philosophical or psychological state of being gripped by Realization, ravished, one could say, by Reason.

On the hike out, we feel small beneath the hot expanse of sky. I become aware of physical annoyances: a few prickly pear tines itch and chafe in my thigh, where (unthinking) I wiped a fruit against my trousers. My right foot begins to ache, the first signs—though I don't know it yet—of plantar fasciitis, an injury that will plague me for months afterwards and end my hopes for competing in an upcoming autumn race. Dave threads his bandanna beneath his cap to shield his neck, which is already sunburned. Dorian sips the warm water and complains that it is so hot it makes one want to puke; I tell her that, miles away, cold water and cold beer both await us in an ice chest in the car. We pass a family, pausing on mountain bikes, and a girl of perhaps nine or ten shows us a dead tarantula she has found in the trail, looking furry and mammalian, though slightly flattened. We exclaim and thank her, and she smiles, flushed with the achievement of demonstration and instruction.

Dead cottonwood trees stand pale and smooth without their bark; a few are lined and shaded by charcoal, signs of fires from some other year. (I think briefly of the tale of the Spanish explorers, lost souls consumed by fire in the river valley.) Dry branches of cholla, weathered down to the hollow, hidden lattice of their bonelike structure, stand in desiccated clumps among the grasses. We pause along the way back to investigate old ruined homesites. There is the Lopez settlement, dating to 1871, including the remains of a Catholic "mission"—two partially standing walls from the rough-beamed church—and a graveyard with hand-carved stones. Back behind these former buildings is a rock-shelter cave with partial masonry walls, reputed to be the Lopez family shelter while the houses were under construction. Farther along, we explore a more recent—though also decaying—structure, with a covered cistern we peer into, hoping for snakes, and a handsome enamel-coated wood cookstove tumbled on the hillside by the house. To our surprise, we run into hunters, young men wearing blaze-orange vests with their rifles slung over their backs. Like the family, they are on bicycles, and we see them first along the river, pedaling through the high, dry grass, away from the tamarisks where they sought—unsuccessfully, evidently—mule deer. I wonder just how these wheeled predators would've handled the carcass, had they been successful. It's a very steep climb to the top, and they'd have to leave their high-tech bikes, perhaps in a little trailside cairn, one atop another, while they struggled upward with the weight of the deer.

We drain the last of our water—all except Dorian—and slowly make the final ascent, back out of the canyon to stony rim above.

In the final days of June the shortgrass plains are delightfully, surprisingly cool and moist. Heavy rains along the Front Range have soaked the soil, and flash flooding has suddenly swelled the little streams outside the concrete-bodied cities in the foothills. Farther east and south, in its valley beneath the Dixie Bluffs, the Purgatoire is muddy and swift but well within its banks. I'm here as a kind of postscript to our autumn visit to the Picket Wire; I want to try to find the little town of Higbee, which the map shows on Highway 109 south of La Junta, along an area of the river called Nine Mile Bottom. Higbee was established in 1866 by a settler most recently from Trinidad, one Uriel Higbee, along with Jesse Nelson and his wife, Susan (a niece of Kit Carson); William and Manuelita Richards; Samuel Smith; and a few others. Soon they joined forces to build an earthen dam along the Purgatoire, for irrigation and flood control; with iron spades and cottonwood shovels they worked from 1868 to 1870 to change the river just enough to allow them agricultural purchase along its banks and floodplain. By the 1930s there was a "ditch caretaker's house" to oversee a more sophisticated diversion channel, paved with stone and cement, and a lock control system. L. C. (Lawrence) Ridennoure was the ditch care-taker by then, and he lived with his family in the stucco house; the building was provided as part of his salary. Born in 1895, he had served as private first class in World War I, and with his wife, Etha Lynn (born 1904), he was now raising children—Betty Jo, Lawrence, Ben, and the baby, Ted—in the valley.

It was Betty Jo who told her high school teacher, Mr. Don Hayes, about the tracks, and shortly afterward MacClary learned of them as well. I gathered this much from reading throughout the winter, leisurely poking around, and when I learned that Betty Jo was still living, I wrote to her in her retirement home in Arizona. She replied to my questions in sentence fragments, some-times only one-word answers, penned right onto my letter. From her I learned of the "ditch house"; she also told me that in 1941 she and MacClary "spent a long time writing about the tracks." But she said, in sometimes spidery writ-ing, changing pens midway from blue to black, she's "not in the best of health"; she was not a loquacious correspondent. So I'm eager to see the spot, to flesh out her story from the spare, historical framework of ink-on-paper.

Right near mile marker 39, on Highway 109, is a turnoff for Nine Mile Bot-tom on the Higbee Road. A dilapidated white wooden sign lists just over a dozen residents, their names and the mileage to their homes. A few of these dangle loosely from the frame, and I wonder whether the people have moved away or just don't have the time or interest to nail back their single-board planks in this lettered landmark. Not far from the turnoff is the Higbee Cemetery, with an iron entrance gate and a cistern beside it spreading out a network of hoses for watering the gravesites. Also near the entrance is a metal sign mapping the burial plots: each grave is marked and the names of the dead handwritten in faded, though no doubt intended to be "permanent," marker: a few are too faint to read. Others are evidently unknown, simply empty locations, sideways U's on the map.

In a cool, light rain (welcome weather for late June!) I wander through the tiny graveyard, noting the large number of veterans (Civil War through Vietnam), the dead infants (most often marked with dateless concrete rectangles, names like Baby Wood or Baby Carson). Barrel cactus and sideoats grama grass punctuate plantings of iris and the occasional hardscrabble rosebush; low, leathery lilacs spread over the Carson family plot. Here, among the irises, are the Ridennoures, three of them (L.C., Etha Lynn, and their son, Ted C., 1934–92). Nearby, neat sheets of Astroturf cover the McGowns, spread like bright green afghans and weighted around their perimeters with rounded river stones. A couple named the Martins, dead before I was born, shares a single piece of petrified wood for their headstone. Several Hispanic families have little wooden fences, chipped figures of Mary, piles of stones and faded plastic flowers to keep company with the gravesite. Here are the names I recognize of founding families: Nelson, Lopez. No Higbees, though, and when I'd asked Betty Jo if there were any Higbee descendants in the valley when she was a child, she wrote, simply, "no." I suppose Uriel himself must have moved on to something else. Overhead, a golden eagle circles the valley, and the air is very quiet.

The road runs southeast, roughly parallel to the river; we're several miles downstream from the dinosaur track site. The morning continues cool, and we drive farther south amidst alfalfa fields and a small stand of irrigated corn. Blue grosbeaks and orioles move between cottonwoods and phone lines; once, in the distance, I see a small group of vultures gazing intently into the field, closely attending something dead, or, perhaps, nearly so. We pass an old adobe-and-stucco ruin, a building that has simply folded in upon itself and is melting back into the ground. And then, high on a rocky knoll, with the Dakota sandstone bluffs above and beyond, unmistakable, is the ditch house, with the muddy Purgatoire waters below. I grin and squint up toward the metal roof weighted against the wind with stones along one side.

In town I visit the Otero County Museum. I want to see whether they have any other images or information on Betty Jo, the dinosaur tracks, the decades of the Dust Bowl. In the cavernous building there are plenty of artifacts to examine: hand-drawn fire hose carts for fighting wildfires; a stage coach from the nineteenth century; a barbed wire collection; a directory for the local ranches' brands. A local man named John Liken donated his arrowhead collection to the museum, along with a careful annotation of where each point was found; most were from out of state, but a few are from the area. Two dark, much-worn points were found in "the vicinity of Dixie Bluffs along the Anderson Arroyo"; an amber-colored, unfinished-looking piece perhaps an inch long "was found south of La Junta"; only one small point was from "the Picketwire River, Godfrey Canyon, Higbee." The collection is neatly and artfully arranged, a geometric pattern of points and their hand-numbered labels, framed behind glass and hanging like a picture on the wall.

In an exhibit dedicated to the early schools of the area, I find a ledger listing each building, its years of use, and the land office deed for the property. On the second page is a description that matches the old, crumpled adobe-and-stucco building along the road, roughly two miles from the highway. The Higbee School, the ledger says, was "constructed as a former saloon and other in the 1880s years," before it assumed its later, less commercially recreational use. "This building evacuated in October year 1962 as school building," declares the ledger, a cramped phrase that sounds, to me, to contain both alacrity and emergency, but I doubt that was the case. And here, in a small plastic frame, are two photos of the students of Higbee in 1933. In the familiar pose of the era, they stand and sit clustered in front of a small stucco building, labeled the Plaza School; the photographs were taken by their teacher, Annabelle Loftis. One shows sixteen students; the other, thirteen. The label says one may have been taken in 1934; the other was Easter, 1933, and reveals a pile of eggs before the gathered children. The pupils' names are recorded in pen on the back, and to my delight, I find three Ridennoures—Betty Jo and her two brothers, Ben and Lawrence. While I'm still gazing at the faces, trying to picture them and this dusty-looking building back in the fields I just drove through, the nineteenth-century walls still standing, the sky dry and sere in those drought-fraught years, the museum attendant introduces me to an elderly woman wearing a volunteer's name tag. She is Mrs. Tillie Autry; she grew up in the Purgatoire Valley and remembers Higbee very well. We sit together in a row of wooden chairs, evidently salvaged from a La Junta school auditorium some years past, and visit. She is a petite, trim woman, with a friendly but poised face; she wears a lovely sapphire and diamond wedding ring that fits loosely on her slender finger.

Tillie Autry tells me she was born a Ballou. Her mother had been raised in Higbee—she was a Richards, a daughter, I later realize, of one of the original settlers of the tiny town, twenty-eight-year-old William and fifteen-year-old Manuelita, married in 1866. Her father's people were from Kansas, but her grandparents had settled with their children in the nineteenth century in the Sunflower Valley, near Trinidad. In 1900 her parents bought a ranch along the Purgatoire where Plum Canyon meets Chacuaco Creek. (Later I study the map carefully and find the spot. As the crow flies, this looks to be eight or ten miles south—and just a tiny bit west—of the track site. It must have been a lovely ranch location, a side canyon of the Purgatoire, with Chacuaco a real stream, not just a seasonal wash in a dry canyon.) Later she and her husband bought a ranch across the river from her parents. Yes, she says, she knew the dinosaur track site very well. It was the ford they all used to cross the river, until the bridge was built down by Higbee. "When was that?" I ask her. She looks thoughtful and closes her eyes, and I wonder whether she is revisiting scenes of the construction work or memories of earlier river crossings, as she works to recover the date. She opens her eyes. "It must have been about 1918," she says. It's only now I realize she's even older than I think.

"And, if I may ask, when were you born?" I ask.

"1912." She smiles. "We called it Rock Crossing," she continues; it was the reliable ford, except for times of very high water. "That was the way we always came in to town," she explains. "My dad always called those the Elephant Tracks."

She tells me a bit more about Higbee. It had a hotel, a garage adjacent to a dance hall, a general store. There were about six families in the town (this explains, I think, how tiny the school is). I ask whether it was just a grade school or whether they went to high school there as well.

"Well," she says, tilting her head slightly, for this is a noteworthy detail. "I went to St. Scholastica Academy in Kansas City."

Five, six hundred miles away, a big-city boarding school for a young rural woman in the 1920s. I think, they must have had some money; more important, education was something her family valued. They drove her there, a two- or three-day trip, most likely, and then returned to pick her up for vacations.

Yes, she said, you could take the train back then, but her parents made the trip by car. I'm beginning to realize that the woman sitting beside me, white-haired and well postured, has had a life remarkable as well as long. I don't know enough to know what I should want to ask her, what I should glean from the near-century of her life. She's just a little younger than my grandparents would have been, rural Oklahoma people—my grandfather walked across France in World War I and came home to marry my grandmother the day after she turned sixteen. Mrs. Autry married an Oklahoma man at age eighteen, in 1930, just in time for the Depression. Oh, yes, she tells me, she remembers dust storms in the valley.

"Sometimes people would wet material and put it over the windows, to keep out the dust, but we never did that." The storms in Otero County weren't as severe as those farther south, around the town of Kim. There, she says, lots of people lost their fields, but "it wasn't that bad here," since this was ranch land and hadn't been plowed up for wheat. Much later, in 1948, Mrs. Autry moved in to La Junta, so that her children—five daughters and two sons—could attend high school in town. "We stayed in town throughout the week, and then went and worked on the ranch on weekends." Only in the 1980s, after her husband's death, did she sell their ranch out in the canyon country just south of the Purgatoire.

Later, back home, I study again the maps of wind erosion and review the records of the relief efforts. By the mid-1930s cattle were starving and suffocating throughout the region; in eastern Colorado rainfall was 45 percent below normal. "The government paid us a dollar a head," Mrs. Autry said of their cattle, "and took them all up and shot them." Her language suggests the emotional damage of the experience; the animals weren't "put down," or some other euphemism. This was destruction, not even a full step ahead of environmental and economic collapse. The Emergency Cattle Purchase Program eventually spent over one and a half million dollars in Colorado; by the decade's end National Grasslands were trying to reclaim the failed wheat fields from blowout and drift. I think, they lost the cattle, but they kept, and kept on, the land. It could, of course, have turned out differently.

Nothing is left of the town where her grandmother grew up. I'd been imagining the place as a rural community, spread out along the Higbee Road, but she said that's not right: the town and its few businesses were clustered right on Highway 109, before you reach the bridge across the Purgatoire. An obelisk now stands near the road, erected of local stone and holding an iron plaque commemorating the centennial of the founding and listing the male settlers: Higbee, Smith, Richards, Jones, Elkins, Carson, Nelson. The memorial is set behind a sturdy barbed wire fence, so I have to use binoculars to make out the words. It looks as though the remnants of a picnic shelter stand behind it, but this is most emphatically private land, and even the horse in the next field is kept out, watching from behind another fence. "Did the town burn?" I asked Mrs. Autry. "Was there a fire?"

"No," she said. "They just tore it down."

As the cool, moist morning brightens slightly, I've descended maybe two hundred feet into Vogel Canyon, and even at noon, a still time of the day, it is full of birds. In shady places the earth is still damp from yesterday's heavy rain, and in the willows along the wash I can see how high flash floodwaters can race, lacing grass and dead branches like remnants of fencing two or three feet above the ground. A few pools linger here, and frog song joins birdcall to fill the canyon's intimate space with aural ephemera. This has been an easy hike, and my malingering foot, shod in sturdy boots, hasn't registered any complaints.

Of course, the easy trail means the place is quite accessible, and even though no one else is visible, there are fresh footprints, boot tracks laid down since yesterday's cloudbursts. Along the northern wall several overhangs shelter rock art, though a few spots are badly damaged by vandalism. Danny R.L. 6/12/04 smirks in black marker. Several round scars in sandstone show where someone has shot at the cliff, and I wonder, spitefully, if the bullets ever ricochet to hit the Dannys or Dicks in the face. Still, beneath the contemporary trash, one can see a few carved human forms and two figures that resemble birdmen, with curved, birdlike heads and torsos that look like crooked wings resting atop tall, stick-figure legs. Zigzag lines like snake tracks in sandy soil. Circles. A rectangular shape with vertical bars is high on a cliff marked with vertical streaks of whitewash from some bird's perch—a marvelous conjunction of form and formalism.

From the rim to canyon floor and back, I make a quick list of the day's bird sightings: a female Say's phoebe, feeding her nest of young; an ash-throated flycatcher; pinyon jays nattering in the trees; two prairie falcons coasting over the cliff top; a canyon wren at the deep, still spring against the cliff; mockingbirds, lark sparrows, western kingbirds. Descendants of dinosaurs, moving quickly through the overcast light and shadows of rock.

And among the petroglyphs are three-toed footprints, carved like crane or turkey feet. Smaller than my hand, if my hand could reach that high, they're aligned perfectly vertical; they hang in the abstract plane of vision; they seem to lead nowhere. They're time-darkened, marked with the desert patina that shows long exposure to bright sun and dry air. They could be allosaur feet, stepping up toward the land long since eroded from above or toward the distant matter of the stars. "The path up and down is one and the same," said Heraclitus, even though the journey back is always a different unfolding of moments, just as other and other waters flow on. A kestrel lands on the cliff above the spring and turns to watch me watch him, while I stand still as the sun moves past noon, on a day in late June that is just barely perceptibly shorter than the one before, while beyond these near cliffs, the river moves silt toward the east and while the phoebe, relieved that I'm no longer trying to find her nest, flips her wings, deposits a bug, and moves off—all of us caught in the day's stride of becoming and disappearing.

DAVID GESSNER

David Gessner is the author of *A Wild, Rank Place: One Year on Cape Cod* (1997) *Under the Devil's Thumb* (1999), *Return of the Osprey: A Season of Flight and Wonder* (2001), *Sick of Nature* (2004), and *The Prophet of Dry Hill: Lessons from a Life in Nature* (2005). *Return of the Osprey* was selected by the Book-of-the-Month Club as one of its best books of the year and cited as one of the Top Ten Nonfiction Books of 2001 by the *Boston Globe*. His essays have appeared in magazines and journals such as *Creative Nonfiction*, *Orion*, and *American Scholar* and been cited in *Best American Essays*; his essay "Benediction: On Being Boswell's Boswell" in the *Georgia Review* won a 2005 Pushcart Prize. He has taught environmental writing as a Briggs-Copeland scholar at Harvard University and currently teaches in the creative writing program at the University of North Carolina at Wilmington, where he is also editor-in-chief of the literary journal *Ecotone*. "Sick of Nature" won the *Literal Latte* Roy Y. Ames Memorial Essay award and is the title essay in *Sick of Nature*.

Why I'm Sick, and What I'm Sick Of

I wrote the essay "Sick of Nature" in a single sitting during a burst of rebellious energy after feeling trapped, for several years, by the label of "Nature Writer." I also wrote it after a long Cape Cod winter, when spring was finally breaking through, the harbor ice melting and the ospreys returning and the herring running, and when I felt something thawing inside me.

I had spent the winter banging my head against a book, and I was tired of just doing and being one thing. "I resist anything better than my own diversity," wrote Whitman, which pretty much sums up my state of mind back then. Like a lot of us, I have at least a dozen personalities, and I was then coming to believe that I was a better human being when I didn't pretend to have only one. Biodiversity, after all, isn't only healthy for the ecosystem. While I claimed to be "sick of nature," in fact I had never felt more connected to place—specifically, to the beach below a bluff near my home on Cape Cod. But what I really was sick of were the grave verities of the nature writing genre. For one thing, so much of the work seemed to be about settling, while my own creative life felt constantly unsettled. Furthermore, I was getting the first inklings that I *liked* the feeling of being unsettled, even thrived on it.

This made sense as the land I walked to every day was wildly unsettled: it shifted between land and water, and it spilled over with life—eiders, coyotes, loggerhead turtles, foxes, even humpback whales. My route led through several ecotones, those dangerous and lively areas of overlap where two separate ecosystems abut. "Life evolves at the edge of chaos," writes Jack Turner, a provocative thinker about the wild, "the area of maximum vitality and risk." The land below the bluff was not a neat place, and this struck a chord. The barnacled rocks were often covered not just with bird cadavers and seaweed but with all sorts of junk thrown up by the tide—Clorox bottles and old boat line and Styrofoam and trash—and it was on that beach that I began to come to terms with my own aesthetic of sloppiness. That sloppiness was reflected in my essays: I tried to throw over the usual earnest, hushed whisper of a nature writer's voice and speak in a voice that sounded more like my own, even if that meant occasionally descending into brashness and bad jokes, not to mention contradiction.

That time period—early spring six years ago on the Cape—also marked the beginning of a break with my literary elders. My new writing was in part a reaction to the fact that two of my literary heroes, Wendell Berry and John Hay, had made "marriage" to their chosen places a primary metaphor in their work. Hay had lived in the same house on top of Dry Hill on Cape Cod for over half a century, while as a young man Berry had returned to settle the land he had loved as a child. In contrast, I was a typical rootless American, of no place and many places, nervous if I stayed still for too long. Not only had I flitted off to Colorado for seven years, but I would soon move a thousand miles south to Carolina, that move motivated by that most pedestrian of reasons: a job.

Talk of settling and geographical marriage made me uneasy. I wasn't ready yet to say a forever "I do" to one town or county (I'm still not), and despite the pressure of my nature writing forefathers, I was beginning to understand that I really didn't have to. For all Wendell Berry's agrarian bullying, his was only one way to be in the world. "Firm ground is not available ground," wrote A. R. Ammons, and so it was for me. I wasn't quite ready to say that I was more comfortable with chaos, just that chaos was what life had dealt me. If Berry had married his land and become its steward, that was fine. But I was beginning to define myself against him as a kind of polygamist of place.

The more complicated truth, however, was that during that time I was not merely rebelling against but also embracing nature writing. One thing living near the bluff had taught me was the importance of pulsing, of tides constantly coming in and going out, and I felt that pulsing inside. If I wasn't quite ready to celebrate the sort of marriage to place the way that Hay and Berry did, that wasn't stopping me from having a love affair with the land below the bluff. This is melodramatic, of course, but also true. I loved the uncertainty of living near that rocky shore in the shadow of that sand cliff pockmarked with the tunnels of bank swallows. And there was human drama too: a huge trophy home was being built on top of the bluff, and when I walked out to the point, I found myself raging against this despoiling, batted between joy at the sheer beauty of the place and rage at that place's destruction.

Sometimes I felt that the bluff existed in Keats's state of "negative capability," that "capability of being in uncertainties, mysteries, doubts, without any irritable reaching after fact and reason." The world of the bluff, always in motion, insisted on openness. It changed constantly, changed with each tide. Ecotones are places of both opportunity and danger, and during the years we were there I found the cadavers of a young coyote, sea turtles—both loggerheads and Kemp's ridleys—many seals, a beautiful gannet with a wingspan wider than I was tall, a brant with a neck like a skin diver's glove, three cormorants, and the usual assortment of gulls and crabs.

But the bluff was a place of composition as well as decomposition. I began to believe that the nearly constant uncertainty of the land was a good thing. The dead/live land gave wordless surprise. And then, after wordless surprise, inevitably, consistently, words came. Words, ideas, sentences, whole books, looking for me when I was looking elsewhere, undermining set plans and projects. Ecotones, the edges between ecosystems, are fertile places, and my time on the edge was a fertile one. In *Imagining the Earth* John Elder has explored the way that poets can inhabit a kind of ecotone of language: "The back and forth movement of an edge . . . is referred to by ecologists as a 'pulse.'" Below the bluff I felt that pulse daily, living with my finger on it.

Moreover, when I say that much of my writing *came* from the bluff, I am not being merely figurative. Walking has always been a large part of the rhythm of the personal essay, and my best thoughts came on the move along that rocky beach. It was during that period that I struck upon a mode of composition that took advantage of my daily marathon walks. Using a microcassette recorder, I would dictate sentences while walking through that inspiring place. Often just bits and pieces would come, but in a few instances the essays came out whole as I walked. Words poured out. As if—and I cringe to hear myself saying this, and wouldn't if it weren't true—as if the place had summoned them.

Barry Lopez writes of how land "compels language," but for me *compels* was too gentle a word. That place insisted, pushed, and practically bullied me into making sentences. At times I felt like I was no more than the bluff's secretary, taking down whatever it instructed me to. While my cynical self might want to once again roll my eyes, even that grim skeptic must admit that during that time it seemed as if all I was doing was simply harvesting words, plucking things that had grown of themselves. Lopez also writes of how relationships with certain landscapes become reciprocal, and while I had made it my practice to spend lots of time in beautiful places, I had never truly felt or believed in this reciprocity until my return to the Cape. I was close to the bluff and beach, intimate even, and if it was going too far to suggest that the land helped me write my defenses of it, it was not going *too* too far. When I first read of Thoreau ecstatically hugging a tree, I rolled my eyes. But while I still never wanted to have sex with plant life, I was tentatively discovering the tree hugger within. It's embarrassing to say, but with regard to the bluff, I could use no other word than *love*.

And so you see I wanted to have it both ways. In the essay "Sick of Nature," and in my life, I wanted to eat my cake and have it too. Specifically, I wanted to both mock the groovy place-loving nature mystics and to be one.

Here's an example. During the summer after that rebellious, thawing spring, I attended a New England writing conference, where I met a famous nature writer I'd long admired. I was throwing a Frisbee around with friends when I saw him walking out of the woods, and I ran over to introduce myself. He shook my hand and then, in a quiet voice—a voice that was exactly that hushed whisper of a nature high priest—he explained what he had been doing (though I hadn't asked).

"I went down to the beaver dam to pay homage," he said solemnly. "I offered up some wood chippings from my home dam back out west."

I couldn't think of the proper way to respond, though it occurred to me that a line from *Annie Hall* might work: "Excuse me, but I'm due back on planet Earth."

Since then I have often retold this story, and when I do the point is how damn seriously nature folk take themselves, how bereft of humor. The story usually gets a laugh, but lately I've come to realize that I'm not being entirely honest when I tell it. Because if I think that this writer's behavior is a little ridiculous, I also admire it. And if I'm ready to mock his offering of sacred chips, I'm just as apt to run out to the bluff and uncover the rocks where I have hidden my coyote bones, taking shamanistic pleasure in fingering my canine stash. In other words, as quick as I was to mock nature mysticism, I am quicker to embrace it. Because the truth is that if you develop a deep relationship with a specific place, you almost can't help conjuring up strange, deep, and, yes, nearly mystical emotions.

So I was—and remain—a big hypocrite. And this extends to my reading, too. If I found, and still find, a lot of nature writing to be pompously earnest and a lot of it to be boringly scientific, it is also says things to me—and excites me—in ways no other type of writing can. So, the truth: far from being sick of nature, I find it the most reliably inspiring part of my life.

Which I hope comes through in the accompanying essay. I tried to write it in a way that reflected these complicated feelings toward my career, my art, and most of all, my place. I guess this is most obvious in the way that nature keeps breaking up through the grid of the essay's argument. The way that, on the way to writing a polemic against the genre, a nature essay broke out.

Sick of Nature

I am sick of nature. Sick of trees, sick of birds, sick of the ocean. It's been almost four years now, four years of sitting quietly in my study and sipping tea and contemplating the migratory patterns of the semipalmated plover. Four years of writing essays praised as "quiet" by quiet magazines. Four years of having neighborhood children ask their fathers why the man down the street comes to the post office dressed in his pajamas ("Doesn't he work, Daddy?") or having those same fathers wonder why, when the man actually does dress, he dons the eccentric costume of an English bird-watcher, complete with binoculars. Four years of being constrained by the gentle straightjacket of genre; that is, four years of writing about the world without being able to say the word *shit*. (While talking a lot of scat.) And let's not forget four years of being the official "nature guy" among my circle of friends. Of going on walks and having them pick up every leaf and newt and turd and asking, "What's this?" and, when I (defenseless unless armed with my field guides and even then a bumbler) admit I don't know, having to shrug and watch the sinking disappointment in their eyes.

Worse still, it's been four years of living within a genre that, for all its wonder and beauty, can be a little like going to Sunday school. A strange Sunday school where I alternate between sitting in the pews (reading nature) and standing at the pulpit (writing nature). And not only do I preach from my pulpit, I preach to the converted. After all, who reads nature books? Fellow nature lovers who already believe that the land shouldn't be destroyed. Meanwhile, my more hardnosed and sensible neighbors on Cape Cod are concerned with more hardnosed and sensible reading material (*People, Time, Playboy*—not a quiet magazine in the house), when occasionally resting from the happy exertion of gobbling up what's left of our neighborhood, selling and subdividing. Being honest (one of the nature writer's supposed virtues), I have to admit that an essay is a much less effective way of protecting the land than a cudgel. In other words, I have to admit to impotence.

Which isn't much fun. Today, the morning after yet another legislative defeat for conservation on Cape Cod, I find myself feeling particularly pessimistic about the possibility of affecting change. The land bank, which marked my first minor foray into volunteer politics, was a modest and sensible proposal for putting aside some money to spare the remaining undeveloped land on the Cape, a still beautiful place that's quickly going the way of the Jersey Shore. But because that money would come from the profits of the sellers of real estate (1 percent on sales over $100,000), conservatives (is there a more tediously ironic word in the language?) decided the time was ripe for another Boston Tea Party. The real issue was that developers and realtors and builders wanted to keep on developing and realting and building, but of course they couldn't come right out and say that. So, they pooled a big pile of money and called in a big telemarketing firm from Washington that proceeded to reframe the debate entirely in terms of that highly original catchphrase "no new taxes" (while also, just for the fun of it, scaring the bejeezus out of the Cape's substantial elderly population).

The standard response to this unfairness of things is to curse and wave our little fists at the wicked telemarketers, but today I have a different reaction. I marvel at their effectiveness. Had the pro–land bank forces called in a team of essayists, what would we have done to help? Assembled, we'd have looked like a reunion of Unabombers: solitary, hollow-eyed, scraggly bearded characters ranting against progress. Likely, our strategy would have been to abandon the phone lines and take to the beaches to wander, alone and aimless, in search of terns and profundities. Not only that, but had we somehow—despite ourselves—won, the victory party wouldn't exactly have been a barrel of laughs. You can bet you wouldn't find a single lampshade-wearing party guy in the group.

Which is part of the problem, or, at least, part of my current problem. Throw an imaginary kegger and fill the room with nature writers throughout history and you'll get the idea. Henry Beston, looking dapper if overdressed, alternates tentative taco dabs at the cheese dip with Aldo Leopold; Barry Lopez sits in the corner whispering to Thoreau about the sacredness of beaver dams; Joseph Wood Krutch stands by the punchbowl and tells Rachel Carson the story of how he first came to the desert as Carson listens earnestly. In fact, everything is done earnestly; the air reeks with earnestness. As usual with this crowd, there's a whole lot of *listening* and *observing* going on, not a lot of merriment. Writers from earlier times drift off alone to scribble notes, modern ones talk into microcassette recorders. You might think Ed Abbey could spark the party to life, but until the booze-to-blood ratio rises, he remains painfully shy. Everyone else merely sips their drinks; buffoonery is in short supply; no one tells bawdy anecdotes. In short, the party is a dud.

Perhaps in real life these writers wouldn't restrict their discussions to the mating habits of the spoonbill roseate (*Ajaia ajaja*). In my present state of mind I'd like to imagine them talking about anything other than nature. Sex maybe. Certainly sex must have played at least a minor role in all their lives, even Thoreau's. Perhaps one reason for the retreat to Walden, unexplored by most critics of American Romanticism, was to have more time and freedom for masturbatory binges. We'll never know. We do know that Thoreau exalted in that most underrated aspect of nature appreciation: pissing outside. "I have watered the red huckleberry, the sand cherry and the nettle tree," he wrote. Hell, maybe Thoreau himself would be just the man to break the ice at my party. "Water is the only drink for the wise man," he said piously, but since I'm imagining, I'll imagine having someone, Abbey maybe, spike his water. Maybe for one night, throwing off his teetotaling ways, he could sing and dance, putting folks at ease by showing that even the great stuffy father figure could tie one on. And with Thoreau—Thoreau of all people, the one they respect the most, their God!—acting the buffoon, the rest of them could let their hair down and start to drink and talk about normal party things like lust or the score of the Celtics' game.

I, a relative neophyte, wouldn't have merited an invitation to the big shindig, but along with the rest of the Corps of Junior Nature Writers, I'd watch Thoreau's wild man antics through the window. And maybe, just maybe,

Henry would stumble out and bullshit with me late at night, and together, just two drunk guys, we could water the sand cherry.

The preceding scenario may suggest that I am losing my grip (on this essay as well as my mind). Maybe so. Not long ago I moved from Colorado to Cape Cod to live in Thoreauvian isolation, and for a while I was convinced solitude was driving me insane. (I'll admit that, unlike Thoreau, I had a wife with me, but we still felt isolated together.) Since coming back, I have been a literary Euell Gibbons, subsisting on a diet of pure nature reading as well as writing. Assuming the mantle of genre, I began my adventure determined to deepen my connection to the natural world, inscribing the front of my journal with Henry Beston's words: "A year in outer nature is the accomplishment of a tremendous ritual." But at some point I cracked. I started writing pieces like this one, tossing aside the stagecraft of birds and bugs and beaches and focusing on what I really cared about—me. Usually I rate about an 8.3 on the narcissism scale, but suddenly, finding myself with long hours to contemplate an empty beach and my own deep thoughts, my rating shot off the charts. Working at a job in the city, it's easy to dream of the rustic life, but actually living it entails dangers. It's not just nature that abhors a vacuum. Deprived of its usual gripes, the imagination creates elaborate dissatisfactions and paints masterpieces of hypochondria. There's a reason Cape Cod, our seaside paradise, has such high suicide and alcoholism rates. Though it isn't fashionable to admit, I wouldn't have made it through the fall without television ("Our only friend," my wife called it). As the sages have long reminded us, when we get away from it all, we still bring our minds along.

As I turned inward, I forgot about the beautiful world outside. Nature became, if not a malevolent presence, at least an irritating one. Gulls shat on my back deck, raccoons rummaged through the trash cans, and the powder post beetles (close cousin to the termite) drilled into the beams day and night with a sharp *tcckk tcckk tcckk* noise that made me feel as if they were burrowing into the meat of my temples. And then, suddenly, I realized that I hated nature, or at least hated writing about it in a quiet and reasonable way. Why? Because the whole enterprise struck me as humorless, which in turn struck me as odd, given that comedy often draws on a strain of wildness. Gary Snyder wrote that those who are comfortable in wilderness are often comfortable in their own subconscious. And it seemed to me that those who are comfortable with the uncertainty of nature should also be comfortable on the same shaky ground of humor. Why was it, then, that so often love of nature seemed to breed earnestness?

And then there was this: with only a couple of obvious exceptions, the modern nature writer is most often praised for his or her "restrained" voice. Restrained as in shackles, it seemed to me. "Quietly subversive" is the phrase usually tossed out by critics when referring to nature writing. Well, while I sit here carving out my quietly subversive prose, the bulldozers down the street at Stone's bluff are loudly subverting the soil. Hollowing out the Cape just as the beetles hollow out our beams.

But I'm not telling the full story (which in this case is a crime since what this essay is really about is the frustration of not telling the full story). When we choose to do a thing, we in effect choose not to do many other things. The same with genre. As I complain about my previous genre's restrictions, I find myself bristling at my present constraints (those of the curmudgeonly personal essayist). Yes, Cape Cod can sometimes seem as desolate as Siberia, and, yes, the sound of hammers banging is never far off, and, yes, there have been plenty of times when, sitting in my cold room listening to the beetles *tcckk tcckk tcckk*-ing I longed for an escape from this drear peninsula. But something else has also happened. After my crack-up in early fall I actually began to settle in. As the year sprawled on, moving slowly, ambling like no year I'd known before, I, despite myself, began to remember some not unpleasant things about Cape Cod. Like October. A month when the tourists finally packed up and cleared out for good. A month when the full moon rose over the pink-blue pastel of the harbor sunset and the blue-gray juniper berries shone with chalky iridescence at dusk, and when masses of speckle-bellied starlings filled the trees (and the air with their squeaky-wheeled sounds). A month when the ocean vacillated between the foreboding slate gray of November and a summery, almost tropical blue (while occasionally hinting at its darker winter shades). Most of all, a month of color, a month when the entire neck caught fire in a hundred shades of red.

And though this is not what I intended to write about, these memories lead to other memories of the fall (a time that's becoming more romantic with each retrospective second). Like the first husky wisps of woodsmoke rising from my neighbor's chimneys or the time I saw the seals playing tag between the offshore rocks or the haze of wood dust in the sunlight as I stacked the logs against the side of the house, fortifying us for winter, or the time I kayaked into the marsh and, sliding in through the channels, low and quiet, caught the great blue heron off guard and watched it walk across the spartina with its funky seventies TV pimp strut, head bobbing forward and back . . .

But there, you see. I'm going off again. Like heroin or nicotine, the nature habit's hard to break. I could, without much prodding, turn this essay into a paean to the beauty of the past year on Cape Cod, on how the year has been a deepening, a wedging into the physical world, a slowing down. If that was my story, then I would, of necessity, edit out certain details (like any mention of those sustained periods when I was sure that the beetles were sending messages to me through the phone lines). It wouldn't be so much lying to exclude these, as much as it would be a genre choice. The sort of choice we make semiconsciously almost any time we open our mouths.

And maybe what I'm sick of isn't the birds and trees and beach or even writing about the birds and trees and beach. Maybe what I'm really sick of is making the same choice over and over again. Of being one thing. Of constraint. Maybe I'm rebelling against my too-safe self. Rebelling against the formulaic in me, the way we squirm uneasily at a too-pat Hollywood movie.

But I'm the one calling the shots, after all, so why keep calling the same shot? Much has been written about the modern tendency toward specialization, and I won't add another long-winded celebration of the amateur. But it is true that from a young age Americans are taught that there's nothing like success and that the way to really succeed is to do one thing well. Having spent a half-dozen years out West, I can say this is particularly true of New Englanders. We proudly celebrate our uptightness. Our heroes as a rule are monomaniacally devoted—Larry Bird, John Irving, Ahab—and whether these heroes focus on basketball, novels, or whales, they are praised for directing their energy toward one thing without wasting time on diversions. But as the good Captain illustrates, this isn't always the surest road to mental health. In my case focusing on one thing (even a thing as seemingly benign as nature writing) was an invitation to those beetles to crawl into my skull.

It is now the middle of February on Cape Cod, a time that I dreaded during the melancholy of late November. The odd thing is that I really am settling in, really starting to enjoy it here. Winter insists on its own pace, dispensing with ambition, and when I do write, I turn to whatever takes my fancy. Specialists may bring home more bacon in our society, but the impulse to variety is healthy, even thrilling. To pursue only one thing eventually grinds down to a grumbling feeling of work and obligation.

In that spirit I have been undergoing a sects change operation, switching genres rather than gender. To support myself I work for half the week as a substitute teacher, and when I go into school the real teachers always greet me with the same question. Wondering which of their peers I'm subbing for, they ask, "Who are you today?" I like the question and have written it down and taped it over my computer. Each day I strive to be a different who. If I feel like writing a haiku about the chickadees at the feeder, that's okay, but if I feel like creating a story about lying naked in a lawn chair, drunk, and blasting the chickadees with a scattergun, that's okay, too. These days I write as I please. To use a simile that would be scorned by my fellow nature writers, it's like watching TV with your thumb on the remote, a hundred channels at your disposal (and, honestly, how long do you ever really rest on the nature shows?—one good chase and kill by the lion and, click, it's off to *Baywatch*). Or to turn to a simile the nature writing Gestapo might like better, the health of the individual, as well as the ecosystem, is in diversity.

"A change is as good as a rest," said Churchill, and I do feel rested these days, jumping from genre to genre. Letting different voices fight it out inside me, I'm ignited by the spark of variety. Tabernash, our adopted stray cat, is never more cuddly than right after he's killed something. The thing that the confirmed specialist neglects is the incredible stores of energy that remain in other parts of us once one part is depleted. Though heretical, it could be suggested that variety isn't only more fun, it's more efficient.

I have already mentioned Ed Abbey (note to New Yorkers: not Edward Albee), and it is thanks in part to his consistent irreverence that I've always been a big fan. One thing a nature essay isn't supposed to be is funny. Or sexual. In this regard I remain a fan of Abbey's, who insisted on constantly broadening the nature corral. Abbey fought against the nature label long before I did, lamenting, "I am not a naturalist," and complaining that what others called nature books were really volumes of personal history, and he has been a kind of patron saint for my own efforts to break free. In his introduction to *Abbey's Road* he complained that critics are always calling some nature writer or other the "Thoreau" of this or that place. He wrote of nature writing that it "should be a broader and happier field" and that, "like vacuum cleaner salesmen, we scramble for exclusive territory on this oversold, swarming, shriveling planet." It's only gotten worse in the years since Abbey's death: as the world grows more crowded, our fiefdoms shrink. Ten years ago Cape Cod had only two living Thoreaus: Robert Finch and John Hay. Now there are a dozen more of us, scrambling and clawing for the remaining turf, happy to be called the Thoreau of East Harwich or the Thoreau of Dennisport. No less than the developers we revile, we try to make a living off the land and scenery, and so it's necessary to subdivide and develop new areas. And it's not only our plots of land that are smaller. Step right up and observe that freakish character—The Incredible Shrinking Nature Writer. If you drew us to scale and made Thoreau a giant, and placed Leopold and Carson at about his shoulder, you could keep drawing us smaller and smaller until you sketched in me and my crop of peers at insect size. It may be, as some suggest, that our time marks a renaissance of nature writing. But it's a renaissance of ants.

Fear has always led to the taming of diversity and wildness, and, in writing as in so many other professions in this increasingly crowded and competitive world, fear breeds specialization. With more and more of us competing for the same food source, it's wise to stick to one genre and to the specific rules of that genre. It makes you identifiable. Marketable. Commodifiable. After all, we don't want to buy Lemon Pledge once and find out it works—"Boy, this stuff can really clean!"—only to buy it again and discover it's transformed itself into an underarm deodorant. That wouldn't be convenient. Or neat. And neatness counts, now more than ever.

So, maybe it's neatness I'm really sick of. A born slob, I admire writers who jump from genre to genre, breakout artists not content to stay in one pasture for long. But I better watch myself: the genre border guards never rest. When I first moved back East, the Cape Cod Museum of Natural History refused to keep my book in stock or let me speak there, apparently fearing both fart jokes and activism. "We really only carry nature books," the manager of the bookstore told me, to which I replied, for once, that mine was a nature book—it even said so on the back cover. "It's really more of a personal narrative, isn't it?" the manager asked in a scolding voice. Particularly damning, it seems, is the fact that some reviewers have used the word *funny* to describe the book.

You don't want to do anything as drastic or volatile as mixing humor with nature; that wouldn't be proper, wouldn't be safe. When I speak to someone else about giving a talk, she tells me, "We only deal with nature here, and we don't want anything political," as if in this day and age, the two could possibly be peeled apart.

For my part I'll take writing that spills sloppily over genre walls, always expanding its borders. We all pay lip service to Whitman and his famous "contradictions," but it's not all that common to see writers contradicting themselves on the page. "My moods hate each other," wrote Emerson. Amen. I love to see Thoreau overcome by an urge to strangle a woodchuck or Abbey take a break from celebrating the stark beauty of the desert to throw a rock at a rabbit or Annie Dillard admitting she wrote of the beauties of nature while locked in her windowless, cinder block study. I admire Rick Bass, for instance, when he interrupts an essay to practically grab readers by the collar and insist that they write their congressman and also admire him for the way his "nature writing" has permeated his fiction. Another writer I admire, Reg Saner, has warned me not to make the natural world a stage for merely personal drama, and these are wise words. He points out that Emerson's little book got this whole mess started. "The trouble with *Nature*," Reg said, "is that there's very little actual nature in it. No rocks or trees or birds." But I like Emerson's self-contradictory title. And I want nature to occasionally act as a stage, as long as it's not only and always that. For instance, I want novels—where personal drama is imperative—set deeply in nature. After all, to write about humans is to naturally write about the things that matter in their world: weather, wind, plants, trees, animals, and water.

But today I want to make a plea not for wilderness but for wildness. For freedom. For sloppiness. For the exhilaration of breaking down the Berlin Wall of genre. A plea for amateurism, variety, danger, spontaneity, and honesty in a world growing increasingly professional, specialized, safe, prepackaged, partitioned, and phony. As novels are set more and more often in lands walled by style and concrete, it has been up to today's nonfiction writers to usurp the themes that have concerned us since the great Romantics, reminding us that writing isn't some impotent, inert thing unrelated to actual life and that stories don't have to all end with some subtle *New Yorker* flicker of hair that subtly signals something few of us get. On the other hand, there's no reason these larger concerns can't be reinvested in fiction, no reason other than prevailing fashion. We have all seen the damage done by the contemporary mania for partitioning. If nature writing is to prove worthy of a new, nobler name, it must become less genteel, and it must expand considerably. It's time to take down the NO TRESPASSING signs. Time for a radical cross-pollination of genres. Why not let farce occasionally bully its way into the nature essay? Or tragedy? Or sex? How about painting and words combined to simulate immersion in the natural world? How about some retrograde essayist who suddenly breaks into verse like the old-timers? How about some African American nature writers? (There are currently more black players in the NHL than in the Nature Writing League.) How about somebody other than Abbey who will admit to drinking in nature? (As if most of us don't tote booze as well as binoculars into the backcountry.) And how about a nature writer who actually seems to have a job? (Almost all seem to be men of leisure, often white guys from Harvard.)

Of course, genres help critics box things (and not incidentally allow us to write), but breaking through genres can be as exhilarating and dangerous as waves crashing over a seawall. And that's where the action is today, when writing spills and splashes over genre barriers. Not just the fictional techniques of today's creative nonfiction—which is exciting in itself—but letting the material go where it will, even if it's "bad" and misbehaves and trespasses in old man McGinty's fictional backyard (and makes our fictional parents mad). Thorny, uncategorizable writing. Of course, this is nothing new. Revealing myself as an Emersonian recidivist, I say let the pages fit the man.

After all, though it gives critics and marketers fits, it's where things get most fuzzy that they're most interesting. There are always those ready to wield the word *autobiographical* like a club, to claim the current interest in memoir signals the end of civilization, but the overlapping of fiction and nonfiction is ultimately freeing. "Consider Philip Roth's *The Facts*—which isn't the facts at all," wrote Wallace Stegner. "*The Facts* is as surely a novel posing as an autobiography as *Zuckerman Unbound* is an autobiography masquerading as a novel." Or as the writer Luis Urrea said: "I tell the truth in my novels and make things up in my non-fiction." Genre confusion, like gender confusion, is disconcerting, but it's overall a happy development, a sign of play and freedom. As Stegner says, it doesn't matter if it's autobiography. It matters if it's art.

But it's time to reel myself in.

I'm willing to write manifestos, but I'd prefer having others act them out. For all my declarations of freedom I, too, am constrained. If genre were an invisible dog fence, I'd have already been jolted by several zaps and would have retreated meekly. So, here comes the traditional twist and summary that marks the end of a personal essay. Of course, I'm not sick of nature at all. Just sick of being boxed in and of the genre itself being too narrowly boxed. In fact, having declared myself done with nature, I suddenly feel the itch of the contrary. Hell, after three days of sitting in the attic typing this too personal essay while listening to an endless loop of the Butthole Surfer's second-to-last album (*Independent Worm Saloon*), I'm ready to get down to the beach and commune with some semipalmated plovers. Maybe even to write about them.

❧ BARBARA HURD

Barbara Hurd is the author of two books of non-
fiction, *Stirring the Mud: On Swamps, Bogs, and
Human Imagination* (2001) and *Entering the Stone:
On Caves and Feeling through the Dark* (2003). She
has also published two books of poems, *Objects in
this Mirror* (1994) and *The Singer's Temple* (2003),
winner of the Bright Hill Press Poetry Book Award.
A past recipient of the NEA Fellowship in Creative
Nonfiction, her writing has won both the Pushcart
Prize and the Sierra Club National Nature Writing
Award and has appeared in *Best American Essays*
as well as in such journals at the *Georgia Review*,
the *Yale Review*, *Orion*, and *Audubon*. She teaches
at Frostburg State University in Maryland and the
Stonecoast MFA Program in Creative Writing of the
University of Southern Maine. "Derichment" is
taken from *Entering the Stone*.

Tipping the Balance

I don't love caves. I never have and probably never will. I don't hate them, either. That I wrote a whole book about caves is a sign not of my passion for them but of my keen interest in what happens to my mind and body when I'm in one. *Entering the Stone* (from which "Derichment" is taken) is a book that arose as a necessary reconfiguring of my response—both mental and physical—to a particular place. I found, in fact, I could not write about the cave without first relearning some things about the body, a relearning that seemed for a while a sufficient impulse for writing. In the end, though, what shaped the book was not my wish to understand my own underground fears but my desire to write the kind of sentences that would help me *make* something of that fear.

The first time I went into a cave, twelve years ago, I had the good fortune of experiencing terror. I'd been teaching creative writing to a group of middle school students at an Outdoor Environmental Camp. The students were scheduled to take a field trip into a nearby cave, and I thought the experience might lead them to interesting writing. I primed them beforehand, talked about caves, the mythologies and kinds of creatures that live in them, and how they were formed. Ultimately, I got so interested I asked the trip leaders if I could tag along. But my own reaction was utterly different from that of my students. They loved the whole ordeal, beginning with squirming on their bellies through a tight entrance, while I had, within ten feet, a complete panic attack that sent me scurrying backwards on hands and knees in a fast, rear-first retreat.

I'm not claustrophobic and not usually afraid of the dark, so that unexpected fear haunted me for a while and finally, mostly, receded. Ten years passed, and then one evening I happened upon some exquisite photographs of Lechuguilla Cave in New Mexico and felt my body tighten again, my heart begin to lurch. Finally, that conflation of terror and beauty became a question too interesting not to pursue: what must the body learn in order to find its way in that particular dark?

It seemed a question I could only attempt to answer underground. I found a couple of guides willing to take me in, able to talk me through the panic and launch me into several years of caving that took me all over the country. During it all I watched how my body moved, how my mind moved, how finally the cave itself became a combination restraining order and stony choreographer dictating the steps that, if followed well, meant at most a few bruises or, if ignored, meant more moments of fear.

To write about a cave meant I could not disregard the limitations of the body. You're inside a rock where ledges, crevices, low ceilings, tight passages, and perpetual darkness all dictate careful squirming, a deliberate bending and crawling. Nothing happens fast in a cave; the body begins to step and twist as in a slow-motion game of hopscotch. You have to concentrate on the placement of each foot and finger. In contrast to the way a lagoon can lull you into a disembodied float, the cave drives you back into your body, will not let you forget how easily you break and bruise.

The body's limitations are what ultimately kill us—an obvious conclusion made even more palpably personal by the fact that both my father and childhood friend were dying as I was writing the book. Perhaps it was watching their bodies weaken and thin, their skin grow pale, during months I was intensively caving that heightened my need for the comforts of physical rhythms. Underground, I learned to move by watching others in my headlamp. I mimicked their reaches and climbs. I thought at first that following their deliberate placement of feet and hands was efficient and safe: if the experts right in front of me were figuring out the best maneuvers, then all I needed to do was duplicate them. I soon found, however, that such step-by-step imitation was more than efficient and safe; it was rhythmically comforting. I sometimes even matched my crawling to theirs, our right knees moving forward at the same time, then our left, in a below-ground synchronicity that helped me feel more like a cog in a larger wheel that would take me safely through. In the dark the body in rhythm with other bodies can soothe, help ease the angst, keep one pushing down a passageway until one begins to trust better one's own flesh and bones.

While the cave certainly provided me with concrete ways of thinking about navigating through the unknown, it also helped me to see how so much of what matters underground has its correlations on the page—those word-holds, sentence textures, cliffs to scale at the end of a sentence, the intimacy with language that might lead to what's hidden.

Another correlation: willingness to head into the unknown. There's an expression cavers use—"Does it go?"—meaning does the opening go anywhere, or are you crawling in the dark toward some dank wall and dead end? How many writers haven't asked themselves that question many times? And the answer is often the same on the page as it is in the cave: there's no way to tell until you head in, stay with it for as long as you can. Even when the passage seems to dead-end, of course, there's a chance that what looks like a wall conceals a small crevice, a tight passage to a larger room. No way to know without placing yourself there.

But it wasn't only physical movement and its compositional analogies that the cave seemed to choreograph for me; it was also the mental flexibility of swinging back and forth between the too imaginative and too rational. Without that flexibility the consequences were immediate: too much musing meant fear and the frantic need to thrash my way out; too much fact meant a lessening of felt experience—the cave as simply an ecosystem that plenty of others have written about. Neither extreme would allow me to write the kind of book that interested me. The dilemma became, then, how—for the sake of physical and mental safety—to stay literal while at the same time to find a way to make something of that mysterious world?

At some point I learned when I was underground to study, for example, a ceiling studded with stalactites for several minutes before I'd allow a few seconds of thinking how bony my friend's shoulders seemed last week. Later, an hour or so with a caver good on hydrology in exchange for a half-hour alone, flashlight off, wondering about the origins of certain mythologies. Back and forth between a mind too full of Poe's stories of being buried alive and a focus too proscribed by the stone and mud just inches from my nose. In such a way

I learned to resolve the dilemma, not by maintaining a static equilibrium but by growing accustomed to the seesawing of fear and curiosity.

The way I ended up writing the book itself was similar, meaning I learned to work back and forth between the psychological and the natural history. When I struggled with shifts among biology, mythologies, and the grief of my father's and friend's deaths, I'd recall the advice of my first caving guide: "Three points of contact," she kept telling me. "Always have three parts of your body—two feet and a hand or a foot, a hand, a hip—in contact with the cave." Less than that, you risk falling. More, you're immobile. It's a book with three foci, I realized—the body in the natural world, the mythological, and the personal. When the movement among those three was off, I risked dull paralysis or its opposite: fast-exit. When the movement was graceful, I could keep going underground, which meant I could keep going on the page, speculating about beauty and death, intimacy and derichment.

It was that tension between the literal and the metaphorical that, for a long time, was the biggest challenge in writing the book. Balance was not, however, the ultimate concern. Aesthetics were—finding the best word, orchestrating the rise and fall of sentences, arranging sounds and rhythms. Just as to be sloppy in a cave is to risk falling or damaging ancient formations, to be sloppy on the page is to risk an insight's evaporating in mid-sentence. For most writers discoveries are elusive and more likely to stay that way unless meticulously chosen words and graceful phrasing converge in a sentence that might get closer to saying what's more true. I learned that getting through a cave sometimes meant finding the body's rhythm—the heft and stretch of arms and legs, matching one's pace to the guide in front—and that, similarly, moving through a paragraph requires a similar attention to rhythm. The act of writing a good sentence becomes the actual way you get somewhere. The sentence itself propels you toward—what? the subject? the better metaphor? Maybe. But more often, simply the next sentence. Whether the sentence marches along or sashays or sidles, whether it's tightly wound or languid, imperative or interrogatory, it's through a concern for rhythm—syntax, sound, texture, and speed—that the writer finds out whether the passage does or doesn't "go."

Though my appreciation of caves' complexities, beauties, and dangers has certainly grown, writing the book didn't, as I've said, make me love them, and they're probably not a place I'll return to time and again, the way I might to the Maine coast or to an upland bog. But now when I drive around my part of western Maryland or upstate New York, southern Virginia, or when I'm traveling in the southwest or the Oregon mountains, I'm aware that they're down there, caverns twisting and winding out of sight. Even if I haven't been in the one that might be underneath me, I can close my eyes and almost see it, almost relive the experience of moving inside what I once thought of as the unfamiliar, even the impenetrable. Such awareness, of course, is only the beginning of what might eventually become art. The mind alert to rhythms and attentive to aesthetics is what tips the balance away from the adventure itself and toward exploration of it by means of language and form.

Derichment

It is this backwards motion toward the source,
against the stream, that most we see ourselves in.

—Robert Frost

In the deepest-known part of a cave in southern Virginia, I turn off my head-lamp and walk slowly forward, straining my eyes, looking for anything, any shadow, any small fluctuation in the amount of darkness, the shape of black against blacker. My right foot bangs against a small rock; my right arm swings out, finds the wet wall, and steadies me. I stand still for a moment, trying to see something, anything. Nothing. Because I'd told her I wanted to see how it was in the dark by myself, Jenny, the guide I'd hired, has left me here, swung the strap of her bag over her shoulder, and disappeared down some passage-way. I'd heard her feet on the cave floor, not the clicking of heels on tile but the grind and shuffle of boot on gravelly, uneven rock. She'd moved away slowly, cautiously, deliberately, as one must in a cave, the beam of her light bobbing in front of her feet, each step a little more muffled and distant until I couldn't hear her at all and only the invisible drip-drip from the ceiling breaks the absolute silence. It's completely, utterly dark in here.

Maybe for every younger twin, the sound of departure means a little soli-tary room at last. Perhaps for me, those thirteen minutes finally alone in the womb with the chance to uncross my arms and stretch out spindly legs have left me forever interested in the moments just after something large has gone.

Surely I must have felt the stillness—my sister has always been more active, more physically alert and responsive, than I—and maybe some lessening of water-muffled noise, her nearby sloshing in the sac gone, leaving me better able to hear my mother's heartbeat or my own. Did I roll around? Turn upside down? Have a few minutes of dizziness? Does a sudden leaving both sensitize and disorient?

Driving to the airport after my father died, I felt my internal compass go haywire. I got lost, headed west when I should have gone east, missed exits off the interstate, couldn't use the sun to figure out direction. It was as if I had always had him as a north pole, a force to set my compass by, a steady North Star for navigation. Deprived of his voice, his presence, his birthday cards and good wishes, the stories of his adventures, I could not, for weeks, get my bearings.

We use landscape and the people in our lives to orient ourselves. We know which window the morning sun comes through; we know on the East Coast that storms usually arrive from the west; Muslims know where Mecca is, Native Americans where the sun rises; we know what the Saturday paper on the doorstep means, what to do about a certain sullenness in the one we love.

Take all that away. Remove the sun, the east-running rivers, the routines and daily reminders. Put yourself in a chamber of absence, where there's nothing that says aim west, offer an apology, schedule an oil change, remember to bring in more firewood. It's dark and empty, unpopulated, its features invisible. Maybe what I want in this cave is some slow-motion, embodied drama of disorientation and adieu, the chance to study in isolated detail how it feels when almost everything's gone: when your twin's born first, when people leave, when the footsteps stop, when the rain ends.

There's a lot that's absent here: changing weather, sun, rain, visible plant life, clouds, sky, the possibility of horizon. It's the same all over the world—in France, China, New Zealand—you go inside a cave and you know that something major is missing. The indigenous creatures, of course, have had thousands of years to adjust, generation by generation, to what remains after the slow washing out, to the water trickling through tiny cracks, widening, carving, dissolving the limestone, carting it away in subterranean streams. For me, however, used to daylight and green, the absence today is sudden, and I turn my light back on to walk farther down the dank passage. The guide had told me that ahead, off to the side and running parallel to the main passage, is a narrow crevice, small enough to twist your ankle, too small in most places to fall bodily in to. I keep my headlamp aimed in front of my feet and swing my flashlight back and forth across the floor. It bounces off boulders, rock-chunks, the muddy floor, searching out a jagged streak, a gash of darker at the edge of dark. "Listen for it," she'd told me. What did she mean by that? I couldn't imagine the sound a crevice might make. Does it creak, like a stone yawn? The ceiling drips, my feet shuffle; everything else is silent.

I'm trying to understand how the mind works when it's subjected to subtraction and absence. Do we become less flexible or more grounded? Bored by the tedium of deletion or less moody? delusional or less superficial? The cave itself is an argument against the claim that growth requires variety and accumulation. It doesn't grow by a flurry of new processes or added weight, substance, or multiplying cells. No huge flood, no volcanic eruption, no earthquake. You can count on a limestone cave's existence being the result of millions of years of the exact same process. The cave is about erasure and exodus, the humdrum routine of taking away. The rain drips through bedrock, dissolves a bit of stone, dissolves a little more.

My children's kindergarten was in a new elementary school. The rooms were all bright, the furniture was bright; bright plastic modular units were frequently moved around on sound-absorbent carpeting to change the shape of the classroom space. There were always new things to touch, to manipulate. My daughter learned about plants by growing moss in a terrarium, about air currents by flying kites. My son studied other cultures by crawling inside life-sized teepees and making masks. It was a rich environment, the school all clean and shiny and colorful and stimulating.

They each left that school after kindergarten to attend a four-room schoolhouse way out in the country. Though part of the public school system, it was run by Mennonites who welcomed all kids grades one through eight, including ones, like my own, who weren't attached to any particular faith. The school was old. Its floors were wooden; the desks were old and wooden and scratched. There was a certain spareness to the atmosphere, a few experiments growing on windowsills, but a lot of white walls, brown floor, big windows, wide spills of uninterrupted light.

And books. Lots and lots of books. If you wanted to learn about other cultures, you read about them in books. About science and math and history, books. Reading was the one steady, repeated, reliable method of teaching and learning. A lot of silent reading periods, a lot of being read to aloud. In subject after subject, written language was the medium. It streamed into their heads, carved patterns in their brains, deepened the neural pathways of language acquisition. The children in the school might not have been whizzes at the video arcade or computer games. The school was, in fact, an argument against excessive variety, against the belief that children learn best in an active, animated atmosphere of constantly changing stimuli.

I suspect what the school did was to teach them to deepen their attention. They learned how it felt not to have various stimuli competing for attention. They learned to bring the whole mind to the task at hand. How to concentrate their mental powers on the one task that required it. I see the lack of this ability in so many of my students today. They want to bring all kinds of rip-rap into their writing, everything that happened to them one night in a bar, in a bed, at the family reunion. Fine, for an early draft, I tell them. But before they bring it to class I want them to pay close attention to what's really going on in the writing. What's the underlying thread? What *doesn't* belong? What's between the noisier lines? What can we not quite hear? Used to handling so many stimuli at once, they struggle to slow the juggling, even to know the value and reward of zeroing in on one subtle idea. I want to bring them into a cave, set them up in a small cranny for a few weeks, get them used to listening to less noise, get them used to focusing their attention.

If they stayed long enough, generation after generation, they'd grow accustomed to the dark. They wouldn't, like nocturnal animals, develop keener eyesight for nighttime hunting. They'd lose it. Their eyes would shrink, atrophy. Their optic nerve would lie in their heads, useless, like an appendix. And then their pigment would go. Their skin, all that honey-colored, coffee, pearly flesh they so love to show off in tank tops and shorts, would fade, grow pallid, blanched. Their shells would thin, their defenses grow delicate. I imagine them, Chad and Danielle and the others, curled with their notebooks in the nooks my headlamp is darting in and out of. I imagine visiting them there, consulting, advising, and departing. They'd feel all this as loss, of course, their world diminished. I wonder what kind of poems they'd offer in exchange.

A few minutes later I hear something, some movement in the stillness. Something low, muffled, but definitely there, and I stumble a little faster, following the noise, until the beam of my flashlight arcs over an edge, a long, scraggy brink. The crevice isn't wide, maybe three feet at the top, but deep. My light finds the bottom and the source of the noise: sixty or seventy feet below, a small stream flows. It's narrow, maybe a foot wide, a few inches deep, though it's hard to tell, flowing down there in the skinny dark.

Hard to tell, too, what's living down there and therefore easy to imagine the need to mythologize. In the seventeenth-century, for example, the people of Slovenia scooped up white, lizard-like creatures from the waters that flowed from nearby caves and believed they were holding the larvae of dragons in their hands. It took years for the stories of cave monsters to settle into the fact of eyeless, albino salamanders, and in this country it wasn't until the mid-1850s that speleobiologists—cave biologists—began to study the adaptations of troglobites—creatures that spend their whole lives in the darkness of a cave. Troglobites have no choice about this; they cannot survive in the sunlit world. They cannot even manage the twilight zone. They need total, constant dark. And they've needed it for generations, been resolute in their avoidance of light, even as their eyes deteriorated, their shells thinned, their bodies gave up what didn't matter anymore in the dark.

The process of loss differs from one species to another. The cave fish *Typhlichthys*, for example, still has remnants of an eye lens but no muscle to move it. The *Amblyopisi* has remnants of eye muscle but no lens and, hence, nothing for the muscle to move. The Ozark blind salamander is actually born with small eyes, but its eyelids soon shut and fuse together. What's trapped beneath may twitch and bulge for a while but will soon give up, begin to shrink. Most likely, generations from now, those short-lived larval eyes will have deteriorated to the point that the embryo no longer develops even them. Some troglobite brains have changed shape, and cave beetles don't even have optic nerves anymore.

Cave-dwelling creatures lose more than eyesight. They lose their thick shells, and they lose their pigment. Above-ground creatures produce shells and pigment as protective strategy. Armor protects not only against other creatures but also against cold and rain, the normal fluctuations of weather. Darker coloring blends in with rocks, mud, tree bark, and underbrush and makes prey less visible to predator. To produce chitin and pigment requires energy, a necessary expenditure in the above-ground, clawed and bitten world, and so the animal world responds in its feathered, scaly, furred, stippled, spotted, hued, and shadowed way.

Heavy protection from unstable weather, however, is irrelevant inside the cave. And camouflage is useless in an environment where nobody can see anybody anyway, and so most troglobites don't waste their energy. Their shells are thin, and most creatures are born pale, even translucent, and spend their whole lives as albinos on dark stone walls, in black underground rivers. The cave crayfish is pearly; the cave fish looks like a cigar-shaped peeled onion with fins. Troglobitic salamanders resemble pale and starving four-legged slugs, while millipedes are as white as the early shoots of nasturtiums unburied in spring gardens.

I confess they're creepy. It's more than their ghostliness. More than the remembered fear of an albino child in our neighborhood when we were young, her pale lashes and other-worldliness, the way she looked too delicate to ride on a school bus and did anyway. It's knowing that their delicacy helps them survive in an environment that would kill a human, that they can, in fact, use their faint ways to outcompete a sighted, thick-skinned competitor for food. I'm used to the merits of heartiness, robustness. If I were looking for a mate, evolutionary biologists tell me, I'd be looking for good size and color, both indicators of health and the ability to protect our offspring. If I had children in mind, I'm less likely to choose a blind male with thin skin, someone inclined to spend his days indoors with the shades drawn. And yet, developing those same qualities—that is, losing the normal indicators of vigor—is what enables the cave-dwellers to survive. They are, in their blind, below-ground world, the contradiction to those accustomed to succeeding in the unstable, fiercely competitive world above ground.

Cave-dwellers compensate for their lack of vision by enhancing their feeling receptors. They grow longer, touch-sensitive antennae. They sprout shorter, chemo-sensitive antennae. On their heads cave fish develop four times the number of sense organs—called neuromasts—as their above-ground counterparts do. And those four-times-as-many organs are all more than twice as sensitive, enabling a blind cave fish to sense a water flea at three times the distance its sighted counterpart can. Troglobites have larger odor sensors, better balance mechanisms, larger vibration receptors in their brains.

In a world without sun, sky, rain, eyeballs, thick skins, and pigment, how do they survive? By knowing what they feel, by a heightened sense of touch. Staying alive in a cave means listening to your skin. Eyesight doesn't help, nor does the brilliance of your plumage, the swell of your chest, whether you can make your throat blush and balloon with mating-croaks. Camouflage means nothing. Nobody who lives here can see a thing. If you stay long enough, you drop it all, the excesses, the decorations, the visible markings we animals use to advertise our potential as mates or to evade our enemies. You grow pale, almost translucent. Loss, in other words, can enhance your sensitivity, make your insides more apparent.

In the troglobitic world it takes thousands of years. After the initial retreat to a cave, a species' devolution is slow, gradual, a gene here, a gene there. It took millions of generations for crayfish to lose their eyes and lengthen their antennae. Who knows how many perished in the first stages of the experiment, unable to see in the dark, unequipped yet with compensatory feelers, starving while some eight-legged meal crept nearby? Or, early on, how many suffered from the too-sudden effects of sensory deprivation, the absence of light, rain, sky. If you take a young rat, a mostly nocturnal creature, and whack off its whiskers, it's unable, as an adult, to master certain learning tasks. It can't compensate for the lack of information its whiskers would normally transmit. If you catch an adult mole, accustomed to life in the dirt, and snip its whiskers off, it becomes not only learning-impaired but neurotic. If you take a human and put him in a sensory deprivation chamber, he's prone to hallucinations and odd behaviors. I knew a man once who volunteered for such an experiment. The researchers put him on a table in a small room, encased his arms and legs in long cardboard tubes, blindfolded him, put earphones on him that issued a steady stream of white noise, turned off the lights, and left him alone for hours. He lay quietly at first, wishing he hadn't been out drinking the night before. And then as the deprivation lengthened, he began to resist it. At first he tried lifting his long cardboard arms and banging them together. Then his legs. Then arm to leg, leg to arm, until nothing seemed enough and small dots of light started to appear. Other subjects reported squiggles, a line of dogs, a procession of open mouths. The speculation is that the brain in such a sensory void eventually begins to compensate, to create images where there are none.

This need to fill in a sudden void is what brainwashers count on. After months of solitary confinement with nothing but propaganda to fill in the blanks, the mind gets confused, has trouble sorting out what's real, what's not. Interrogators in prisoner-of-war camps know this, as do cult leaders, maybe even some proponents of prolonged meditation. Reducing external stimuli can produce altered states of consciousness, including visual and auditory illusions, and sometimes feelings of expansiveness, great waves of love and tranquility. Who knows what happened in the small minds of those first cave-dwelling creatures, what kind of hallucinatory compensation they might have experienced?

I think of Emily Dickinson, not blind but pale and delicate, a white-dressed recluse in her room, a woman who seldom left Amherst, increasingly avoided the excesses of ocean, the populations and panoply of nearby Boston, who gradually intensified her austere seclusion and knew every inch of the heart's interior. Every nuance, every side passage and hidden crevice of the emotional underworld, a world she mined for poems so startlingly clear they read like beacons in a once-shrouded landscape.

One afternoon Jeanne lay on her bed and told me everything she didn't do anymore. Some of them were things she couldn't, physically, manage: her career as a statistical expert for the National Science Foundation, travel to China, the weeds in the garden, washing the car. But some things she stopped because she simply didn't wish to do them anymore. She no longer answered her phone, e-mails, letters. She didn't watch television or look through her dozens of fat photo albums. We'd shared a great love of reading all our lives, but on most afternoons now, she told me, she simply lay in bed with the book on her lap. "Do you go back over your life?" I asked. "Think about regrets or good moments?" "Sometimes," she answered. "But more often, even on good days, I just lie here and don't think about anything. I just lie here." She smiled. "I'm just here." I knew she wanted me to understand this, how it feels to know it's time to put things down, to stop. I knew, too, that I couldn't understand that, or I couldn't feel it as she felt it. I did, however, know that I was in the presence of some big thing happening. Being with a woman who has, after a long battle, accepted the fact that her death is imminent made me feel how much I deny mine, made me feel how achingly I want years ahead of me, how naïve and stubborn and defiant I can feel. She was dying, and she felt her end, which she didn't resist anymore. She wasn't bitter, no longer angry. I wanted to talk about junior high school, how Belinda Izzi lit up a cigarette in the school library. Remember that? Or the way Mr. Bell warned us about liking boys too much? I asked her. I want our memories, like a transfusion, to keep our lives going, to keep us alive together, as if a stream of remembered images could somehow get inside her body, dissolve the tumors, leave her rinsed and ready for another twenty years.

She smiled at me. Her body was crowded with cancer and fluids and drugs. Her mind was astonishingly clear. If she wanted anything, it was to give away. "Here," she said, handing me a small jeweled box from Thailand, "take this. And this." She was, it seemed, being rinsed after all. While her body broke down, her mind was somehow growing more uncluttered. Sitting with her, I could almost feel that she'd grown more unjumbled, more smooth, fluid; I could almost sense something untangling itself, running unimpeded now, out of her, away from her. It wasn't that flowing thing that felt so rarified; it was what remained, how the leaving has created in her such thinned, almost pure space. I was sure she must know things now that none of us not face-to-face with our deaths can know. *What?* I wanted to ask her. *Tell me.* But I didn't, couldn't. Probably wouldn't have understood even if she could have answered.

A week later I opened the gate at the entrance of a crevice-cave in New England and stepped into a stream that rushed toward me, eddied around my boots, flowed on behind me, year after year, out of the cave, out of the mountain, that tumbled away, down over its slopes. Even in wool socks, my feet got cold. I walked into the cave against the stream's current, back and back in the dark between high, narrow walls the water had cut over thousands of years. I was walking toward something, I didn't know what. Toward the source of water? There was no source. There was only the knee-deep water that ran in a current and had, some time ago, seeped through from the ground above and, before that, fallen as rain and before that evaporated from the oceans and before that run in riverbeds, in streams, inside caves, maybe had even been in that one before. I walked and walked; the cave became chasm; it twisted and wound, and the walls got narrower; I could stretch out my arms and touch them on both sides. There were few formations, and the stream was still cold.

Monotony is the backdrop of most meditations. You sit on your cushion, and you sit and sit and sit. Nothing happens. You watch your thoughts; you let them go. Monks all over the East have for thousands of years meditated in caves. In 1976 an Englishwoman climbed into a cave in the Himalayas, and for twelve years she mostly sat. She ate rice and lentils, a few vegetables, a bit of bread, a few bites of *tsampa*. She sat and sat, and the cave stayed cold, and the stream stayed cold, but the chasm deepened, and this, I suppose, is what meditation is about. You learn to watch and let go, watch and let go.

No more bullshit, Jeanne says.

A deriched environment? Maybe. Certainly, Jeanne isn't accumulating anymore, materially or physically. She's discarding, letting go, letting things slough off. But she's not turning airy, ethereal, wraithlike. In fact, the more frail her body becomes, the more grounded her mind seems, more able to sort what matters from what doesn't. She grows tired of my need for memories, wants me to just sit and hold her hand. I do this for hours, watching her fade and return. She loves the feel of my fingers on her palm, her thin arms. Her dying doesn't disorient me nor free up a little more room nor offer hope for some new beginning. Part of me feels carried along on her slow, cell-by-cell closing down and flowing out, and part of me has one hand on the stone and clay in a cave that I love, walking farther in, following the stream to its source, hunting albino shrimp, a sightless salamander.

I can hear Jenny's footsteps for a full five minutes before I see her light. She's been exploring some side rooms but wants to take me now to a specific passage in the cavern. I lift my pack to my shoulders, and we walk and walk. The cavern twists and narrows, grows wide, grows low. Sometimes we scramble; sometimes we walk fairly easily. I have no idea where we are. Fifteen minutes later she leads me around a bend and into a side passage, and suddenly my hair, light and curly in the humidity, lifts away from my ears. I look at her in amazement and then turn and face it—what?—directly. Wisps of her hair lift off her neck too. There's a light wind here, deep below the surface, a wind that smells distinctively *old*, meaning, perhaps, that it's been underground a while, like the air in catacombs, mausoleums, underground parking garages with poor ventilation. Jenny grins and shines her flashlight at me, watching the wispy tendrils puff around my head. Then it stops. Then I feel it from behind, as if someone has circled behind me and is breathing down my neck, sending tendrils forward over my ears, surrounding my face like a wimple. "This is a breathing cave," she tells me. A breathing cave? We stand still; in a couple of minutes my hair reverses direction again, lifts away from my forehead now.

We are standing in the entrance of the small passageway, maybe four feet wide. The muddy stone walls lean toward us. Changes in barometric pressure or wind turbulence near the cave's main entrance often cause the air to move even deep inside a cave. Sometimes you barely notice it. Sometimes the right configuration of multiple entrances produces a breeze you can feel lightly on your skin. There are even blowing caves where winds whip out the entrance at forty miles an hour. In a breathing cave, however, air moving across the entrance to a smaller passage, such as the one Jenny and I are standing in, acts the way your breath does if you position your lips just so and blow into a Coke bottle. The movement of air across the bottle's narrow neck produces high-frequency sound waves. You hear the bottle hum. Down here the high volume of air moving across the entrance to this smaller passage produces low-frequency waves, which means no sound, just the periodic flow reversals, oscillations that resemble breathing and lift my hair one way and then the other.

No wonder so many yogis meditated in caves. You can imagine their deep breathing in here, feel the slow, deep inhalations. I remember my Indian guide Sunithi trying to teach me about breath and its relation to wind. Hindus, she explained, have arranged the five elements in hierarchical order. At the bottom is earth, which we can touch, see, hear, taste, and shape. Next up is water, which we can touch, see, hear, taste, but not shape. And then fire, which we can neither touch nor shape. And then wind, which we can only feel; and finally space, which we cannot see, feel, touch, taste, or shape but whose existence we cannot deny. Through fasting, that ancient Eastern practice of nutritional derichment, she explained, one might realize the power of the body and ascend the hierarchy of elements. It is through that ascension, leaving behind earth, water, fire, and concentrating on wind and space, that one might, she said, approach the divine.

With the breath first on my face, then the back of my neck, I don't know much about the divine, unless it's those moments, alone or with another, when defenses crumble and you feel transparent, your interiors exposed, when to inch ahead is not even a matter of vision, when you go on and on, led only by what you feel, and what you feel if you're lucky is some enormous expansiveness, an upswelling and the swoosh of what can drop away, leaving you exposed, every part of your body both alert and permeable, and what you want most, finally, is to give it all away. Here, you say, *take this and this*, and then I don't know if this is how Jeanne feels, dying, or whether when my father died he'd handed over the invisible compass I didn't know how to use on my own, left me disoriented, headed in all the wrong ways. *Take this and this*, and finally I did, I took it, and west settled back into west and east, east, and now I'm interested again in wind, how even my rudimentary understanding of what causes the breathing doesn't erase my sense that the cave *is* breathing and that though I love the mind at work, its theories and tangents, its draw to paradox, I'm interested now in the opposite too: the unadorned, distilled, pared down to what I thought was the core, the thing itself without its layers of hiding and flesh. Peel away the layers and layers of an onion, and what you get down to is something oblong and pearly, not a core, a seed, or a bone that says the beginning but the last layer of succulence, a cluster of veined petals, a nest of opalescence.

The cave breathes. My hair lifts one way and then the other. There's no fire in here, no earth we can shape. No sun, no moon, no green, no day. The beings who live here survive because of how they've adapted to what they've lost. Blind, transparent, they rely on highly tuned receptors. They survive by knowing what they feel. "Touch me," the poet Stanley Kunitz pleads, "remind me who I am." "Hold my hand," Jeanne says again.

In the bottom waters of this cave stream, Jenny confirms, blind, albino shrimp wiggle their way underground. Their shells have thinned over thousands of years, their antennae grown long. All over their backs, their sides, hundreds of small receptors keep their bodies alert. I think of the photograph at home of a troglobitic cave shrimp. It looks like a transparent ghost with many feelers, an oblong made of Saran wrap. Inside it, clearly visible, an orangy mass that must be its brain, maybe its heart.

❧ LISA KNOPP

Lisa Knopp is a widely published essayist whose writing has appeared in such journals as the *Missouri Review*, *Shenandoah*, *Cream City Review*, ISLE, *Michigan Quarterly Review*, and *Creative Nonfiction*. She is the author of a collection of essays, *Field of Vision* (1996), a memoir about growing up in Iowa, *Flight Dreams: A Life in the Midwestern Landscape* (1998), and a collection centered on Nebraska, *The Nature of Home: A Lexicon and Essays* (2002). She is on the faculty of the Master's of Fine Arts in Creative Nonfiction Program at Goucher College in Baltimore, Maryland, and also teaches at the University of Nebraska at Omaha.

Writing "A Salt Marsh Reclamation"

> An environmental value requires its antithesis for definition. . . . "Home" is a mean-
> ingless word apart from "journey" and "foreign country"; claustrophobia implies
> agoraphilia; the virtues of the countryside require their anti-image, the city, for the
> sharpening of focus, and vice versa.
>
> Yi-Fu Tuan, *Topophilia: A Study of Environmental Perception*

When I set out to write about Arbor Lake Salt Marsh, a wildlife area managed by the Nebraska Game and Parks Commission, I didn't know why it was
considered a salt marsh rather than the soggy, neglected field that it appeared
to be. I didn't know what forces had created or maintained it. Nor had I ever
read anyone else's perceptions of this place. But I had heard that an inland salt
marsh is the rarest and most endangered type of natural community on the
Great Plains. That surprised and intrigued me.

A couple of miles south of this rare landscape is its antithesis, an utterly
common, dreary landscape that I know too well: a new commercial strip near
the city limits with a dozen or so big-box retailers, strip malls, car dealerships, motels, apartment complexes, and a flurry of fast-food restaurants. I
knew how to see this place. After all, every Wal-Mart looks like every other
Wal-Mart; every Carlos O'Kelly's looks like every other Carlos O'Kelly's. And
I knew what social and economic forces created and sustained this part of the
city. Even though traffic is always heavy there, and people shop, work, and eat

there all hours of the day and night, most of us see this part of the city as ugly, stressful, and uninhabitable.

Because the contrast between the salt marsh and the nearby commercial strip was so sharp and unsettling, I felt compelled to write about it. But before I wrote, I had to learn to see the marsh. That required collecting information about it from books, magazines, and newspapers as well as from conversations with people who knew something about it. Equally important, I had to collect information in the field by paying close attention.

Since I prefer meeting a place with innocence, before I read anything about Arbor Lake, I spent an early-spring morning there, just strolling and sitting, watching, listening, and loafing. I took my binoculars; Robbins, Bruun, and Zim's *Birds of North America*; and my notebook, in which I recorded the following details:

chocolaty water

LES [Lincoln Electric Service] windmills

huge dragonflies—helicopter-like

low grass side—more birds

crunchy grass

taller cord grass

a bathing grackle—wing snapping

circles of darker grasses (what kind? why in circles?)

sandpipers?—too low down for identifying characteristics

man sitting on ground near boardwalk, drinks from brown bottle

chow dog near house

6–9 black terns, ashen wings, diving surface, basting surface with invisible thread, facing wind, hovering over water, all facing wind, same direction, wings long & slender, swallow-like, forked tails. Like a squeak toy without the second, let-go sound.

fast, white butterfly

yellow-headed blackbirds

sandpipers—are they playing with my binoculars?

meadowlark ch**

tall, segmented, square stem, hollow, grows near sedges

nodes

3-sided stems (sedges?)

mouse skull on ground near sedges

ticks

killdeers

small gray ducks with black necks and white faces (what kind?)

lots of Canada geese

These notes reveal that during my first encounter with the marsh, I was preoccupied with singling out objects, with identifying and naming them. But one notation, "circles of darker grasses (what kind? why in circles?)," suggests a desire to understand patterns and relationships. After this observation I went to the library to discover where salt marshes come from, how they work, what patterns mean, and how people have used and want to use marshes. What I saw at Arbor Lake directed my research; what I learned from books directed my attention at Arbor Lake.

The library part of my research presented a challenge. My search under *inland salt marshes* yielded nothing. When I searched *salt marshes*, I was directed to two books on "tidemarsh ecology." Neither was helpful, since coastal salt marshes are formed and maintained by different processes than inland salt marshes. Next, I searched *wetlands*. This yielded many dozens of books and articles, but since fresh and salt water wetlands host different plant communities, these sources were only marginally useful. Then I tried a smaller category: *halophytes*, plants adapted to growing in salty conditions. The one article I found on this subject was quite specific and contained information that belonged in my essay. But I wasn't yet ready to focus on the small parts. It was the "big picture" I sought.

When I stopped thinking vertically (i.e., larger and smaller categories of biological information) and started thinking laterally (who, other than biologists, are interested in salt marshes?), I found plenty of good information. Nineteenth-century speculators in southeastern Nebraska had attempted to profit from the manufacture of salt. Each failed. But some of these salt boilers and miners left records about those geological features that account for the presence of salt marshes in Lancaster and Saline counties, the quality of the soil, the way the basin looked and smelled, and why it flooded with brine twice a day. When I stopped searching under biological subject headings and started searching under Nebraska history, I saw the big picture. When I returned to Arbor Lake, the past seemed very near.

Some information that I needed was delivered directly to my front door. While I was researching salt marshes off and on during 1999 and 2000, the Nebraska Game and Parks Commission was involved in the long and contentious process of adding saltwort (*Salicornia rubra*), a halophyte, and the Salt Creek Tiger Beetle (*Cicindela nevadica lincolnia*) to Nebraska's list of endangered species. The latter is one of the rarest insects in North America (during the 1990s the total population of this species fluctuated between one hundred and six thousand) and has such a highly restricted range that it basks in the sun and burrows in the sand in no other place in the world but the salt marsh remnants of Lancaster County, Nebraska. Yet because these salt marshes are in areas that are in great demand for new housing subdivisions, the move to extend protection to this species was fought by local house builders. About the same time as the endangered species debate, the Lincoln City Council was considering whether to rezone the land on which a salt marsh was located from agricultural to highway-commercial to accommodate the owner of a car dealership who wanted to build an even larger lot than he presently owned on a salt marsh near the edge of the city. Consequently, numerous articles and letters to the editor appeared in the newspaper about ecologically based development restrictions versus the rights of private property owners, about the long-term effects of protecting the habitat of endangered species versus the long-term effects of tax revenues from new houses and businesses—issues being debated in cities and counties across the country, the only difference being the species and land forms at stake. The different sides in the controversy offered different visions of how the land now covered by salt marshes will look in another five or ten or fifty years. When I returned to Arbor Lake, the future seemed very near.

Research answered my questions about what a salt marsh is, how it functions, and why it matters, ecologically. Yet, too, my absorption in the facts, concepts, and abstractions that I encountered in book, magazines, and newspapers led me to forget that what I was writing about is a *living* organism. To move me out of my head and into my own heartfelt sense of why the salt marsh mattered, I turned to freewriting. I wrote about the salt marsh not while I was there, sitting on the observation deck, but while I was at home at my desk so that I had to rely on memory and emotions as I evoked and reflected upon the essence of the place. I wrote about the grief I felt over the likelihood that in another decade or two, almost all of the salt marshes would be drained and covered with suburban sprawl. I wrote about the joy I felt in the presence of the wind and the birds moving across the grasses and sky. I recorded two dreams I had had about the place: one, a frightening dream about my efforts to find a salt marsh aster in a world covered with asphalt; the other, a crazy, wonderful dream about people dismantling the Cracker Barrel Restaurant at its present site, adjacent to a small, unnamed salt marsh, home to fifty-eight Salt Creek tiger beetles, and carrying it downtown, where they reassembled the restaurant at a new location. As I was writing about these dreams, it occurred to me that the salt marsh had entered my subconscious. When I returned to Arbor Lake, I saw that it was mine.

I face two difficulties when writing about natural places. One is that when I focus entirely on the flora, fauna, weather, water, and landforms, my writing makes for dull reading. To remedy this, I bring people into the essay: a landscape with figures, as Robert Root says. Of course, it is easier to people landscapes that I've known for a long time, especially those in which childhood memories are set. When writing about Flint Creek near Burlington, Iowa, my growing-up place (see "This Creek," *Cimarron Review* 144 [Summer 2003]: 26–37), I wrote about my grandmother, who told me stories about the landowners who lived near the creek, and my mother, who took her biology students there for field trips. I wrote in more detail about my father, who, as a child, spent summer vacations there with his buddies and who, as an adult, took his own children, my brothers and me, to play in the creek. I wrote about hiking the steep, hardwood-covered, cave-studded hills with my son and daughter and nephews. I wrote about how in the 1920s family members of the ecologist and nature writer Aldo Leopold sought to preserve this place, where as a child Aldo had fished, waded, watched birds, caught tadpoles, explored the caves in the limestone bluff, and searched for arrowheads—the very things that my family did at the creek. My problem when writing about such highly charged landscapes as Flint Creek is that they are so layered with human presences and stories that it requires a great act of will for me to see past the people to the flora, fauna, water, wind, soil, rocks, and sky.

Because I hadn't known the salt marsh long enough for it to be layered or embedded with personal stories, I had to invent ways to include people. Again, I turned to books, journals, and newspapers. I wove in the words, ideas, and actions of nineteenth-century salt boilers, a local wetland biologist, a city planner, a city council member, an attorney for the Home Builders Association of Lincoln, nature writers Gary Snyder, Bill McKibben, Aldo Leopold, and others. And I wrote about Rich Weise, Richard Powell, and Sue Kuck, who used their own money to initiate a project to buy a salt marsh, a project that snowballed, gathering financial contributions from local businesses, residents, and developers. Wiese and his partners bought the land, now home to saltwort and Salt Creek tiger beetles, and transferred ownership of it to the Lower Platte South Natural Resources District. Theirs is a good story to tell.

A second problem I encounter when writing about natural places is my tendency to deliver ecological sermons about how we humans can live more harmoniously and respectfully with our nonhuman neighbors by lessening our consumption of material goods and living more simply. Two earlier drafts of "A Salt Marsh Reclamation" reveal my attempts to minimize my didacticism. In one draft, "Wild Dreams: A Salt Marsh Reclamation," I placed more emphasis, as the title states, on dreams—the dreams of salt boilers, the dreams of developers, the dreams of ecologists, the dreams each of us imposes on the land, the two dreams I had about the marsh. In another draft, "Brine," which was more about me than the place, I included a personal story about how the first time I observed at the marsh, I was accompanied by my then eight-year-old daughter, who helped me take notes about what we saw, and a man who called my attention to things I would not have seen if left with my own preoccupations, a man with whom I would part ways in a few months. Both of these approaches, communicating my ecological fears and remedies through dreams and the imposition of personal story onto the terrain, felt contrived. What I really wanted to do was to delve into the current controversies surrounding the salt marshes of Lancaster County, take a side, and speak to the issues. And speak to the issues I did, though as much as possible, I let other people's words and stories speak for me.

Four years have passed since I "finished" "A Salt Marsh Reclamation." In that time my feelings about the place have become more complex. For that reason I would like to rewrite the essay. I would like to write about the irony of having a son who is a landscaper, paid to plant and tend the nonnative shrubs,

A Salt Marsh Reclamation

1. How to Get There from Here

I cross Cornhusker Highway and drive north on North 27th Street. Ten years ago this spring I bought worms in a dark fish-bait shop at this intersection. Beyond the shop were fields. Now the site of the former bait shop is occupied by a Super KMart, where the father of one of my daughter's friends works third shift.

I follow North 27th past a dazzling, mega–hardware store, over Salt Creek, past another hardware store, a furniture warehouse, Wal-Mart, a grocery, Payless Shoes, Jumbo Sport, the various fast-food franchises, office buildings, drive-through banks, an industrial park, and the farthest strip mall, where the major tenants are Toys 'R Us, Petsmart, and Slumberland.

Farms do not begin where the businesses thin out. Rather, this is land adjacent to Interstate 80 and Highway 77, a place of new apartment complexes and motels and signs announcing the future construction of more motels. Backhoes wait across the street from the Cracker Barrel Restaurant and a new Phillips 66 station. Behind the restaurant, a new road traces a wetland. Here even soggy land commands high prices. I follow North 27th over the interstate. On the right side of the road is Arbor Lake, a wildlife area, a salt marsh managed by the Nebraska Game and Parks Commission.

Once about sixteen thousand acres of saline wetlands were included within Nebraska's borders, most of which were in Lancaster and Saunders counties. Now about one thousand acres remain. Thus Arbor Lake, located only one mile north of Lincoln's present city limit, represents the rarest and most

endangered natural community in the entire Great Plains. While this particular salt marsh is safe from destruction for the time being, it is too close to the
edge to provide the sanctuary it did even five years ago.

I climb the steps to the observation platform. In the winter, all but the center of the marsh is dry. Where the marsh is crusted with salt, vegetation is
sparse. But following the spring rains, most of the twenty-acre depression is a
watery patchwork of greens: tall dark circles of slough grass, short, pale inland
salt grass, bright wavy blades of pondweed. To the left of the marsh is a farmhouse where a chained chow dog watches and barks from the other side of a
fence. To the right of the marsh is a cornfield. Ahead Lincoln Electric Service's
white fiberglass windmills spin and blink above Interstate 80.

I filter out the rumble of semitrucks, the farm dog's barking, and the rolling, sky-scraping roar of a plane preparing to land at the airport just a few
miles west of the marsh. The sounds of the marsh move through me. The
bubbling *kon-ka-lee* of red-winged blackbirds. The barking of Canada geese.
The rasp and falling buzz of yellow-headed blackbirds. The grunts and cackles
of American coots, as ungraceful as their lobed toes. The buzz and rattle of
marsh wrens. The *tsu-wee* of plovers. The wing *snap-snap* of a bathing grackle.
The high scream of a red-tailed hawk. The swelling of male frogs' vocal sacks:
the earth's pulse.

As I watch wind bend the light-filled salt grass, as I watch black terns rise
and fall, I believe that I have dreamed this place where everything is moving
toward me. But when the wind that ripples the water surface, that bends the
salt grasses, that ruffles the terns' feathers, moves around but not through me,
I know that this place is real.

II. Other Oceans

Dakota sandstone lies beneath much of eastern Nebraska. The porous, rust-
colored layers of sand and clay are visible around the base of some of the
steeper slopes on the Salt Creek's west bank and some road cuts. Water made
salty by deposits from the continental seas that once covered southeastern
Nebraska springs up or seeps out of this sandstone.

Gravity decrees that the brine flow into the shallow, wind-hollowed basins
in the flood plain. In "Nebraska Salt Marshes: Last of the Least" John Farrar
and Richard Gersib explain that where the soil does not drain, the evaporating
water leaves behind salty compounds. As the cycle of seepage and evaporation

is repeated, a white crust accumulates, "concentr[ating] salt in flood-plain soils, setting the stage for the formation of saline wetlands."

Just as coastal salt marshes are ocean fed, so too are inland salt marshes.

III. The Recent History of Salt in This Place

"The discovery of salt deposits west of the Appalachian Mountains was one the most important factors in the westward advance of the American frontier," writes Agnes Horton in her 1959 study of the history of Nebraska's saline land grant. In the absence of inland salt deposits, people from earlier centuries would have been limited to coastal areas by their need for salt to preserve meat, antisepticize wounds, tan leather, make soap, regulate the water balance, maintain normal heart rhythms, conduct nerve impulses, contract muscles, and achieve the correct acid-base balance in their own bodies and that of their livestock.

The absence of trees and the presence of salt were the first things that Euro-Americans noticed when they came to what is now Lancaster County, Nebraska. Of his arrival at the salt basin stretching along the west side of Salt Creek in 1861, William Cox wrote: "There was something enchanting about the scene that met our eyes. The fresh breeze sweeping over the salt basins reminded us of the morning breezes at the ocean beach. This basin was as smooth as glass, and resembled a slab of highly polished, cloudy, marble." Augustus F. Harvey, who made the first survey and plat of the town site of Lincoln, reported that "twice a day, like clockwork, the basin flooded with brine to a depth of two to three inches. When the 'tide' receded, the brine would disappear into the cracks, leaving a white crystalline film behind from solar evaporation. Over the course of days or weeks, this would accumulate to a depth of three to four inches and could simply be scraped up and used without further refinement."

When some saw the salt lake, they dreamed of fortunes to be made. Indeed, people from as far away as Iowa, Kansas, and Missouri were willing to trade meat, eggs, butter, fruit, potatoes, equivalent amounts of flour, new sets of clothes, live chickens, cast-iron stoves, sorghum pans, and money for Lancaster County salt. By 1860 several salt manufacturers were established in the area of what is now Lincoln. In 1864 J. S. Gregory Jr. manufactured salt to sell to the Indians and those traversing the Overland Trail.

But the dreamers did not foresee the difficulties they would encounter in extracting salt from water for large-scale use. In the mid-nineteenth century, the prairie was whole and vital enough to prevent the encroachment of trees. In *Lincoln: The Prairie Capital* James McKee writes that those in the salt business couldn't find enough fuel to feed the fires beneath the big kettles where they had hoped to boil the water from the salts. The solar method—pumping brine into a system of wooden vats or reservoirs and allowing the sun and wind to evaporate the water—was too slow. J. Sterling Morton of Nebraska City believed that these methods were unnecessary, since "the best and finest article of table salt" could simply be scraped from the banks of the Salt Creek. However, Sterling's son, Joy, founder of the Morton Salt Company, made his fortune not from Lancaster County salt but from salt caves in Kansas and Michigan, where he found the mineral to be more easily extracted. By the late 1880s all efforts at making a living directly from salt production in Lancaster County ended.

Yet there was money to be made indirectly from salt. The Lloyd Mineral Well of Union, Nebraska, bottled and sold salt water. The sulpho-saline baths in the basement of the Lincoln Sanitarium were, according to Erwin Hinckley Barbour, who was the Nebraska state geologist from 1891 to 1921, "deservedly popular and enjoyed a local reputation, especially among those afflicted with rheumatism." In 1895 a pair of entrepreneurs dammed the east end of the salt basin and rerouted Oak Creek so that its waters created a permanent lake, then called Burlington Beach, since the Burlington Railroad shuttled customers from Lincoln and the surrounding areas there and back. An 1897 photograph of the lake shows still waters, two sailboats, a man in a rowboat, and a strip of beach in the foreground. In the background is a pillared structure—the dam, I guess. At the end of a long pier is a pavilion, perhaps for refreshments or dancing or bathing in the supposedly medicinal waters. In 1906 the new owner named the lake Capital Beach (later Capitol Beach). For the next several decades it continued to offer swimming and a midway. Now the lake is rimmed with private residences on streets named Surfside, Sailside, and Lakeside Drive.

More recently, Lancaster County salt marshes have become the sites of several garbage dumps, have been drained for the construction of Interstate 80, for industrial parks, car dealerships, the Capitol Parkway West bypass, a hemorrhage of housing subdivisions, and one of two new high schools to be completed by 2003.

In the absence of salt, Lancaster County probably would not have been chosen as the site of the state capital and now be home to almost a quarter of a million people, making it the second most populous county in Nebraska. Nor would it have suffered such rapid and violent changes in the natural environment.

In the yellow heat of a late May afternoon at the salt marsh, I remove my black sun hat. A white ring marks the inside brim. I bend down and take a pinch of the gray clay. The salt in the soil stings my tongue.

iv. Transients

I spend the afternoon at Arbor Lake watching the black terns through my binoculars. At first I thought the birds were swallows because of their deeply forked tails. But the black terns are larger, less colorful birds, and instead of twittering like swallows, they utter calls similar to the sound made by rubber squeak toys. Nor do they dive toward the water surface from great heights like swallows. Rather, they erratically drop to the water, rise, hang in the air, then drop again. What they are doing is hovering, then swooping down to peck insects from the water surface. Occasionally one hawks an insect in midair.

Perhaps these terns can use any salt marsh as a motel, campground, nursery, or wayside eatery upon their vernal return from the tropics. Or perhaps their presence here is deliberate. The same black terns and their offspring return to Arbor Lake because it is their place of origin and the site of several millennia-worth of annual family reunions. For these birds there is no other cattail stand in which to build their nest.

v. Who Can't Live without It

Red-winged blackbirds, great blue herons, and red-tailed hawks are year-round residents at Arbor Lake. I know that coyote hunt here because I've seen their scat. In the cold part of the year frogs, snakes, salamanders, newts, and turtles sleep in the mud. The eggs of other permanent residents—dragonflies, grasshoppers, spiders, beetles, flies, mosquitoes, and ticks—are everywhere. Thousands of single-celled protozoa, fungi, and bacteria dwell in a single handful of soil. Last winter, near a stand of sedges, I found a skull, perhaps of a white-footed mouse, which from the orange tip of its two top incisors to the back of its skull is the length of my thumb, tip to first joint. I keep this relic, a representative of the millions of organisms who call Arbor Lake their one and only home, nestled in a bed of gauze in an earring box on my altar.

That pondweed, marsh elder, spearscale, foxtail barley, cattails, bulrushes, cordgrasses, and sedges can grow on such seemingly hostile, poisonous soils is remarkable. Gerry Steinauer, wetland biologist for the Nebraska Game and Parks Commission, writes that because many halophytes (plants adapted to grow on salty soils) "concentrate salts in their cell sap, [they] can draw soil water into their roots, since water generally flows from areas of low salt concentration to areas of higher salt concentration." Other adaptations include a shallow root system, which allows plants to exploit the less saline water found in upper soil layers after a rain, and special glands in the leaves that excrete salts before they reach toxic levels. Some halophytes—saltwort, sea blite, and saltmarsh aster—are reported in Nebraska only on the salt marshes. But other species such as inland salt grass is found throughout the Great Plains. On the dry, salt-encrusted outer rim of the salt flat, the salt grass might only reach a few inches in height and be sparsely spaced. But at the less saline salt flat-prairie transition zone, it grows in thick clumps, reaching eight to ten inches in height. What I like best about this wiry grass is that it crunches when I walk on it.

After a June evening at the salt marsh, I dream that I am searching for the tiny yellow corollas and pastel disks of the saltmarsh aster. I look in the pavement cracks in the island in the middle of the street, on the banks of a concrete-lined creek, beneath a colony of billboards, along the chain-link fence separating this parking lot from that one. My anxiety deepens. I run hard, searching for the edge where the asphalt ends and the grasses begin.

vi. Reckoning

Shortly after Arbor Lake was set aside as a protected place in 1992, my children and I stopped along the margin for a look. Though I had read about what a unique ecosystem this was, honestly, I saw nothing but straw-colored grass, dried cattails, a few crows, shotgun shell casings, and a CLOSED TO HUNTING sign. I couldn't yet see why Thoreau called wetlands "tender places on the earth's surface." But after six years spent hiking in Iowa, Illinois, Nebraska, and Kansas with field guides and people who know and see more than I do, I returned to Arbor Lake. Now I spend entire afternoons at the salt marsh, absorbed in the birds, the grasses, the dragonflies and beetles, the complicated webs of interdependencies, the nearness of the Cretaceous period and the as yet unnamed geologic periods that will follow our own.

Some people see nothing of value in a marsh. For them, "reclaiming" wetlands means draining them, filling them, and turning them toward human ends. In the twentieth century in the Rainwater Basin of south-central Nebraska, a critical stopover on the mid-continental spring migration route for seven to nine million ducks and geese and a half-million sandhill cranes, over 80 percent of the original wetlands have been "reclaimed" primarily for the irrigated, mechanized, chemically controlled production of soy beans, corn, sorghum, and wheat.

In March of 1999 the Lincoln City Council rezoned a salt marsh from agricultural to highway commercial, despite objections from the Lincoln Planning Department. Speaking for the majority, Councilman Curt Donaldson said that Lincoln did not need to add another layer of wetland protection to guidelines established by the federal government. But city planner Nicole Fleck-Tooze said that federal restrictions did not preclude the marsh from being filled in. For the majority of the city council members, immediate economic gain outweighed long-term ecological stability. "To build a road is much simpler than to think about what the country really needs," Aldo Leopold observed over a half-century ago.

The loudest opposition to the 17 March 2000 inclusion of the Salt Creek tiger beetle on Nebraska's endangered species list came from David Thompson, attorney for the Home Builders Association of Lincoln. Of the plan to protect this beetle, which has experienced a 90 percent loss of habitat in recent years and whose total population fluctuates between one hundred and six hundred individuals, making it the most endangered insect in the United States, Thompson said: "There's a concern that it can lead to tying up land. It can prevent landowners from using their land the way they want." Thompson and the 532 house builders that he represents appear to be motivated by the same philosophy as the nineteenth-century salt boilers: the land and the biotic community are there for them to use any way they want.

The only objections I've heard voiced against plans to build a new high school on a salt marsh north of the city is that this particular parcel of land is more costly than other available land in the area. The irony in this situation infuriates me. Over the years my children have received numerous lessons in the public schools about the threatened tropical rain forests, yet those who

make decisions on behalf of the local public schools demonstrate no awareness of or regard for the threatened ecological communities in and near their
own city.

Perhaps some can so easily alter wild landscapes because they believe that
temporary homes aren't as valuable or as necessary as permanent homes. One
day they visit the marsh and it's aflutter with black terns, sandpipers, avocets,
shovelers, and snow geese. They come back in January and no one is home
but the crows. "Preserve this?" they ask of a place that seems the same as any
other soggy field. And, too, salt marshes are neither permanent nor stable. As
salinity and moisture levels fluctuate, plant zones widen or narrow and blend.
During the extreme drought of 2000 Arbor Lake was dry, a pool of pale green
grass occupying the usually submerged center, and not a tern, shorebird, or
waterfowl in sight. Farrar and Gersib write that some salt marshes are on their
way to becoming solid ground; others have became so diluted by freshwater
that they are no longer saline. Salt marshes are always on their way to becoming something else.

But for those of us who find beauty, complexity, and a sustaining body of
metaphors at the marsh, reclamation means returning the land to a condition
in which it hosts a greater diversity of life forms. On the west bank of the Salt
Creek this means plugging drainage tiles, filling ditches and dugout pits, rip-
ping up asphalt and concrete, and enforcing limits on the growth of our cities,
towns, suburbs, and, most importantly, our human population. Because of
agricultural runoff, invading plant species, silt deposition, and alteration of
watersheds, the marsh cannot return to what it was when the Pawnee jour-
neyed there to scrape salt or when bison herds paused there to lick the white
crust. But it can become healthier, wilder, more alive. Thus reclamation is an
act of redemption.

Such reclamation will not happen with any frequency until there is a shift
in our collective mind-set. I cannot say how this shift will occur, but I can say
that it will move us to see the consumption of place as an act of deep disre-
spect, even violence, since it renders homeless countless organisms who have
fewer and fewer places to go—if they can go. This shift will move us to accept
radical changes in what we eat, where we live, how we travel and spend our
leisure time, and who we vote into and out of public office, so that these fragments of biodiversity are less vulnerable, so that there are near places where

we can observe and pay homage to what Gary Snyder calls "the pathless world of wild nature."

Some have already made the shift. Capitol Beach resident Rich Wiese, a seventy-one-year-old retired pipe fitter, dreamed of buying 117 acres of salt marsh near Capitol Beach Lake from the housing developer who had planned to drain it, build houses upon it, and dig canals linking the houses with the lake. In the early 1990s Wiese, who had no experience with conservation work, and two of his neighbors, Richard Powell and Sue Kuck, each donated $2,500 of their own money to initiate a project to purchase the marsh. When they couldn't get support from county, state, or federal governments, they appealed to local businesses, residents, and developers who contributed a total of $260,000. The U.S. Fish and Wildlife Service donated an additional $75,000. Wiese and his partners bought the land and immediately transferred the ownership of it to the Lower Platte South Natural Resources District in perpetuity. Since then, the local Audubon chapter has identified about two hundred bird species on this marsh and two of Nebraska's endangered species, saltwort and the Salt Creek tiger beetle.

Of course, there are compelling reasons not to make the shift from disregard to respect. In a culture in which happiness is sought through the consumption of more and more material things, knowing and loving a wild place demands a counterculture philosophy and lifestyle. It demands, in Bill McKibben's words, "an all-out drive for deep thrift, for self-restraint, for smaller families . . . smaller homes, more food grown locally, repair instead of replacement." It demands knowing how much is enough.

Knowing and loving a wild place also means living with an, at times, uncomfortable range and depth of emotions. To love a salt marsh, for instance, is to live with sadness. I am mindful of the fifteen thousand acres of salt marsh that no longer exist and the fragility of the approximately one thousand acres that do exist. Each year more and more nonnative plants assume spots once held by the native marsh plants. Each year more and more birds descend upon Arbor Lake because other wetlands in the area have been drained. Even though Arbor Lake lacks trees, restrooms, water fountains, wood-chip paths, and picnic tables, more and more people use it as a park. Sometimes I share the marsh with people eating their lunches on the observation deck or exercising their dogs or drinking beer in cars or trucks, thumping and rattling from the volume of the stereo. Always I find evidence of human use—broken glass and cigarette butts at the edge of the marsh, fireworks, fast-food and condom wrappers in the parking lot. Given the current rate at which the cornfields, pastures, and salt marshes north of Lincoln are being paved over or planted in bluegrass or fescue, I predict that within the next decade a two-lane street will replace the gravel road near the marsh; power lines will be strung overhead; and landscaped, half-acre backyards, three-car garages, and houses the size of small castles will surround Arbor Lake on culs-de-sac and winding streets named Salt Marsh Circle and Avocet Lane. Then, will migrating birds still come to Arbor Lake? If I can't find birds and solitude, will I?

To love the marsh is to live with hope. I hope that those office and retail sales workers who eat their lunches at the marsh see the birds and other creatures that dwell there. I hope that they know something of the human and natural history of this place. I hope that they yearn to see one of the agile, long-legged, and elusive Salt Creek tiger beetles. I hope that they consider which extravagances they can forgo in order to protect wild places for those who dwell there and for those of us who can't live without them. I hope that one day they'll initiate or support a grassroots reclamation or preservation project of an inland salt marsh or a native grassland or a stretch along the Niobrara or Platte River. Above all, I hope that this place and those who dwell there will be permitted to endure.

But also, to love the salt marsh is to be overwhelmed by joy. In the absence of water in the fall and winter I find a nest, perhaps a black tern's, anchored near the base of a cattail stand. On a late afternoon in winter I follow the silent flight of a short-eared owl above the winterkilled, wind-bent tufts of salt grass. In the spring and summer I watch dark-headed, adult black terns and the white-headed juveniles rise and fall from the water surface. As the wind ripples the water and the inland salt grasses, as the wind flutters the delicate, awl-shaped leaves and pale lavender rays of the saltmarsh asters, as the wind bends the ribbonlike cattail leaves, my heart and throat open with love and gratitude for the rich and fragile beauty before me.

JOHN HANSON MITCHELL

John Hanson Mitchell is the winner of the 1994 John Burroughs Essay Award. His books include several works centered on Concord, Massachusetts: *Ceremonial Time: Fifteen Thousand Years on One Square Mile* (1984), *Living at the End of Time* (1990), *Walking to Walden: A Pilgrimage in Search of Place* (1995), *Trespassing: A Inquiry into the Private Ownership of Land* (1998). He has also written about his travels in Europe in *The Wildest Place on Earth: Italian Gardens and the Invention of Wilderness* (2001) and *Following the Sun: A Bicycle Pilgrimage from Andalusia to the Hebrides* (2002). His latest book is *Looking for Mr. Gilbert: The Reimagined Life of an African American* (2005), the story of his quest to uncover the life of the first African-American landscape photographer, a heretofore unknown assistant to the nineteenth-century ornithologist, William Brewster. He is the editor of *Sanctuary*, the magazine of the Massachusetts Audubon Society. "The Kingdom of Ice" is taken from *Ceremonial Time*, his first book set on Scratch Flat.

Scratch Flat and the Invention of Place

Location

The place is a square mile of anomalous land, characterized in the main by farmlands and woodlots and a long snakelike, slow-moving stream that winds lazily through wide cattail marshes. Sometime in the early nineteenth century, for reasons that are recorded only in local folklore, the tract came to be known as Scratch Flat, although in our time, if you ask anyone about its location you will draw blank stares.

Scratch Flat lies thirty-five miles west of Boston, Massachusetts, and is set down in a vast region of low, rolling hills east of the Appalachians known to geologists as the Schooley Peneplain. If you care to look it up, you can also find it on the U.S. Department of the Interior Geological Survey map of 1966 in the Westford Quadrangle for Massachusetts, Middlesex County, 7.5 series. Or you can experience the place in person by following the state highway known locally as the Great Road, which runs northwest from Concord, Massachusetts, through the Nashobah Valley and thence northwest to southern New Hampshire and the rising ground known as Monadnock. You can also see it, or part of it at least, if you are driving north or south along the great ring road that circles Boston known as Route 495. Look west after you pass the exit for Groton, and you will see there a low hill, very like a whale. That hill lies more or less on the eastern edge of the square mile.

Superficially, at least, from a driver's point of view, the landscape here is generally pleasing. If you follow the Great Road west you will cross over the winding cattail marshes of Beaver Brook. West of the brook you will pass over the low rise of a wooded drumlin and drop down into a flat of cultivated lands. There were six working farms in this section thirty years ago, but now only two remain, although lined up one after the other, like the fastfood joints of less fortunate communities, you will see three farmstands selling—in season—local produce. North of the Great Road the land rolls up to a wooded ridge where the last bear in this region was killed in a hemlock grove in 1811. Northwest of this woods, behind a working dairy farm, is a lake that was the site of one of the best Indian fishing weirs in the region for as many as ten thousand years and which now demarcates, roughly speaking, the northern end of the tract. The western end is marked by a stand of larch trees, the south by a ring of low hills, and the east is bounded by the winding marshes of Beaver Brook.

Until 1995 Beaver Brook was a wild country of reed canary grass, cattails, and unhoused, wooded banks. Development has now invaded the uplands along some sections, but if you canoe the interior of the marshes in mid-June when the grass are high, you can still get a sense of the wilderness that characterized Scratch Flat over its fifteen-thousand-year history. Somewhere along Beaver Brook the old Pawtucket man known as Tom Doublet maintained a fish weir. He inherited the weir from his father, who, according to the local histories, was killed at the spot by a party of raiding Mohawks sometime around 1632. Tom Doublet was a major player in the King Philip's War in 1675, but after the war, as a result of an insult from the General Court, he reportedly cursed the land just east of the brook. The farms in that section, and plans for three major economic ventures, two of them backed by international funding, have failed at the site. The farms of Scratch Flat, by contrast, survived well into the twentieth century. Some have been continuously cultivated since agriculture first moved to the region.

I came into this country in 1974 and began walking the square-mile tract the day I moved in. It was all farms and fields then and woodlots where you could find ironic beds of daffodils, old peonies, foundations, stone walls, cairns, and the skeletons of Model t Fords. The hay fields were ill tended, the woods were littered with the remnants of time, and it was clear that this was a country that had once been lived in, had once been cultivated, perhaps loved, or more likely, simply used, first to grow food for the Puritan families who settled here in 1676, then to grow food to sell to those Puritan families who had settled so densely that they no longer had land to grow their own food. In fact, the land had already been cultivated, as I learned, for some three or four thousand years before the Puritans arrived. The original natives of the place had developed a primitive form of agriculture that required only that trees be felled on a given plot of suitable land. The brush and trunks were burned or used for wickiups, and the land between the stumps was broken with clamshell hoes, planted to corn, beans, and squash, and then watched over by women and children posted to keep the crows and raccoons away.

I learned too that this area had once been the site of a village of Indians who, under the tutelage and protection of one John Eliot, the so-called prophet of the Indians, had converted to Christianity. They cut their hair, stopped sending their women out to menstrual huts each month, began to wear shoes, and learned to sing hymns in Algonquian. In exchange they were granted—outright—a tract of land some sixteen miles square, the northwest portion of which included the aforesaid Scratch Flat. The grant, as with so many later treaties, was temporary. In 1675, with the advent of the uprising of King Philip, the Puritans went to war, and the presence of Indians, even Christian Indians, was unnerving. One morning the peaceable Indians, believing themselves under the protection of Christ and his vested associate, John Eliot, were rounded up, roped by the neck, and taken to a stockade in Concord. After that they were deported to Deer Island in Boston Harbor for the duration of the war. It was February; they were ill supplied with food and eked out their days digging clams and plucking mussels from the rocky shores. Very few of them returned to Scratch Flat after the war save for a powerful woman named Sarah Doublet, the purported Saunk, or female chief, of her remnant people. Sarah lived to a very old age and died in 1735, whereupon she turned the land over to a pair of cousins from Concord, thus ending the eight- to ten-thousand-year sojourn of Asian people in that section of the northeastern coast of the land now known as North America.

Following Sarah's death, even before it actually, Puritan families from nearby Concord, Groton, and the coastal town of Ipswich began to settle in the area west of the Beaver Brook. The glacier had left behind a deep layer of alluvial soil in that section of the community, and in time the place acquired the sobriquet Scratch Flat. There are two theories on the origin of the name. One is that the soils and the farming were good and the settlers there were forever scratching the soils with the plow. The second is that for a few years in the eighteenth century a strange cutaneous itch affected those living on the flat and they would appear in the town, constantly scratching themselves. I dug all this out from a popular history of the town written in the late nineteenth century. In my time I only met one old farmer who even remembered the name: "They don't call it that no more," he said.

By the turn of the nineteenth century there were some six working farms on Scratch Flat plus a working poor farm, an early version of a town-supported social program that cared for wanderers and homeless people. The farmers were Yankees of English origin, most of them having come over from Kent in the early seventeenth century, and having some familiarity with fruit cultivation, established apple orchards in the region. By the turn of the twentieth century immigrant farmers from Greece and Italy began to buy up some of the farms. By the turn of the twenty-first century there were only two of these farms left, one run by one of the oldest Yankee families in the town and the other held by a hardworking Greek family. The last in the Greek line was a ninety-two-year-old man from Sparta named Tasso, who ran the place with his grandniece. In general, by the late twentieth century the fields had languished, had grown up to birch and red osier dogwood and alder, and eventually, one by one, lot by lot, had been sold off for housing. Now some of the thousand-year-old farms support immense palazzi with faux Palladian windows and two to three floors of rooms, most of them empty most of the time. Scratch Flat for all intents and purposes had disappeared.

But who cares, really? Why bother to spend twenty-five years digging for the deep and singular history of this otherwise unremarkable stretch of farmland and woods?

I came up to New England out of family that had very deep roots on the Eastern Shore of Maryland. I spent summers there, dragged "down home," as my exiled parents referred to the region even after thirty years' absence. My strongest memories of that section of the world were of summer nights on old front porches, the hooting of owls, and the slow, languorous conversation of the family and friends who would gather every evening, to rock and smoke and chat. Stories would begin like a small stream and then head for the sea, gathering many tributaries and asides and counter-stories until they came to the shores. When the tale was told there would be a silence, except for the creak of the rocking chairs, followed, after decent interval, by the beginning of another story. All this was tedious business for a restless ten-year-old, but it had its effect. Looking back, I realize now that there was not one story re-counted on those summer nights whose action was played out independent of land. Nothing was free from the bonds of setting. Stories would take place in a given section of named territory, an intimate, known part of their world, which, having been named, carried with it a full burden of associations, of history, of other stories and events. Nothing that lived—neither dog nor horse nor human—existed independent of place.

By the time I got to the town in which Scratch Flat is located, the vicis-situdes of the mid-twentieth century had wreaked havoc. A major highway, Route 495, had sliced through the town; small tracts of housing had been built in the forested lands; good fields had been lost; the orchards, which were once the mainstay of the economic life of the community, had been plowed un-der. Only on Scratch Flat was there any active agriculture. In town, at a small shopping plaza wherein lay a grocery store selling produce from Florida and California, the local people were not certain where Beaver Brook was, were not aware of the fact that there were still otters there, let alone sora rails, let alone the deep Indian heritage that was at the foundation of the town. No one sat on front porches in the evening—there were no front porches. No one told stories. No one had stories to tell save, perhaps, for accounts of places they had come from. The older farm families, whom I later met, did have some tales. But to find out about them I had to make phone calls, go to their houses, and, at an appointed hour, sit in enclosed living rooms—sometimes with the coun-ter-stories of the omnipresent television competing. I had to work to draw out their tales. They still farmed, still had perhaps a love for the land, but they were in effect a displaced people—not displaced by war, as with the Indians or the immigrant families who were moving in. They had been displaced by their own culture, by our own culture. American mobility got the better of their psyches, and they felt they were living as aftereffects.

I was too, of course. So were my parents. Faced with the economic realities of the Depression and the opportunity of work, my father sold his family farm and fled to New Jersey and spoke of "down home" for the rest of his life. I was set free after a certain amount of requisite education and began wander-ing—in the American style—living abroad, living in the cauldron of New York City, living in the remnants of wilderness in the 1960s, and then finally, in the 1970s, living on Scratch Flat.

Ultimately, Scratch Flat was an invention. A creation, or re-creation, of my own version of the mythic center. In time this singular tract of land, with its deep historical shadows, its farms, and its resident wildlife, became for me a metaphorical hunting ground. One book was not enough to explore the hollows and empty quarters and people that seemed to characterize the place. I spent two years living in an unheated cottage sans electricity to get closer to the story of the land. I wrote a book about the natural history of my own backyard while I was living there. I used to go to the old Christian Indian village that was located on Scratch Flat to explore the question of the meaning, origin, and uses of the curious Western concept of private property. I used Scratch Flat as the jumping-off point for a pilgrimage to Concord in which I undertook an exploration of the whole idea of place, of whether who we are has anything to do with where we are or where we are from. I even explored the curious interconnection between the Renaissance Italian gardens and the invention of the American wilderness by constructing a pseudo-Italian garden, complete with hedge maze, on land that, according to twenty-first-century American law, I am told that I actually "own" (whatever that means).

In short, I became a traveler on my own land, and I never got very far beyond my own square-mile myth. But at least I found a place.

The Kingdom of Ice

For fifty thousand years, give or take an interglacial period or two, the area known as Scratch Flat was buried under a mantle of ice one mile deep. There was a world before the onset of the glaciers; that is to say, there was dry land in the area, and there were plants and animals, life and death, trees and rocks and all the other things that make up an ecosystem. In fact, geologists have theorized that the landscape that existed in the area was far more dramatic in aspect than the landscape of today. In the valley of the Beaver Brook which runs along the eastern edge of Scratch Flat, there was a vast uplifted fault running north and south for fifty or sixty miles. Living things grew or foraged above and below these immense cliff faces. But the fact remains that everything that existed in the area before the glacier—the landscape, the soils, the living things, and for that matter the entire world—was obliterated by ice.

The last ice age began sixty to seventy thousand years ago. It came on slowly, to be sure, but it came on inexorably, a long winter one year, a slightly longer one the next, until finally there was nothing but winter for fifty thousand years. Snows piled on snows, compressing the bottom layers into ice packs; the ice packs moved out from under the incredible weight of year-after-year of snow, crushing the very rocks and soils beneath, so that finally, unable to withstand the downward pressure, the whole mass moved southward like a hideous all-encompassing plow. No living thing could endure these timeless winters, and as the ice moved southward, generation after generation of plants and animals were forced into the more benign climates of south-central North

America. Although there may have been two or three interglacial periods of warming, the world at Scratch Flat was dead and would remain dead until history wrote it into existence.

This interminable season of ice is the overriding reality of the landscape of Scratch Flat, and indeed of the entire northern half of North America. The record of the glacier, and most specifically the record of its departure, is inscribed on the land; you can see it in the rounded drumlins of Scratch Flat, in the streams and ponds, and in the boulders, the numerous stone walls, and the deep beds of gravel. There is no escaping its presence once you are aware of it; if God had a hand, it was the glacier.

This overbearing reality, the fifty thousand–year reign of ice, is lost on the general public in the Scratch Flat region. Beaver Brook, the drumlin, the flat farmlands, might just as well have been created by the hand of a giant as by the hand of ice. I can't say that I blame the public for not appreciating the great timeless scales of the ice ages. The coming and going of the glacier is an event which has almost mystical overtones. Geologists glibly throw off statistics as if they were comprehensible—the glacier endured for fifty thousand years, they will tell you; the sheet of ice was one mile deep and locked up one-quarter of the earth's water. Such statistics are beyond comprehension in some ways, mere figures with no apparent base in reality. And yet over the past few years, and through a variety of methods, I think I have come to understand something of the way in which the piece of land I am writing about was formed.

The traditional view of the creation of Scratch Flat, its birth by ice, comes for the most part from a friend of mine whom, for years, my wife and I have called the Red Cowboy, simply because he comes from Colorado and has flaming red hair. The Red Cowboy (his real name is Vernon Stafford) loves glaciers; he has studied them for some ten years, first at Harvard, then at various universities in this country and in Europe. He has traveled to many of the existing glaciers of the world, has camped for weeks on their backs, has descended icy crevices into the very core of their bodies and emerged alive; and, fortunately for me, he has spent a few weeks at Scratch Flat walking over the land and describing to me the events which must have taken place.

According to geologists, Vern Stafford included, about fifteen to sixteen thousand years ago the "summer" seasons began to lengthen, the long advance halted, and the glacier began to draw back. As it did so, it released into the world untold cubic miles of water which had been stored in its body. Among other things that water caused world sea levels to rise dramatically. It also created innumerable lakes which endured on the North American continent for centuries after the glacier retreated. It appears that one of those lakes, a rather small one, sat over Scratch Flat for a period of time—exactly how long, no one is able to say.

The glacier was not a monolithic front stretching east and west for thousands of miles. There must have been a front, obviously—that is, a general latitude where the snows melted every year—but current theories suggest that there was so much variation and there were so many ice ages or mini–ice ages during the great glaciations of the past fifty thousand years that it is difficult to say any one thing about the whole process. During the final millennia of its existence however—that is, during the recessional centuries when it did most of its handiwork on the land—at its forefront the glacier seems to have been nothing more than a series of towering blocks of ice, some of them as much as one hundred to two hundred miles square and others no larger than a ten-acre pond. For centuries, for a thousand years, for who knows how long, it appears that one of these blocks sat on top of Scratch Flat, slowly wasting away. Vast rushing streams poured down the face of the block of ice and rushed out from underneath, carrying with them sand and gravel, boulders and similar debris. About twenty miles south of Scratch Flat this detritus created a dam of ice, gravel, and rock so that water backed up, creating a shallow and lifeless lake.

My friend the Red Cowboy says that the tops of the glacial fields were not necessarily smooth stretches of ice or snow. There were crevices in the melting surface, and, among other things, there were deep gurgling holes, swirling with water, which would sink into the nothingness of the body of the glacier. Nineteenth-century geologists referred to these holes as "moulins," or "mills," after the tub mills of the period. The Red Cowboy has a more graphic term. When I pressed him for a description, he thought for a minute. "You know what a toilet's like? Well imagine a huge toilet. Only this toilet is stuck and keeps flushing, flushes maybe for ten years, maybe a hundred." According to the Red Cowboy, these toilets, or moulins, played an interesting part in the creation of part of the local landscape.

Scratch Flat today is more or less surrounded by water. There is the wide stream to the east and northeast, there is the lake to the north and northwest, and in the middle there is a geological formation known as a drumlin, an elongated hill of perhaps a half a mile, with its steep end to the southeast and a sloping end to the northwest. The lake to the north is a remnant of the glacial lake, and the stream may be a remnant of a large outwash stream that rushed out from beneath the block of ice. But there are a couple of anomalies in this simplified description. One is a series of mounds or hills on the west edge of the stream, and the other is a sharp, almost conical formation that once sat on the floodplain of Beaver Brook.

If you look at the old maps of Scratch Flat, you will see, marked in the wonderful old hand of the eighteenth- and nineteenth-century scribes, a place at the edge of Beaver Brook called Cobble Hill. One day in 1960 a couple of men in boots and khaki approached Ted Demogenes, the man who, according to twentieth-century legal documents, "owned" Cobble Hill. The men in khaki were from the Massachusetts Division of Public Works, and after some negotiation and discussion, they offered to buy Cobble Hill outright, buy the gravel and the sand, that is. It seems that a major highway was coming through, and the engineers needed the gravel for the roadbed. Before the bulldozers and the payloaders moved in, one of the engineers stopped the work for a while and called a geologist to have a look at Cobble Hill—there was something about it that was interesting. Ted Demogenes, who told me this story, didn't know what it was, didn't think to ask, or couldn't remember what they said if he did. But after a little research my friend Vern thinks that he has figured it out. He did so by looking at earlier geological survey maps that show Cobble Hill.

Basically, he said, the conical hill was created by one of the moulins and, were it still in existence, would be known technically as a "kame." The detritus of rocks, sand, and gravel that was flushed down the toilet of the glacier was deposited in the place that was Cobble Hill in a regular form. Kames often occur in the outwash plains of the glacier; there are similar formations to the south of Scratch Flat, and there are others to the north. Vern says that if you look carefully at the maps, and if you know what to look for, you can see the actual footprints of the glacier as it tracked back across Scratch Flat to the north and northwest, flushing its icy toilets all the way.

The other curious geological formation on Scratch Flat is a series of mounds maybe fifteen yards high and twenty or twenty-five yards in circumference. These mounds occur irregularly along the banks of Beaver Brook on the eastern edge of the stream and are covered over with a thick growth of white pine. One wet March day while the Red Cowboy was staying at our house, I managed to get him down to the mounds to have him explain them to me. By that time he had come to know the geology of the area fairly well, and once he had made a few preliminary digs, he was able to say how the hills were created. Conveniently, there was a woodchuck hole on the top of one of the hillocks; the Red Cowboy took advantage of it, began to dig deeper into it with his trenching shovel, and after a few minutes reached in and pulled up a handful of fine sand, as clean and white as the sand on a Florida beach. He rolled it around in his fingers for a few seconds, took out a lens and looked at the grains, then stood and looked across the wooded landscape at the random scattering of hills and mounds. "Dunes," he said after a few minutes, "you all have got some fine sand dunes here."

What had happened, he explained, was that the dam that created the lake had broken and the water had drained out, leaving a wasteland of mud, sand, gravel, and jumbled rocks. The open treeless landscape was exposed to the wind, and as the lake bed dried, fine particles of sand were picked up, swirled across the flatlands, and deposited in a line along the edge of the outwash stream. He told me that he could tell that the sand was wind-deposited because the grains were small and uniform; had there been diversity of grain size or if the mounds had gravel in them, they would have been something else, he said.

With the receding waters of the lake, the place that is Scratch Flat was, for the first time in fifty thousand years, open to the sky, and the land onto which so much human and natural history was to play itself out was formed. You can see the resulting hills and ridges as you drive past on Route 495. Beaver Brook winds twice beneath the highway, and the flat lake bottoms surround the drumlin that sits in the center of this little world. All of these land formations are subtle. This is no country of dramatic vistas, great scarps, or rushing cataracts. Everything is rounded and smoothed, worn down by ice and shaped and reshaped by human hands. Time, not space, is the dominant feature of the landscape in these parts: the place is defined by human perceptions and human use.

This version of the creation of Scratch Flat is not quite as simple as I have described it. There were elements of guesswork involved, and in fact some of the geologists I have talked to dispute the Red Cowboy's interpretation of the maps. But then there are other geologists who will dispute his critics. The more you question, the more confusing the story becomes. There is, however, another version of the formation of Scratch Flat, one that is completely at odds with what the Red Cowboy and all the other geologists tell me.

There were human beings living on the American continent at the time of the retreat of the glacier. These people begat descendants who are still living in the place the Europeans came to call America. Nompenekit is one of these people; through him I have met others, and it was from one of them that I learned about these alternative versions.

One of Nompenekit's friends was a woman named Linda Waters, a Wampanoag who had gained respect in the Indian community as a shaman, or medicine woman. Linda Waters was about forty-five years old when I first met her. She had rounded features, brownish skin, and a thick braid of oily black hair running down her back. She was slightly overweight, dressed in shopping center clothes, and in spite of her mystical leanings, used to smoke a lot of cigarettes and apparently used to drink a lot of whiskey. She once worked in the mills at Lowell but was unemployed when I knew her and would receive money from the federal government to support her one child, a teen-age boy named Steve, who liked fast cars, who also smoked a lot of cigarettes, and who expressed little or no interest in Indian affairs. Steve's father had left Linda when Steve was about a year old and had yet to return, although divorce proceedings were never carried out.

Linda spent her childhood on Cape Cod and had been steeped in what was left of Wampanoag traditions by her grandmother. When she was younger, she said, she loved nature, would spend days in the summer picking blueberries with her grandmother and listening to the old legends and stories of the Wampanoag people and other Indians. After her husband left her, Linda began to think more about her past, went back to Mashpee on Cape Cod, and began, as she explained it, "to walk alone." "One day," Linda said, "I heard my grandmother's voice in the pine trees. The voice said, 'Linda, don't forget what I told you.' I didn't know what that meant then. But later I knew that I am Wampanoag, and I knew that she was saying that I had special powers. My grandmother could talk to birds."

After her experience Linda came back to Lowell and took a job in the mills. She began attending meetings of a local Indian affairs group and attending ceremonies and festivals of some of the Indian groups around New England. Nompenekit told me that at one point people began to worry about her again; she was dancing a little too hard, living her Indianness a little too intensely;

and then in the midst of her "rebirth" she disappeared. When she came back a second time, she said that she had visited her uncle, an old man in Maine, and had had a vision. She said that she had been given power there and now could "see through things," or as she told me on another occasion, "see into things." She changed her name to Tonupasqua, or Turtle Woman, and, according to Nompenekit, calmed down considerably.

I met her one night at Nompenekit's house in Lowell. I had asked him specifically if he knew anyone who could travel in time, go back into the past and see things as they were then. He said, in his enigmatic way, that maybe he did and maybe he didn't, and one afternoon a few weeks later, he called and invited me to come up to his house. There were a lot of people there sitting around the kitchen table drinking beer, some of them dressed in cowboy clothes such as you would see at a cheap western outfitter shop. I was introduced and in the course of the evening got to ask a lot of questions about the Indian view of time and history, how people might have lived, and how a place like Scratch Flat might have come into existence. Tonupasqua was there, but she stayed with the other women and never contributed to the discussion. Just before I left, she came up and asked me why I wanted to know all these things. I told her that I wanted to write an account of the way things really happened; I said I knew one version of the history of the area but that I wanted to make sure that I included everything about the place and that since it appeared from what I had learned so far that Indians had lived in the area for a long time, I wanted to get that part too. "Well, I can see different times," she said offhandedly and gave me a napkin with a telephone number on it.

I got to know Tonupasqua after that and would meet with her on occasion, sometimes at her house, sometimes in Nompenekit's kitchen, and whenever I wanted an alternative view of history, I got into the habit of asking her. Sometimes she would become subtly abusive of white people, white versions of history, and indirectly of me. She would rail at the archaeologists who "steal" her people's tools or the anthropologists who dig into her people's secrets. Usually, she lumped me grossly with all the other white exploiters, but since I must have given her the sense that I was simply interested in everybody's version of history—white, black, Indian, and anyone else who cared to share information—at least she came to tolerate me.

One day after fairly elaborate arrangements, I got her to come down to Scratch Flat. I wanted to get her to walk over the land with me, look at some of the sites where, according to the records, Indians had once gathered. We ended up driving around the land in my car, stopping at various points while I described some of the events that had taken place. Sometimes she would get out and look around, but mostly she sat in the car, smoking cigarettes and grunting positively at my stories. "I know, I know," she would say, or "right, right." She spoke as if she had seen it all before and was bored or anxious to get back to Lowell.

I called her a few days after her first visit and asked her if she had thought at all about Scratch Flat and how such a place might have come into existence. I had already told her the story of the Red Cowboy and the glacier and wanted to know if she thought that's what might have happened. She said that she was thinking about it and that she would call me when she had "seen." Late one night she finally telephoned to say that she had the story and that I should come up the next day if I wanted to hear it.

"This Red Cowboy?" she asked me when I got there. "He is a man who has read a lot of books?" Yes, I said, he read books and even taught geology at a university in the West. "Well he don't know things. He don't know every-thing. I talked to my uncle about this, and I can tell you now how that place there came to be like it is."

Turtle Woman explained that Scratch Flat was created long ago, in a time when a thing called the stiff-legged bear walked the land and Crow and Wolf played hide-and-seek in the hills. She said there was a "being" who lived there with the people, whose name was Glooscap. Glooscap could do a lot of tricks, she said, and sometimes he helped the people, although sometimes, too, he played tricks on them. One day a horrible thing came out of the earth, a mon-ster snake. This snake came to the village of the people who lived near Scratch Flat. If anyone strayed from the village at night, Snake would eat them, and the more people he ate, the hungrier he got, so that sometimes the people could see his head swaying over the top of the stockade that surrounded the village. All the people were worried about Snake, so they called a council and decided to send for Glooscap to see if he could help them. They sent Crow over the hills, above the head of Snake, to fetch him. A few days later Glooscap came to the village, and the sachems told him about the monster. Glooscap could make things of metal, Tonupasqua said, and he taught the people to melt rocks, and from the melted rocks he made a thing like a bell. One night Glooscap took the bell out and tied it to Snake's tail while he was asleep. Then he stabbed Snake in the tail with a spear and told him to run. Hobomacho, a terrible monster who also stalked the forests in those times, was right behind him, Glooscap said, ready to eat Snake alive. Snake slithered off, but as he moved, the bell rang out like the voice of Hobomacho. Snake slithered faster, and soon he was moving so fast that he dug a groove in the ground. Finally, in desperation, he forced his way into a cave and disappeared into the earth forever. Tonupasqua said that the groove that Snake dug is now the course of Beaver Brook and the hole that he went down became the lake that lies on the north side of Scratch Flat.

A few months after I began to think of the glacier in terms of human history, it occurred to me that I too am a descendant of a people who hunted along the edge of the glacier during its recessional years. These people lived on a different continent and were of a different race than Tonupasqua's people, and over the past few hundred years, my people have developed another means of understanding time and events that took place in what we call the past. But that is not to say that Tonupasqua and Nompenekit and my people are different from each other; in fact, since we both experienced the realities of the glacier, the long winters, and the joy and terrors of the hunt, we may be more alike than we believe. Only recently have we gone our separate ways in terms of our views on time, and so when Tonupasqua told me one night that it is possible that I once personally visited the glacier that sat over New England fifteen thousand years ago, I was willing to believe her.

When I was about seven years old, I was given, I think from my two older brothers, an all too graphic description of a hideous entity known as the glacier. It was a great wall of ice shaped like a huge curving snowplow, caked and pitted with chunks of stone, and what is more—and this is the terrifying aspect of it—the thing moved. I was told, in all honesty, that it moved slowly, but to my mind *slowly* meant about as fast as you could walk, and, of course, if you ever tripped or got stuck, it would sweep over you. It was immense and unstoppable; this plow of ice would crush whole houses, crumple automobiles, snap trees and fences, crush dogs, cows, bicycles, toys, and anything else that was left in its path. And, of course, it was coming back. It had come before, I was told, and it would return; it was just a question of time.

Such is the stuff of nightmares, and inevitably one night I had a dream about the glacier. Fortunately, it was not really a nightmare; it was more of a universal dream, filled with a sublime, though terrible, landscape. I was standing at the very top of the edge of the glacier, high above the surrounding land. Behind me I could see the ice fields rucked and pitted with jagged up-lifted slabs of ice interspersed with smooth plains of snow and all of it flat, flat beyond imagining, and stretching interminably backward. Ahead of me were houses, streets, dogs on the sidewalks, and everything else that is a part of the world of a seven-year-old; behind me was the ice, stretching backward into darkness. That, fortunately perhaps, is all I remember, except for one other thing, and that was the inevitability of this dream, the underlying reality of the return of the glacier.

I related the dream one night to Nompenekit and Tonupasqua and asked them what they thought about it. I described to them the incredible clarity that had characterized the experience.

"You still remember this thing?" Tonupasqua asked.

"Yes," I said, "I can still see the fields of ice."

"Well, it may have been a dream. But my uncle would say that if that hap-pened to me, I was there. You can travel in your sleep, you know. You live here now when you are awake, but then, when you sleep, you can go away to other times. This has happened to me. One night I dreamed that I could talk to the birds like my grandmother. I say I can talk to birds now. So maybe you went there to this glacier in dreamtime. Maybe you saw all these things."

"But you believe I was there?" I asked.

"I believe you could go there. You believe what you want," she said.

A few years ago, armed with a lot more knowledge of what the actual glacier was like, I went back again in time. I am in the habit of walking out in Scratch Flat in foul weather; I find that the old adage about the weather being bad only from the inside holds a certain amount of truth, and so periodically, during sleet or snows or rain, I get dressed in the proper gear and venture out. One January night about three years ago, after a particularly heavy snowfall, I strapped on some snowshoes and waddled down the east side of the drumlin to the marshes of Beaver Brook. In spite of the fact that the snow was a foot and a half deep, it was crusted over, and it was easygoing all the way—I was, after all, headed downhill. It was one of those crystal nights that sometimes occur in New England. There was a brilliant ice-cold moon, a clear black sky, and a biting wind that swept down out of the northwest with a deep-throated growl. All around me the trees were cracking and swaying, and little drifts of snow were working themselves loose in the open hayfields and stacking themselves up against the windbreaks of the stone walls. It was an exhilarating night for a walk, and all went well for the first half-hour or so. Then about a half-mile from my house, in a field about at the edge of the marshes of Beaver Brook, I stepped suddenly into a wilderness that might as well have been ten thousand miles from the nearest human settlement. I did not go abruptly into that wilderness of night; I went there in a series of excruciatingly slow steps. The strap on my left snowshoe broke and somehow, before I was aware of it, came off altogether and got buried somewhere behind me. I went back to look for it, but although I found part of the strap, the critical crosspiece was lost, and I found myself one-footed and alone in the emptiness of winter. My first reaction, of course, was to go home, so I turned around and began to make my way up the hill toward the house. I set as my first goal a large glacial boulder that sits in the middle of Charlie Lignos's hayfields.

It was hard traveling from the start. The crust broke through with every step, and I would sink to my shins in the deep powder. I found that I could move forward, after a fashion, by pushing off with the snowshoe, stepping into the deep snow with my other foot, and then repeating the process, but it was slow going, and by the time I reached the shelter of the boulder, I was exhausted and somewhat concerned. I was warm enough, to be sure—the effort of walking had seen to that—but in the near-zero-degree air I began to chill quickly and got up to move again. About a hundred yards uphill from the boulder something like panic flashed in. I realized that there was the distinct possibility that I might not make it home at this rate, that I might die no more than a mile from my kitchen stove. In a half-hour's time I had traveled maybe two hundred or three hundred yards; I was close to total exhaustion; I was cold, my cheeks were beginning to sting, and I still had at least a half-mile to make. It wasn't exactly panic that I felt; it was more a sense of excitement or revelation. But fear was at the root of it—a deep, primal fear. Ahead of me was the huge nothingness of drifting snow; behind me was the dark line of the woods with the open marshes below. There were no roads, no trails, no fellow human beings out for a stroll; there seemed, in fact, to be no life at all, as if I had been thrust back into the very heart of the glacial reign. I witnessed then, briefly, the essence of timelessness. I saw Scratch Flat as it must have been fifteen thousand years ago, saw the fields of ice, the heartless whip of blowing snow, the endless winters, and, at the base of it all, the insignificance of the human experiment. The place that I saw, the Scratch Flat that had endured for some fifty thousand years, was neither cruel nor kind; it was simply inhuman, totally devoid of meaning. Never mind that on the heels of this revelation I realized that it was easier to go downhill than it was to go up, and never mind that I half-slid, half-dove down to Beaver Brook and managed to walk to the Great Road on the wind-cleared ice. The essence of the experience, brief though it was, was that I had seen into the heart of the glacier.

SIMONE POIRIER-BURES

Simone Poirier-Bures is the author of an autobiographical novel, *Candyman* (1994), set in Halifax, Nova Scotia, and *Nicole* (2000), a collection of short narratives about growing up female and Acadian. Her travel memoir, *This Shining Place* (1995), about her experiences in Crete in the 1960s, won the 1996 Evelyn Richardson Award in Canada. She teaches at Virginia Polytechnic Institute and State University in Blacksburg. Her essays and stories have appeared in numerous anthologies and more than thirty journals in the United States, Canada, Australia, and England. The essay "The Shepherds" is taken from her work-in-progress about Kyrgyzstan.

Writing about Place

Whenever I travel to a new place, always hovering in my mind is the question: what would it be like to live here permanently? To see those mountains every day, to look at that sky, to feel the presence of that river, to eat these foods? How would the way I see and experience the world be different from the way I see and experience it at home? What small, hidden parts of my self would open up and bloom in this landscape? What parts would recede or go dormant? Place, I have found, deeply affects my experience and shapes my consciousness. When I write about place, everything is filtered through my sensibility. For me, writing about place means examining the intersection of place with self.

The four places I have written about most are those to which I've felt both an affinity and a sense of belonging. Two have been "home" for long periods of time—the province of Nova Scotia, where I grew up, and southwestern Virginia, where I now live—and two, the island of Crete and Kyrgyzstan, have been temporary homes.

During the last years of my growing up in Nova Scotia, I longed to be anywhere but there. My grandfather and great-grandfather had been sea captains; perhaps the same restlessness ran through my blood, or perhaps it was simply adolescent malaise. After I left—years later—I longed to return. My novel, *Candyman*, and its sister book *Nicole*, both set in Nova Scotia, were the result of that longing. The books are loosely autobiographical, so the writing of those books was very much a "return," not just to the place but also to the self

I had been while I lived there—the self-conscious girl with large but unshaped dreams, struggling to find an identity, coming to terms with her French Acadian ancestry in a province where the dominant culture was English. My family's roots in Nova Scotia run deep. My mother's ancestors arrived in 1632, when "Acadie" was French territory; my father's people came a little later; so there was a lot to sort out. Much about the province had changed since I'd left, but so had I. I had to paint a picture of what the place was like in the 1940s and 1950s, how it shaped my life and the life of the Acadian family I wrote about. The writing helped me "reclaim" both the place and my childhood self.

The self that emerged when I lived and taught on the island of Crete in the mid-1960s, when I was twenty-one, is also inextricably bound with my experience of that place. The island thrummed with passion and sensuality. The intense blue sky, the rich, warm light, the seductive music, the picturesque buildings, the food, the faces—were unlike anything I had ever experienced. I had come to that vibrant place from a cold northern climate, from a gray city muffled by blue laws and excessive self-restraint. It was an extraordinary liberation. Everything inside me exploded. I became consciously aware of the impact of place on self, of the many choices one could make about how to live. My months there became a time of great experimentation—how to live simply and joyfully with the fewest creature comforts possible. But I also felt the darker undercurrents present both in that place and in myself—a sense of chaos and order being held in a delicate balance. When I wrote about my life in Crete and a return visit twenty-five years later (in my memoir *That Shining Place*), I had to revisit that younger, braver, more idealistic self. I imagined her lurking in the corners, ready to reproach me. Revisiting that place both literally and figuratively was an intense and illuminating experience.

Apart from a few interludes, southwestern Virginia has been my home for the past twenty-three years. Predictably, the landscape here calls out a different part of my "self." Here, I'm much more aware of the nonhuman living world than I am or have been anywhere else. Nature is a strong presence in this part of Virginia—the vegetation is lush, the wildlife plentiful. I have a cottage by the New River, where I go in the summers to write, and while there I feel part of something larger, part of the community of all living beings, not just human. I've written a whole series of short essays about encounters with various creatures—spiders, lizards, feral geese, a possum, a wounded crow, deer in the garden, and so on—which I would probably never have written had I lived elsewhere. This place speaks to me in a way no other place has and becomes the muse for a certain kind of writing.

Kyrgyzstan, where I lived recently for eight months, affected my psyche in a profound and unexpected way. The country is 94 percent mountainous and sparsely populated, with perhaps the most starkly beautiful and dramatic landscapes I've ever seen. The highest mountains are snow-covered year round, and most are not treed. In the spring and summer the lower mountains turn velvety green, then brown, so you have vast expanses of great bare-shouldered mountains leaning against a bright blue, cloudless sky. Georgia O'Keeffe would have loved Kyrgyzstan. The landscape seems stripped down, unclut-tered, starkly simple and clean, yet full of surprises. I found myself resonating intensely to this landscape. It seemed to draw out and to mirror what I long for at this stage of my life—strong lines, simplicity, things pared down to the essentials. I wrote several articles about Kyrgyzstan and recently completed a memoir, "Where the Mountains Meet the Sky," about my experiences there. The piece included here, "The Shepherds," is an excerpt from that memoir.

Establishing a sense of place in writing involves much more than simply de-scribing the landscape. Landscape, of course, is very important: what the sky looks like, the vegetation (or lack of it), the horizon. Weather is important too, as it affects a person's experience of place in profound ways. But place is much more than this. To write about place means also to write about the people who inhabit that place, who have been formed by it—what they look like, how they dress, their food, customs, the sounds, the smells, the language. All these things are part of "place." When I lived in Greece, the passionate nature of the Greeks really struck me. They seemed part of the intense blue sky, the sunlight, the olive groves, the aromatic hills. The lives of the ethnic Kyrgyz also seem to match their surroundings. Once they were nomadic herd-ers who lived in yurts. Many still live the old way from May to October, when they take their herds of horses and sheep to the high mountain pastures. The Kyrgyz are a quiet, watchful people, as you would expect of those who live mostly outdoors. As a group, the traditional Kyrgyz are far less materialistic than we are in the West; their "riches" are family, fresh air, the mountains, their animals, rather than "things." Their relatively simple life seems to mir-ror the uncluttered landscape.

History and myth are also important in experiencing and rendering place—what happened there, the stories. When I lived in Greece, I was always aware of both the mythology and the history of Greece in general and Crete in particular. How can you live on the island of Crete and not know the stories of King Minos and the Minotaur? My experience of Crete was filtered through the lens of Mary Renault's book *The Bull from the Sea* as well as my studies of Greek history and myth. The same goes with Kyrgyzstan. Wherever we traveled, I felt the ghosts of the many people who had inhabited the land. I would look out over the vast panorama of mountains and sky and imagine the great camel caravans of the old Silk Road days that once lumbered over those mountains. I'd stand at the highest point of a mountain pass and imagine the Mongolian hordes that once swept down from the north and east. I'd picture the great Kyrgyz clans making their seasonal migrations with their animals and their yurts, carrying everything they owned. The past lives on in the present. The stories are there, in the land, the rocks, the air.

Writing about place, for me, always requires distance, both physical and temporal. You have to hold something away a little in order to see it properly. This was especially true with my memoir of Greece but also for my two books set in Nova Scotia. Only years later was I able to "hold away" those times and places in such a way as to "see" them clearly.

I tried to write about Kyrgyzstan while I was there. However, I found it hard to complete anything. I sketched out a few pieces, but changed them a lot after I got home. Part of the problem was that I didn't always know what things meant. I was trying to write about the old nomad culture, what remained of it, how it bubbled up into the now. You can tease a number of meanings out of a particular situation, but it often takes the magic of distance to really understand. To put something in perspective means to see it in terms of a larger whole, to see it from the outside, to see it from a distance. Often I would write my impressions of some event, then learn something that would make me see the earlier experience in a different light. As a result, I hesitated to try for any kind of closure.

Even after I got home, I had an exceedingly hard time shaping my material, deciding what to include, what to exclude. First I had to render the entire experience in language, then sift and sort. The act of writing, of course, is always a clarifying. You don't always see things until you write about them. Words distance. They make something into an object, separate it from you. In one of

Gabrielle Roy's novels an Inuit character says, "When we see things clearly in our heads, it is because we no longer hold them in our hands." "Separation" is the price you pay for clarity. Something is gained, but something is also lost.

While physical and/or temporal distance helps to distill and clarify how we see and write about place, the process is not without problems. For one, you forget things. When I wrote about my early days in Crete, I relied largely on memory, then used letters I had written home as a kind of check. When I reread those letters more than twenty-five years later, I found references to people and events I absolutely could not remember. Even though I had written about them vividly to my mother, they were completely gone from my memory.

Physical distance posed a special kind of problem in writing about Kyrgyzstan. Once home, I discovered many gaps in my notes. And because Kyrgyzstan is so little known in the West, I couldn't just look up facts on the Internet, and I couldn't just pop over and check. For example, I'd written a chapter on the still widely practiced custom of bride-kidnapping, based on conversations with my friend Zina, who was herself bride-kidnapped. But her narrative went only so far. When I returned to Kyrgyzstan a second time, after an interval of ten months, I learned many more details about this custom that I needed to include in my book.

Interestingly, I learned and experienced a good deal more of everything during that second stay, though it was considerably shorter than the first. I'd had time to digest the earlier experiences, to wonder about things. So, when I returned, I was ready to absorb more. Also, the fact that my husband and I had gone there not once but twice seemed to make a huge difference to the people. We were treated more like "insiders." We were shown things, allowed below the surface, so we saw much more deeply.

My process of writing was quite different for each place. As I mentioned earlier, when I wrote about Crete, I wrote about my early experiences largely from memory. Since so much time had passed, the process of "reconstructing" that period was an amazing journey, one I chronicle in the afterword to the memoir. On my return visit to Crete twenty-five years later, I kept a journal to record my impressions, and used those extensively in the writing.

When I wrote about Nova Scotia, I also relied a good deal on memory. But my family still lives there, and I travel back and forth regularly to visit them, so I was able to do a lot of firsthand observing as I was doing the writing. I was also able to check things with my siblings and do some research during my visits.

Writing about Kyrgyzstan involved a different process altogether. I went there with the intention of writing about it. This changed the way I experienced it as well as the way I wrote about it. A kind of longing had precipitated and propelled my writing about both Crete and Nova Scotia, a longing to make meaning out of a period of my life spent in those places. I lived in those places first then wrote about them. Because I set out to write about Kyrgyzstan to begin with, I had my writing antennae on alert the whole time I was there. I kept copious journals. I wrote down many, many specifics—names of things, places, people, facts, dates—the sorts of things I tend to forget. I also wrote little narratives of various experiences and transcribed whole conversations shortly after they occurred. In a few instances I even tape-recorded conversations on my small recorder. I also wrote a series of "newsletters" that I sent via email to family and friends. All these things helped me begin the process of characterizing the place and shaping narratives. Because my focus was more on the place than on any significant thing that happened to me there, this book is unlike the others I have written on place. Still, my observations were very much determined by my interests and the strong affinity I felt with the people and the landscape.

The Kyrgyz singer Rosa Amanova sings a love song called "I Want to Long for You." The speaker of the song wants to see her beloved from a distance, wants to feel the exquisite state of longing. It took that kind of "longing"—being separated from the beloved—for me to be able, finally, to complete my book.

The Shepherds

Zina is planning an excursion in the country for us. We will go to the mountains and make *shashlik*.

"What shall I bring?" I ask.

"Nothing. I will bring everything. You don't have to worry about anything."

Finally, I've learned how it works. Back home, if a hostess is asked, "What shall I bring?" she might suggest something. Here, it would offend the laws of hospitality to ask a guest to bring anything. We buy a half-dozen of the raisin rolls we know Zina likes, a kilo of huge ripe cherries, and another of apricots. These fruits, just now coming into the markets, are still expensive for locals, so they'll be a special treat. We also bring a bottle of vodka, mineral water, and five small plastic tumblers. In the Kyrgyz code of host and guest these items will be considered "gifts" rather than contributions to the meal.

We all pack into the old Lada, Allen and I, Zina and Kalubek, their son Kubanich, and both grandsons, six-year-old Semetey and three-year-old Jomart. The trunk is loaded with cucumbers and tomatoes and onions and rice and a covered enamel bowl with about ten pounds of raw mutton.

"We will go to a village," Zina tells us. "It is in the mountains. We have a relative there."

"Are they expecting us?"

"No," Zina says, "but it is okay. Relatives can come any time." Though the clans are not as strong as in the old nomadic days, they still have a powerful hold; kinsmen are always welcome, whatever the circumstances.

The village, called Arashan, is about a half-hour's drive from Bishkek and consists of several dozen shabby houses sprawled along rutted dirt roads. Zina calls out at the gate, and a woman emerges from the house looking enormously picturesque with her big smile, half of her teeth missing, the other half studded with gold. A colorful kerchief covers her head, and she wears a mismatched vest and old woolen skirt. The man who appears behind her in a short-sleeved shirt and dark trousers looks much more urban, like a professional man from Bishkek. They are Batima and Johlchu, both sixty-six. We follow them into the house, an old Russian cottage made of plastered adobe, pausing to remove our shoes in a primitive anteroom which serves as the kitchen and storage area. Among the sacks of flour and grain, enameled bowls and glass jars hold various milk products—sour cream, clotted cream, fresh milk, *ayran* (a yogurt drink), butter. A thick wolf pelt hangs on the wall near a hearth with a huge wok-like *kazan*.

Johlchu leads us into the main room, where we are to sit on long quilted mats arranged on the floor around an eating cloth, while Zina and Batima make tea. I know there will be more than tea, and I want to watch the preparations, so I go out and join the women. Batima has made a fire using patties of dried cow dung and small pieces of wood. Now she will make bread. I watch her slice off a chunk of dough from a large mound in one of the enameled bowls, roll out a round flat loaf, and place it in the hot *kazan*. There's no oil; the dough cooks like pizza in an oven. As the bottom browns, she flips the bread over and punches it down.

As I hover over Batima, she turns and grins at me. "You very beautiful woman," she says, my blue eyes and fair complexion exotic here next to their bronze skin and Asian eyes. But how refreshing, this spontaneity! She says what she thinks, with an impish face.

Her husband comes in and watches her bustling around. "She is my beautiful girl," he says. She laughs and gives him a playful look. "He, my chocolate."

"Forty-six years," he says, "we are together."

Batima slices off another hunk of dough for *kattama*, a delicacy. She rolls it into a wider, thinner circle, smears it with butter, rolls it up, flattens it, butters it again, then rolls it out like the other loaf. This one, though, is filled with half a pound of country butter.

The first loaf is now cooked, so Batima puts the *kattama* in its place. Zina, meanwhile, prepares the salad. There's no running water, and I watch how efficiently she rinses the cucumbers, tomatoes, and radishes in a shallow pan half-filled with water. Inside, the cloth is laden with bowls of *ayran*, fresh clotted cream and the fruit. Zina carries in the tea and salad. Everything is in two's, even the cherries and apricots. The warm bread, by itself or dipped into the cream, is absolutely wonderful.

Kalubek pours out drinks, vodka for the men and brandy for the women. It's time, now, for the formalities. Johlchu holds up his glass. "I am Muselman," he says. "No drink, no smoke." This is to let us know that though he holds a filled glass for the toast, he will not drink it, and we are not to be offended. Batima raises her glass and cackles. "I am American woman." Though her husband does not drink, she does.

Johlchu pauses, recalling the English words he learned during his university days. Zina has told him that Allen and I were in Kyrgyzstan once before, that we had become good friends. "Guests are sacred to the Muslim people," he says, measuring his words carefully. "When they come for the first time, they are the dearest guests. When they come the second time, they are relatives. So, let us drink to relativeness."

It's a lovely toast, and as we raise our glasses, Batima chimes in to Allen, "Your wife very beautiful. Many Kyrgyz men want to marry her."

"I'm already taken," I say. We all laugh and drink to the toast.

Our host and hostess, we learn, spend their winters in the city and their summers here. During the Soviet period Johlchu worked in Bishkek for the KGB, which accounts for his citified mien. He retired eleven years ago, when he was fifty-five. I can't help but remember the stories we've heard about the KGB and wonder what kind of man Johlchu might have been then. Most likely, there were as many functionaries as there were thugs, I remind myself, and those old things are best forgotten.

Batima is more interesting to me, this quintessential country woman who does everything with such joy and zest. According to Zina, she spent a year at the university in Osh; then she and Johlchu married, and she quit. They have eight children and thirteen grandchildren. How did they come to have this house? I ask Zina. Was one of them born here? No, Zina reminds me, they are from Toktogul. Of course: Johlchu is Zina's uncle; all of Zina and Kalubek's friends and relatives are from Toktogul. Batima and Johlchu have this house because Batima was a shepherdess here. During the Soviet period everyone had a job. This was her job. She and her eight children took care of three hundred sheep, and the house came with the job. In the summer they took the sheep to the high mountain pastures and slept in a yurt; in the winter they slept here. Johlchu had a car and commuted to and from Bishkek.

I still have many questions about the Soviet period, about the whole system of communism versus privatism, how things were for villagers in particular. What happened to the sheep? How did they get to market? There were no markets, Zina says. The state made a plan for a region, say, how many sheep they were supposed to produce. A man would come and take the sheep, and the meat would be given to the people. Could they keep some of it for themselves? Of course, and they had their own animals, too. And did they grow crops for their own use? A few. Not so many. But they kept turkeys and some horses. The other things, they got in Bishkek.

It's hard to figure out how the whole food distribution thing worked, how people got what they needed. There were shortages, Zina confirms. "Some things we could not buy. There was no black tea, for example, only green. Then we had plenty of money but nothing to buy. Now we have not much money but many things to buy!"

"I hate money," Batima says with her impish grin. Zina laughs. "Our families and our friends are our riches," Zina says. "Money is not so important to Kyrgyz people." I am reminded again of the traditional Kyrgyz aversion to buying and selling. The old way, bartering, was like a system of gifts: this gift given, that one returned, a system that sustained the Kyrgyz for most of their long history. During the Soviet period most things were provided, so they didn't have to worry about money. Now they must learn an entirely new system.

Batima and Johlchu have sixty sheep, thirty goats, six cows, and many chickens. A few dozen hens, a huge King rooster, and several clutches of chicks freely roam the yard. Every summer their children and grandchildren come at various times to visit; when they go home to the city, they take with them fresh milk and butter and eggs, sour cream, and *ayran*—the tastes of the country, redolent of fresh air and high meadows, the other "riches" of the Kyrgyz.

Kalubek and Kubanich go outside to prepare the fire pit and *shashlik*, while the rest of us linger.

"She is also a wonderful craftswoman," Zina says. "Her *yurta*, which she made herself, was the most beautiful in all of Kyrgyzstan. It is now in a museum in Turkey."

Batima shows us several bundles of wool, some the natural color, some dyed yellow and red, and a long, beautifully woven band intended to encircle the top of a yurt. She also shows us several long patchwork cushions in the making and colorful diamonds of felt to be stitched together for *shirdaks*, the traditional floor coverings of a yurt.

"She is making a *yurta* for her daughter," Zina explains.

"How did her yurt end up in a Turkish museum?"

"They put it in an exhibition in Bishkek. It was 1993. An important Turkish minister was visiting. They gave it to him. They did not ask her permission, exactly. They asked her in such a way that she could not refuse. But they paid for her to go there for a ceremony and gave a two-room flat in Bishkek in exchange. It's where they live now, in the winter."

"Was she happy with that?" I ask, ready to sniff out an injustice.

"It was okay," says Zina.

Batima says something which Zina translates. "She would like to make something and present it to you. Perhaps you would like a small *shirdak*?"

A felt mat—far too generous a gift, it seems to me, given their means. But it would offend the laws of hospitality to refuse altogether. Something more modest attracts my attention. An exquisite woven triangle about six inches long, fringed and colorful—a needle holder to hang inside a yurt. "One of those," I say. "That would be wonderful."

"Good. She will make another and present it to you."

Batima beams. "I love you," she says to me. "You are my girl."

I hug her. "Your old girl," I say, noting that I am only ten years younger than she is. She finds this enormously funny. "My old girl," she says and laughs and laughs.

Outside, the fire in the small pit has died down to coals, and the smell of the roasting meat is irresistible. Our host and Zina gather up the skewers—sapling branches stripped of bark and threaded with mutton—and Kalubek brings the brandy and vodka and glasses. Someone else carries a bowl with the remains of the salad and one spoon, and we head out for the foothills, the two grandsons trailing behind us. The hills are covered with wildflowers, thousands and thousands of bright red poppies, studded with bluebells and small orange flowers.

As we walk, Batima orders: "Sing song." I sing a few verses of "Old McDonald Had a Farm." She listens, unimpressed. "It's a children's song," I explain. "Sing love song," she says. I sing "The Water Is Wide," an old folk song. She nods her approval.

By now we have arrived at a particularly beautiful spot, and we stand among the poppies eating the *shashlik*, pulling off the meat with our fingers. There are no napkins or plates. Johlchu passes around spoonfuls of the salad, which Allen and I decline (that common spoon, going into everyone's mouth), but no one else seems to mind. We drink a few more toasts, and Batima announces: "I sing song." She sings first a song about love, then one about the motherland. Her voice is rich and beautiful, like the rich, heavy cream we dipped our bread into. She sings for the sheer joy of it, as if the beauty of this place called forth her song. I'm reminded again how much the Kyrgyz love music, how much they love nature, how both are part of the Kyrgyz identity.

The boys, meanwhile, wander around gathering flowers and poking and inspecting small stones and insects. On their wrists they wear bracelets with small black and white beads similar to the blue and white "evil eyes" of the Turks, evidence of their common origin as Turkic people. Children here also sometimes wear an owl or hawk's feather to keep away evil or a wolf's claw or tooth, the most powerful "protection." Kubanich has a wolf's claw hanging from the inside mirror of his car. A small link to the old consciousness, something I hadn't noticed when we were here before.

Batima sits and spreads out her apron, which turns out to be a wraparound skirt, under which she wears what look like sweatpants ("I am American woman," she cackles again), and invites me to sit with her. She is clearly in her element here, surrounded by all this beauty—the velvety green lower mountains, the snow-covered ones higher up, the foothills shimmering with luminous red poppies. Below us a handful of cows graze. Above us a chestnut mare hovers over her foal, the grass almost iridescent behind them. It feels like a kind of heaven, like the idyll of the great pastoral poems: come with me and be my love, and we will all the pleasures prove . . . . It's the idyll of the Kyrgyz nomad, too, the *jiloh* of their dreams, for which they spurned sedentary life.

"Was this your *jiloh* in the old days?" I ask.

"This good *jiloh*." She points to the higher mountains. "There is better." Always, the Kyrgyz prefer the highest places, close to Tenir, the god of high places.

We look and look, utterly content. Days could fly by. Years. There is no past, no future. Only the now, heavy with timelessness.

"I will sleep," Batima says suddenly. She wraps her apron around herself and lies down in the poppies for a nap.

Johlchu leaves to check on the sheep, and Zina heads down to check on the boys. Kalubek and Allen and I wander up over the next hill. In the distance a flotilla of hang gliders suddenly appears over the crest of the mountains, wafting down like enormous red and yellow birds. Tourists from Bishkek, we conclude, and such an incongruous sight—a reminder of the twenty-first century, in this place that seems to belong to a much earlier time. Behind them the sky has begun to darken, and we can hear the deep rumble of thunder. A mountain storm is brewing. We head back to the house as the first sputtering drops begin to fall.

Zina has begun making *plov* in the big *kazan*. She fries what's left of the mutton then adds onions and garlic, followed by rinsed Uzgen rice. Aside from the bread and dairy products supplied by our hosts and the fruit that Allen and I contributed, Zina brought everything for the meals. When you arrive unannounced, it seems the safe thing to do.

She needs more cow dung for fuel, and I volunteer to get it. I find a pile of dried patties by the barn and marvel as I fill the bucket. I could never have imagined myself handling dried cow dung like this. But it's not offensive. It doesn't smell, and it's both an efficient fuel and a good way to use the dung, as wood is scarce. When I return, Zina hands me another bucket to get some water. I ask Zina's son Kubanich where to find it, and he takes the bucket without a word. I follow him.

The way to the spring is through a neighbor's yard, but a big yellow dog is lying in the path. Everyone here has a healthy respect for dogs, and Kubanich does not forge ahead. Instead, he stops about fifteen feet away, fixes his eyes on the dog, and begins making soft, barely audible clicking and whistling sounds. The dog watches him over its shoulder, its ears twitching. This goes on for several minutes, Kubanich making his small noises, the dog watching him warily. Then the dog gets up and slinks off toward his house. It's as if Kubanich, this young man of few words, has just conjured the dog. I can't help but think of the old descriptions I've read of Native American guides: how silent and alert they were. Kubanich is like that. He rarely makes eye contact yet seems completely aware of what is going on around him. He, like his father, spent his boyhood summers in *jiloh*, tending sheep and horses under the wide blue sky. Perhaps that is why he seems to know things.

At the spring Kubanich rinses the bucket then fills it with fresh, clear water. Except for the fact that we carry a tin bucket instead of a bag made from an animal skin, things have not changed much in hundreds of years.

On our way back, it begins to rain in earnest, and we make it to the cooking room just as it begins to pour. The rain beats down on the corrugated roof. Semetey listens and says something that delights Zina: "He is saying, 'The rain sings a song,'" she tells us.

Johlchu comes down the path from the mountain, where he had been checking on the sheep. He walks at his normal pace, though the rain is pelting down. He has on an old shepherd's vest made of thick, coarse wool and holds a heavy quilted mat over his head like a small umbrella. The shepherd's mat: to sit and recline on in the pasture, to use as shelter when it rains.

The *plov* is soon ready, so we all go into the main room for the last meal of the day. And it seems once more that we have been catapulted back to an earlier time. Everyone eats directly from the two platters of *plov*, no little plates and forks—that is for modern times and with strangers; we are "relatives" now. Though Allen and I use spoons to scoop up the rice, the others use their fingers and hands, the old way. It's easy to imagine ourselves in a yurt a hundred years ago.

Suddenly it's time to go. It has stopped raining, and Johlchu must attend to the sheep. We say the *omin*, then quickly gather up all the pieces of bread, for it must be treated with reverence. Batima carries the rest of the food to the kitchen, and Zina rolls up the eating cloth. In a few minutes we are at the back door. Johlchu dons his shepherd's vest, still a bit damp from earlier, puts on his kalpak, and heads out to the hills. The KGB man turned shepherd, content with his life. We say our good-byes to Batima, who smiles and hugs us fervently, then leave her to the mountains, the poppies, the green grass—everything washed clean now, the way it has always been, after a spring rain.

◄► ROBERT ROOT

Robert Root is the author of the memoir *Recovering Ruth: A Biographer's Tale* (2003) and several works on nonfiction writing, including *E. B. White: The Emergence of an Essayist* (1999) and *Working at Writing: Columnists and Critics Composing* (1994). He is the coeditor, with Michael Steinberg, of *The Fourth Genre: Contemporary Writers of/on Creative Nonfiction*, 4th ed. (2007), and interview/roundtable editor of the journal *Fourth Genre: Explorations in Nonfiction*. An emeritus professor at Central Michigan University, he has published and presented widely on nonfiction and composition and is the author of a writing text, *Wordsmithery: A Guide to Working at Writing*, 2nd ed. (1998). His essays have appeared in such journals as *Ascent, River Review/Revue Riviere, Rivendell*, the *Concord Saunterer, divide, Ecotone*, and *North Dakota Quarterly*, where "Anasazi" first appeared.

Discovering Place

All my writing has been a means of discovery, whether I intended it or not. Whatever I write turns out to be about something different or to have meant something different than what I initially supposed it would. Writers can't escape their individual perspectives, which always filter the images they perceive. The composing itself may be an attempt to see past the filters, to slide the interfering surfaces out of the way, but it usually only reveals the nature of the filters, particularly the ones that can't be removed, and the result is not so much "This is the way the world is" but "This is the way the world appears to me and why I see it that way." That is, the subject ends up being not *the way the world is* but *the way certain filters affect the way the world appears to be to the author.*

When I write about place I'm discovering not only the place but also the reasons I'm writing about it. When I write in my journal at home, I'm not writing about home as a place but, rather, what's on my mind about my work or my life or, less often, events occurring in the world. When I write in my journal as I travel, I may be equally mundane, simply recording what I did or saw or ate and who was with me. But sometimes in the travel journal I find myself being more exploratory, more observant, more reflective—I sense that something's happening to me because of where I am and wonder why I'm still responding to the experience long after I've recorded the details. The clincher comes when I find myself writing about the place at home. The only way to get it off my mind may be to write about it until I can't write about it anymore.

That's the way it began with "Anasazi," the essay that follows. As its opening sentence indicates, when my wife and I returned from our trip to the Four Corners area, I felt haunted by the Anasazi. We'd visited Anasazi ruins in places like Mesa Verde and Chaco Canyon, and the experience seemed to color everything else we saw as we traveled. There's a kind of synchronicity that seems to be at work in some writing projects, a sense that everything you encounter is somehow connected to some essential core. Much of the composing is an effort to discover how much is truly connected, no matter how tangential it may at first appear, and how much isn't truly connected, no matter whether it happened at the same time and in the same place or not. Sometimes the connections are wildly disparate, part of a random and felicitous design; sometimes they are intimately related, fundamental and inseparable. At the risk of putting too much of a mystical spin on this feeling, I'd say that very often the writer's job is not to impose order on scattered material but, instead, to let the work in progress tell the writer what it wants to be, what order or structure it should have—what it means.

At the time of that Southwest trip I was writing brief essays, three or four pages long, to run four or five minutes on a local public radio station. A couple of scripts came out of our travels, including one about the darkness at the back of caves and watching the flames in campfires, and another about the Anasazi. But three pages weren't long enough to satisfy whatever need I felt. In some ways I was so attached to Mesa Verde and Chaco that I wanted to be there still, not back in Michigan starting another school year. In my reading—pamphlets, brochures, guidebooks, Tony Hillerman and Nevada Barr mysteries, picture books—and above all in my writing I *was* still there. Eventually, I worked through the discovery of what lay beneath my fascination with this lost culture—the note on which the essay ends was a primal epiphany for me. I also discovered something about myself as a writer.

I came away from the experience of "Anasazi" hoping to do more essays of place, what I often refer to as intersecting histories, explorations of places where my personal history intersects with cultural history and natural history. If you're looking for places of intersecting personal, cultural, and natural histories, you theoretically could find them everywhere. Some places seem to readily provoke that urge in me, for example, the Habitation at Port Royal in Nova Scotia or Isle Royale way out in Lake Superior; others seem to have no effect of that kind on me. I love Paris and Venice but can't imagine writing about them. I can travel comfortably in Rome or Chicago or London, but as much as I enjoy the art and architecture and ambiance or atmosphere, nothing about them gives me, in John Jerome's phrase, "gear teeth for my interest"—as a writer, anyway. And that was even truer of the place I lived most of my adult life—the center of Michigan's lower peninsula, to which I felt largely unconnected and detached in spite of nearly thirty years' residence there.

Though I would love to be an insider, I think I mostly start out as an outsider and write my way into place. In my earliest essays of place, the places usually surprised me, and the essays grew organically out of engagement and surprise. Three weeks in the Southwest, a week in the Bitterroot Mountains, a week in Nova Scotia—all generated essays I hadn't intended to write. Even my first book of creative nonfiction, *Recovering Ruth*, grew out of an unexpected fascination with place, Isle Royale, as much as out of an unexpected obligation to research the life of a nineteenth-century woman whose diary I was editing. But lately I've been trying to predict what projects will fascinate me and electing to launch myself into the nonfiction of place deliberately, rather than find myself already afloat and very much at sea.

I carefully designed the project that became the essay "The Ponds" (though I certainly didn't design the way the essay ended up). "The Ponds" is about Great Pond in Belgrade Lakes, Maine, and Walden Pond in Concord, Massachusetts, and I traveled to them in order to discover what I could recognize about them from having read great nonfiction inspired by them, E. B. White's essay "Once More to the Lake" and Thoreau's book *Walden*.

A long project I am engaged with—perhaps the most challenging work I've undertaken—is a lyrical meditation on the Hudson and Rhine rivers. I was familiar with neither locale before I started, and both of them have been difficult to write about because I don't have constant easy access to them. I can't be on-site long enough to write copiously enough while I'm there to have discovery drafts to draw on when I get back home. There are other problems with the rivers book as well—for example, the scale of it is so large and the number of segments and sections I have to deal with so varied that I'm often at a loss for which item to concentrate on when—but clearly I'd have an easier time of it if I lived on the Hudson or the Rhine or both instead of where I do live, which for now is Colorado.

My second long project, instigated by my need to acclimate myself to an unfamiliar landscape, is somewhat easier in terms of proximity. It sets me in search of intersecting histories again by making me follow the trail of Isabella Bird's 1873 travels around the Front Range of the Rocky Mountains, all of her destinations within a day's drive of where I live now. She wrote her first draft in letters to her sister about her experiences as she lived them; it took her three months. I expect my first draft will take longer, but I also expect to get a great deal more on-site exposure to the place of this nonfiction than I have anywhere else.

Sometimes a place sneaks up on you. You don't know you're going to write about it or even that you're going to be in a particular place, and it's the disorientation of the first encounter that sets the writing in motion. Because I usually travel with at least one journal and one daybook, I usually intend to record my experiences, if only so I can remember a particular restaurant or particular hiking trail later on or know the dates I was in a particular place. In those instances the eventual essay (if an essay surfaces) builds from the journal entries. One essay started after I'd been hiking while attending a writing conference near the Bitterroot Mountains. After a while I recognized a pattern or an arc to these events, something to explore in writing, and because I had nightly journal entries to help me remember, I was able to reconstruct the experiences. Something similar happened with "Anasazi," though in that case I did more background reading as I wrote the essay for accuracy about the information in the draft. Often I will turn to other resources to be certain I correctly identify the flora and fauna, the geology and topography, the history and culture of a place. In the Bitterroots essay, which ends with a view of distant mountains, I checked maps and regional geology to be certain I was naming the formations and the locations correctly. In "Anasazi" I was more focused on up-to-date research in anthropology, geography, and botany.

While I usually carry a journal or a daybook—the daybook is a small blank book that I can stick in a pocket and write in anywhere—I write in them impulsively rather than systematically. I seem to have a fear of being alone somewhere with nothing to read and nothing to write on. But if I intend to go somewhere in particular, especially if there's a chance I'll write about it, I'll do some homework, read up on the place, get hold of some maps or other writing about the location, and arm myself with project-specific journals. For the visits to the Hudson and Rhine rivers I traveled with a special daybook, which I thought of as a traveler's log, and a special journal. As much as possible I wrote daily in both, recording immediate experience in the daybook and reflecting on locations and events in the journal. In practice I'm more faithful to the daybook than to the journal. Because on one trip east to work on the Hudson I was also going to Maine and Massachusetts to work on the project involving Great Pond and Walden Pond, I kept separate journals and daybooks for each project, effectively compartmentalizing my life—the rivers project here, the ponds project here, the personal life here. I often remind myself of a trail guide in James West Davison and John Rugge's *Great Heart* who kept two separate journals; in conscious allusion to him I often write in one journal, as he did, "See other book," to redirect myself to something I've recorded elsewhere. Emerson, when he traveled in Europe, apparently had a notebook for expenses and similar items, a different journal for each country he visited, and an overall travel journal—he was a great compartmentalizer and always aware that everything he wrote was potentially work-in-progress.

Of course, even though I make field notes and journal entries and take photographs I'm always learning on the spot or, especially, when I'm writing a journal entry or a rough draft, finding out just what it is I don't really know or should have known before I arrived. Sometimes you get the knowledge to fill in what you should have known, and then you can go back and try to see the place again from your new vantage point; sometimes the new knowledge is enough to help you reconstruct the experience. I'm always trying to write myself back into the place I'm writing about.

Writing about place while you're in place provides a sense of immediacy to the writing. From the reader's perspective that sense of immediacy isn't dependent upon the writer's having composed the essay on the spot; for the writer—or at least for me—it always helps to have launched the writing in place. It makes it a little easier to recapture that sense of immediacy later on, which is better than having to invent the sense of immediacy from scratch. This acknowledges that immediacy is partly a literary device—one of my favorite and most often repeated comments by Oscar Wilde is his remark that he revises everything eleven times, ten times to get everything right, and the eleventh time to put in that touch of spontaneity that everyone admires about his writing. Immediacy isn't simply something you start with; it usually is something you painstakingly preserve or consciously construct over many revisions.

But since it's often the writing itself that reveals or uncovers the significance of the experience or the locale for the writer—sometimes over many drafts, with excruciating slowness—it's difficult to complete the writing in place, especially if it's not a place you live. In order to deal with the distance in time or space from the actual moment in a specific place, I try to record as much as I can when I'm there—in daybooks, journals, notes, photographs—and then expect to find ways to relive or reenter the experience when I'm writing. Once, when I was writing short essays for the radio, I went camping at a state park and wrote a letter to a friend while sitting on a sand dune watching the sunset over Lake Michigan. I didn't take notes or pictures, since I wasn't expecting to write an essay about the experience, but later on, when further reflection made me realize I could write something, I was able to recapture the experience by imagining myself back on that dune at sunset writing that letter to my friend. Of course, I could have asked to borrow the letter—that's what the Victorian writer Mary Kingsley did when she was writing *Travels in West Africa*; she called in those voluminous letters she had written from the field and recovered a lot of information about her adventures and their background—but I found that remembering the sand dune and the sunset was enough to get back in the moment.

Writing records ideas and language in your memory as well as on the page, and the secret is to find a way to access those memories. One of my students once wrote a journal entry about a photograph of her and her friends getting on a gondola in Venice at the start of a tour of the city, and that opened her up enough to the memory of the tour that she eventually wrote a whole essay about it. The key is finding the trigger for memory. When my wife and I were sailing on the Rhine, the cruise vessel played the opening of Schumann's Third Symphony, generally known as the Rhenish, or Rhine, Symphony, each time it left a dock, and now, at home, all I need to do is play the symphony to conjure up that trip.

If these strategies are not enough, I'll read background sources. For the book on the Hudson and Rhine, for example, I want to know the geology of the Palisades or the Loreley Rock, and I'll find a way to fold the information into the narrative; for my book about Isle Royale I read a great deal about the copper mining industry and toured old mines in hopes of being able to translate my experience into the unrecorded experiences of historical figures. No matter how much writing gets done in place, it is always necessary, for me at least, to look something up, to consult a field guide or a history or some other resource to add specific background details, to make the experience richer and more concrete than it was at the moment I lived it.

I don't want to misrepresent or exaggerate the role of place in my writing. If I continue the family memoir I started years ago, I will have to evoke place—Lockport, New York, in the 1940s and 1950s—but the core of the work will be family, character, narrative moments. As a memoirist I will need to know the degree to which place affects outlook, but the emphasis will have to be on personality. As I work on the Colorado project, I will be more centered on place—how certain locations appeared to Isabella Bird and her contemporaries in the 1870s and how they appear to me in the 2000s—but I will also be centered on time, how when we perceive these sites influences the nature of our perceptions. It's another project about intersecting histories. But then, so is the memoir.

Maybe it's only a matter of shifts in emphasis, this project more subjective, more personal, more intimate, that project more objective, more historical, more analytical. There's a sliding scale here, but at bottom maybe all I'm writing is a nonfiction of place.

In my writing I want to be accurate enough, detailed enough, descriptive enough, that the reader can breathe the air of the place I'm writing about, can go to the place in my essay or memoir or travel narrative and have the sensation of feeling that she's been there before. Before that can happen, of course, I have to bring it alive for myself. And that's what I'm trying above all to do.

Anasazi

I am haunted by the ghosts of the Anasazi, the ancient ones of the Mesa Verde cliff dwellings, the Chaco Canyon pueblos, and thousands of other sites scattered across the Four Corners. I am haunted by the spirits of those who peopled the Cliff Palace, Pueblo Bonito, the primitive pithouses on Chapin Mesa, and the Great Kiva of Casa Rinconada. Once I gazed at a stark, sheer wall of Cliff Canyon only to discover the shattered ruins of an Anasazi house secreted in a niche under a massive overhang—saw it emerging in my vision like a spirit photograph; now I browse coffeetable books of western landscape photography half-expecting to discover in the scenery a telltale set of handholds in rock overhangs, props beneath great boulders, the remnants of a wall, or the outline of a buried kiva. Like buildings taking sudden shape upon a bare canyon wall or a city of clay and stone rising from a desolate desert, the Anasazi seem to be just beyond my vision, perhaps drawn back down the Great Sipapu from which in the beginning mankind first emerged, and I am haunted by a sense of their imminent presence.

That August Sue and I had crammed clothing, camping gear, and all kinds of guidebooks into a Chevette and left Missouri for the Southwest, first sweltering through the prairie heat of Kansas and then steaming through the mountain rain of southern Colorado. Yet when we turned off U.S. 160 between Mancos and Cortez onto the road to Mesa Verde National Park, we were not too weary to be startled by the flat cylinder of rock rising from the pine forest.

We drove cautiously up the steep, winding entrance road carved out of the side of the mesa, two lowland midwesterners both awed and unnerved by the tortuous twists and turns, the magnificent view unfolding ever farther below us, the sheer drop seeming always to be only inches away.

Morfield Campground, located in a basin surrounded by further heights of the mesa, had over five hundred campsites, but each campsite was isolated from the others by piñon pine and juniper and tall grass. When we began setting up the tent, the only ones who watched us were a mule deer doe and her twins, kibitzing at the border of the trees. Near sunset dozens of deer slipped out to browse in the high grass; campers strolling around the campground in the fading light stopped in the road to watch them, and the deer stared back warily while they ate.

The night turned cool and the campground quieted and the sky was clear and dazzlingly brilliant with stars. We found our way to the campground amphitheater to listen to a talk on astronomy. One of the park rangers had set up a telescope and helped us locate Mars, Jupiter, four of Jupiter's moons, and some constellations. On our return the lights of lanterns and woodfires were absorbed by the surrounding vegetation, and the campground seemed sparsely populated, even though we knew it was nearly full. We were only aware of that dazzling overcrowded sky, for the first time in our lives appearing before us unobstructed, in its full glory. We fell asleep looking up at that dense canopy of stars, feeling absolutely alone except for the company of the universe.

In the morning we drove off toward the ruins. Mesa Verde, the "green table" aptly named by early Spanish-speaking visitors to the region, spreads out to the south in long peninsulas separated by deep, narrow canyons. The Anasazi ruins most visitors see are on Chapin Mesa, some sixteen miles south of the campground. There, at Mesa Top Ruins, the neatly laid out archaeological evidence follows the path of development that culminated in the magnificent cliff dwellings built in the twelfth century CE and abandoned mysteriously soon after. The peoples who wandered onto Mesa Verde from unknown origins around six hundred CE were Modified Basket Makers. They found in the climate of the mesa a place to develop their agriculture of corn and squash and supplemented it by hunting the plentiful game with spears, using an atlatl, or spear-thrower, for greater force. Mesa Verde rises seven to eight thousand feet above sea level; its rains are more plentiful than in the surrounding area, and the Anasazi soon learned how to capitalize on the rainfall by building abundant dams and irrigation channels—the remains of Mummy Lake, one of their reservoirs, is still visible at Far View Ruins.

In time their population grew. At first they built pithouses by excavating earthen circles, strengthening the walls, and covering it all with a raised roof of sticks and wattle. The entrance was through the smokehole on the roof. Originally pithouses were single-family dwellings and single rooms; eventually anterooms were added for storage. Then, as the population grew, the pithouses were replaced by pueblos, multi-room dwellings built above ground of single-course masonry, a row of stones mortared with mud. The pithouse, which had been not only a dwelling place but a place of ceremonial events, survived in the communal kiva, a large circular pit whose common elements included a firepit in the center, supporting pilasters, or pillars, a banquette or bench encircling the room, niches in the wall for ceremonial objects, and a ladder leading to the roof by which clan members entered or exited. Ventilation shafts were added to bring in fresh air by another source than the smokehole/entrance, and a stone slab was added to deflect the airflow and circulate it around the room. Each kiva also had a small circular hole in the floor, the sipapu, a symbolic reminder of the Great Sipapu, the hole in the earth leading to the underworld from which, according to myth, mankind had first appeared in this world.

The development from pithouse to pueblo was a matter of centuries, a time of growing population, stable and increasing food supply, and expanding trade with other Indian cultures. From the world outside Mesa Verde came beans, a more reliable crop; the improved hunting technology of the bow and arrow; pottery, which the Anasazi adopted and enhanced with their own unique black and white designs; and better techniques of construction, apparently developed in the pueblos of the Chaco culture to the south.

The Chaco culture had developed in ways similar to Mesa Verde throughout the same period. Chaco Canyon, in west-central New Mexico, is a broad desert rimmed with low mesas. There the Anasazi developed an extensive culture of interrelated towns and outposts. Roads were developed, trade routes established, lookout towers constructed with some system of communication between outposts and central pueblos. At the center was Pueblo Bonito, an enormous planned city of over six hundred rooms and thirty-three kivas, terraced up to five stories high and supporting an estimated population of a thousand people. The desert Anasazi had an influence on the Anasazi of Mesa Verde, particularly in the method of stone construction of pueblos, and the trade between them must have been vigorous.

But in the twelfth century, almost at the height of their prosperity, the Chaco Anasazi abandoned Pueblo Bonito and vanished, their extensive culture withered, and their buildings were left to the ravages of time. And at Mesa Verde the Anasazi began to construct their dwellings in sandstone overhangs on canyon walls, leaving the mesa tops for the cultivation of crops but living their lives in cliff dwellings that sometimes reached astonishing size. They came and went from the dwellings by means of hand and toeholds scraped in the sheer cliff face, descending a hundred feet from the rim to buildings often perched hundreds of feet above the canyon floor. It was a precarious, if well-protected, existence.

And then, at the end of the century, following twenty-three years of drought, dated by tree ring dendrochronology as 1276–99, the mountain Anasazi too disappeared, abandoned their cliff dwellings, left no traces of where they went. When nomadic tribes such as the Utes, the Navajos, and the Apaches wandered into the region, they avoided the deserted buildings. Today the Ute reservation surrounds Mesa Verde on three sides, and the Navajo reservation to the west of Chaco Canyon occupies an area larger than New England, stretching across New Mexico, Arizona, and Utah, much of it dotted with Anasazi ruins.

There are mysteries here, about both the origins of the Anasazi and their fate and about the decisions they made concerning the culture they created in the five centuries in which their culture is recorded. The pueblos and cliff dwellings seem to be defensive measures, particularly the double-course masonry that replaced simpler construction in later centuries, but there is no historical evidence of warfare or invaders—the known nomadic tribes came much later. We understand little about the relationship between such towns as Pueblo Bonito and Cliff Palace and their outlying communities and outposts. What little we assume about the religious and ceremonial activities in the kivas we interpolate from studying modern Pueblo ceremonies—surely, the Anasazi were the ancestors of the modern Pueblo peoples, though shifts of population among ancient Indian peoples are not so simply explained as that. One interpretation of their demise sees it as an ecological warning, an example of how overpopulation and counterproductive agricultural practices can leave a culture with no means of survival; the counterargument is that twenty-five years of drought surely would wreak more havoc on a primitive agriculture than the devastation wrought on a more advanced agriculture in the few short years that created the twentieth-century dustbowl. Moreover, Chaco was deserted before the great drought at Mesa Verde began, while the rain was still falling.

These are issues we may never resolve. The Anasazi left only abstract designs and some few petroglyphs—no written language, no hieroglyphics or cuneiform tablets, no Rosetta stone. And yet we still can feel their presence in the cliff dwellings of Mesa Verde.

The white man's first significant encounter with the cliff dwellings of Mesa Verde occurred just over a hundred years ago, on 18 December 1888, when two drovers hunting in the snow for lost cattle happened deep into one of the canyons outlining the mesa and discovered, in a single day, the ruins we now call Spruce Tree House, Square Tower House, and the Cliff Palace. The modern traveler sometimes recaptures that experience by standing on the rim of the mesa, taking in the stark beauty of one of its canyons, measuring the plunge to the canyon floor, slowly surveying the kaleidoscopic changes in rugged grandeur along its walls, and then, suddenly, realizing that among the sandstone shapes, tucked into a long, narrow niche, shadowed in part by the massive stone overhang and perched impossibly in the midst of a sheer rockface, are a series of stone walls, perhaps the telltale shape of a window or doorway. He squints and focuses on the sandstone-colored ruin, searching in vain for a discernible path or road to the building, and turns to tell his wife. But when he looks once more, the harsh sunlight disguises the building again; as he scours the ledges and overhangs, the dark lines and shadowy openings, he seems to find it suddenly but farther south than he remembered and somehow missing a wall or two. His wife has meanwhile found a ruin herself, this one north of where he began pointing, and as he follows her arm he rediscovers the first ruin and almost simultaneously sights the third one, the one she had found.

One of them is well preserved, perhaps restored in part by the National Parks Service, and well protected by a large overhang; the ledge it sits upon seems level and secure. Another is an eroding remnant of a building of several rooms; over the centuries the ledge to which it clings obviously has broken away as far back as the very center of the house itself, perhaps carried down into the canyon by the fall of a portion of the cliff face that had overhung the house originally—lines of fracture are still visible on the rock above the building. The condition of the third is somewhere in between the other two, still secure on the cliff face but crumbled and hobbled by its own debris. And even as he marvels aloud that buildings could be constructed on ledges seemingly inaccessible to mountain goats, he discerns the regularly spaced indentations in the cliff face that mark the handholds the Anasazi used to descend to those buildings, and he feels a thrill of acrophobia run through him.

In such a discovery the visitor replicates the surprise of those two cowboys a century ago, an unnerving realization that these steep, rocky canyons harbor the ghosts of a culture long vanished. Often, having turned away from the view of the canyon, the visitor has to search again to find the cliff dwellings. Standing on the rim of the mesa, just off the modern blacktop road that winds through gambel oak and thick dry grasses, he may feel a sense of isolation on his side of the canyon, until he discovers that nearby the National Parks Service has installed a stairway down the canyon wall and that a hundred feet directly below him, unheard and unseen, dozens of campers and day visitors like him are scrambling among ruins more extensive than those he searches for in the distance.

We descended to the Cliff Palace on such a stairway, twisting its way down the cliff face and threading through fractures and around debris, now a manmade series of steps, then a footpath along a ledge. The approach allows a panoramic view of the Cliff Palace, and the result is awesome. Under a massive lowering brow of rock stand the remnants of a prehistoric city of interconnected apartments, terraces, towers, and pits. At its most extensive it had had over 217 rooms and 23 kivas and an estimated population of 200 to 250 people. Deep within the overhang a ledge, now inaccessible, shelters walls where food was stored; entrance would have been gained by means of a ladder on the roof of a four-story building, now no longer so high. Much of the Cliff Palace is similarly gone, the debris cleared for visitors, some walls restored or repaired in the Anasazi manner, but the general sense of the place remains. Here was a city of streets and plazas, private dwellings and communal buildings, all tightly linked together and demanding a complicated sense of social order.

We moved along the terraces, gazing through T-shaped doorways at dark, square rooms, peering into the kivas where clans met to carry on the ceremonies that were responsible for keeping the Anasazi in harmony with the universe. Where walls had fallen and roofs collapsed we could see the quality of construction, the overlapping of stone and mud mortar, the bracing up with wooden beams.

From an upper terrace we could look down into one of the open kivas. At Spruce Tree House, another ruin, we had been allowed to descend into a kiva with its roof intact. We had felt the coolness of the semidarkness, the overarching weight of the roof and the mesa above—it had made us feel for a moment closer to the Underworld. Sitting on a bench built into the wall, gazing around the kiva, we had heard the bustle of people outside and begun to imagine it was the bustle of Anasazi society. Then we had emerged into sunlight and summer warmth and the twentieth century, into the viewfinders of European and Asian and American photographers and a babel of conversation. At Cliff Palace, gazing into the open kiva, it wasn't hard to imagine these buildings restored and active.

The climb out of the canyon, by another way than the path in, was steep and tiring but gradual and safe, nothing like the hand-over-hand scramble up the rock face the Anasazi had faced daily to ascend to the agriculture of the mesa top or descend to the springs at the base of the canyon. Our climb gave us yet another panorama of the Cliff Palace, gleaming in the sun, and yet when we turned to look back a few feet farther up, it was gone, and behind us the canyon seemed silent and empty.

Throughout our stay we wandered the ruins of Chapin Mesa, often descending arduously to investigate features of various dwellings. We strolled the mesa rim searching for inaccessible sites nearly invisible in both glaring sunlight and shadow and occasionally clambered across the walls of mesa top ruins like the Sun Temple or Far View Pueblo. Once we drove to Park Point, around eighty-six hundred feet above sea level, nearly two thousand feet above the rest of the mesa, four thousand feet above the surrounding Delores Plateau from which the mesa rises. The view extends for 360 degrees, to the easily identified figure of Sleeping Ute Mountain in the west and the Delores Peaks and Mt. Wilson in the north, across the Mancos Valley to the east, toward the singular volcanic shape of Shiprock in the south. The unaided eye could barely discern the sparse sprinkling of communities in the lowlands, and the distances were great enough that it was easy to believe that the world beyond Mesa Verde was unpopulated, that the tent and RV dwellers of the

Morfield Campground were somehow the last outpost of the Anasazi, taking refuge on the overgrown mesa while the buildings of the ancient ones continued to crumble and those of the less ancient ones we had fled had already begun to decay.

One evening, because I hadn't had enough of that magnificent view, I walked alone from the campground out the Knife Edge Trail to watch the sunset over the Montezuma Valley. A modern road had once extended along the western cliff face of the mesa, but the farther you walked the more evidence you found of how the mesa had rejected it, like an incompatible transplanted organ. Massive boulders littered the road from above, and the eroded cliff face had torn away chunks of it from below until the road itself disappeared into the earth. The sun sank behind Sleeping Ute Mountain, its glow incarnadining the mesa wall and casting its craggy face into red relief. I watched it as long as I could, then started back before the absolute darkness of the mesa night could catch me on the trail.

As usual, the mule deer were moving in the thickets and rustling through the undergrowth on the bluff above the trail. Rounding a boulder, I surprised a trio—a buck with the downy beginnings of antlers and two young does—on the trail and tried to pass them casually, without putting them to flight. All three watched me for a moment without moving then bolted for the bluff. I was startled by their sudden movement but continued on my way until I heard a sound behind me. Turning, I saw the young buck following me cautiously. My movement sent him toward the bluff again, but he clearly had no intention of dashing into hiding. Instead, he took a parallel route halfway up the rise, made his way ahead of me, and then stopped, watching me all the while. Behind me, visible but safe at the top of the bluff, the two does watched us. Expecting skittishness, I was unsettled by the buck's belligerence. I started walking again, keeping one eye on the buck and the other on the uncertain footing of the trail. He moved parallel with me, his progress on the loose shale noisy and often graceless, until a boulder in his path made him pause. I continued along the trail around it and heard him come down to the slope to level ground. Voices drifted up from ahead of me on the trail. I stopped and looked back at the mule deer. He stopped and kept his head low. In the faint gleam in his eyes I thought I could see the spirit of a powerful stag with a full rack, but he seemed satisfied that he had escorted me out of his neighborhood—when I went off toward the campground, he stayed behind. In the dimmer light away from the western rim I could see other dark shapes moving in the underbrush and hear their rustling all the way back to our tent.

That night I lay awake, thinking of the Anasazi, imagining them here, before they abandoned the mesa to the mule deer, when they would have seen those shapes in the darkness. I thought of the progression from single families living in a hole in the ground to a complex society building a culture, discovering irrigation, ventilation, and architecture virtually on their own, occupying such monuments as the Cliff Palace and Pueblo Bonito and making the complicated social structure to sustain them virtually out of whole cloth. I thought of their disappearance, their moving out and abandoning their culture for reasons as yet uncertain, their blending and merging with the descendants of Hohokam and Mogollon cultures and the nomadic peoples who entered the area long after the Anasazi had disappeared. I thought of the long centuries when the Anasazi were lost to time, their buildings crumbling in the canyon crevices and worn away by the winds and rains of the mesa, the brilliant sunlight of the days giving way to inevitable, impenetrable night, the sky ablaze with innumerable stars, all unseen.

The night was without a moon, and the sky was densely packed with stars of every magnitude and configuration. Lying in the tent, staring through the tent flap, dazzled by the shining immensity of the universe, I fell asleep pondering how such a universe would have seemed to a primitive man on a planet blanketed in impenetrable darkness, a man seeing that spectacle through a square window or T-shaped doorway or a kiva smokehole deep in the recesses of an overhang on the side of a cliff, a man living like a rock dove or a cliff swallow and believing that he and his kind are newcomers to the light, having recently emerged through the Great Sipapu from the underworld.

The ghosts of the Anasazi traveled with us when we left Mesa Verde the next day. They haunted the whole of the Four Corners Area, the canyons and mesas and deserts and mountains. We looked for them in Chaco Canyon, lurching over washboard dirt roads past Navajo hogans to get there, and found them in the sprawling ruins of Pueblo Bonito and the neighboring ruins of Casa Chiquita and Kin Kletso. They were in the straight footpaths across the desert and up the canyon walls to carefully positioned towers and to other ruined villages and family dwellings; they were in the large pueblo of Chetro Ketl farther down Chaco Wash and, across from it, in the elaborate kiva at Casa

Rinconada, looking in its restored but still roofless state like a primitive gladi-atorial arena; they were in the petroglyphs above Una Vida.

Even after we left Chaco, turning our attention away from archaeology, we still found ourselves among the ghosts of the Southwest, ever among the vanished. At Natural Bridges National Monument vanished rivers had left the eroded shapes that included Sipapu Arch; in the Guadalupe Mountains a vanished sea had left the coral reefs of El Capitan, the fossil-littered floor of McKittrick Canyon, the limestone recesses of Carlsbad Caverns; in Taos and Santa Fe we walked among buildings indebted to Pueblo Indians and Spanish missionaries—in Santa Fe's central marketplace, at a festival of Indian artists, Sue bought a poster of corn kachinas, and later, in Taos, I bought one of La Noche de Zozobra, both celebrations of past rituals. On our night in Santa Fe we took in a movie about the near past and clannish young men who used a Baltimore diner for a kind of communal kiva.

In Bandelier National Monument we hiked through Frijole Canyon, passing the basalt flows and rhyolite tuff tent rocks that gave evidence to the vanished volcanoes nearby. It was our last day in the Southwest. I left our campsite to take a trail across the desert that would bring me out above Frijole Canyon. I watched my footing most of the way, in part because the trail crossed rugged outcroppings of rock close to the canyon rim, in part because I wanted to obey federal warning signs and not "molest" any rattlesnakes, especially inadver-tently. Suddenly I was at the edge of the mesa, and I could see the tent rocks in the distance. But, unexpectedly, I found myself looking down on Tyuoni Pueblo, Anasazi ruins laid out below me like a stone diagram on the floor of Frijoles Canyon. Nothing was left of the pueblo but the base of its walls, dry-ing in the sun after a brief afternoon rain. In a thicket nearby I could see mule deer moving cautiously, peering out across the empty canyon floor.

In the ways we talk about cultural heritage the Anasazi may matter very little. They seem to be all but untraceable in the modern Pueblo cultures, had no impact on the European heritage that dominates modern American culture, can have no role in the changes a nonwhite, non-European world will make in the cultures of the twenty-first century. And yet they matter still, perhaps because of the changes to come.

We are all Anasazi, always in transition, either in ascent or decline, chang-ing in our agriculture and architecture and art, adding intricacy to our ceremonies and our society, making our inauspicious debut before the footlights of history or mingling undetected among a new troupe of players for a final crowd scene. Our cultures are only kinds of mud wattle, varieties of adobe or stones and mortar, ever in need of repair, restoration, replacement. Culture doesn't solidify like cooled magma; it is always fluid, metamorphic, protean, and even the hardest rock eventually wears away.

In America we like to see ourselves as forever young, a mere two hundred years old and still growing up; we like to think that the destiny of the planet is indistinguishable from our own national future. But the "American Century" is ending, and it will be the only one we get. To our amazement and chagrin all history was not simply a prologue to the American moment, and the past was not only a European past. Here on our own continent others came before us—Hohokam, Mogollon, Hopewell, Anasazi, and countless others—cliff dwellers and mound builders just like us, if on a different scale. Like them, we too are caught in the flow of history—in our turn we are becoming prologue.

Our history is one of deserted dwellings, places recording the different ways we shut off our view of the universe in the recesses of caves and cliffs, pueblos and tenements. The electric canopies that shroud our cities in gray haze hide from us the brilliance and immensity of the night sky, the oldest, most awesome memory of our kind, but we are all Anasazi, newly emergent—once again—from the Great Sipapu, fresh from the underworld of our past lives, fugitives from its ruins.

SCOTT RUSSELL SANDERS

Scott Russell Sanders has been frequently reprinted and cited in *The Best American Essays* annual collections and has published a number of books of nonfiction, including *The Paradise of Bombs* (1987), winner of the Associated Writing Programs Award for Creative Nonfiction, *Secrets of the Universe: Scenes from the Journey Home* (1991), *Staying Put: Making a Home in a Restless World* (1993), *Writing from the Center* (1995), *Hunting for Hope: A Father's Journeys* (1998), *The Country of Language* (1999), *The Force of Spirit* (2000), and *A Private History of Awe* (2006). He is also the editor of *Audubon Reader: The Best Writings of John James Audubon* (1986) and author of a number of novels and children's books. He teaches at Indiana University in Bloomington. "After the Flood" is taken from *Staying Put* and "Buckeye" from *Writing from the Center*.

On "After the Flood" and "Buckeye"

Like many another willing or unwilling migrant, I learned the importance of place from having been uprooted. My first uprooting, from a farm in Tennessee, occurred before I was old enough to realize what I had lost, but my exile from the land I came to know while growing up in Ohio left a deep and lasting ache. How lasting? The exile began in 1963, and I was still writing about it three decades later, in "After the Flood" and "Buckeye," a pair of essays composed in the early 1990s. When I read those essays now, after yet another decade has passed, the loss of my childhood landscape still feels fresh.

My family moved from Tennessee to Portage County, Ohio, when I was five, and we stayed there twelve years, until the summer following my high school graduation. We lived first inside a military arsenal where bombs were made, then on a farm nearby, then once more inside the arsenal. We made that final move after being forced to sell our farm to the government to clear the way for the building of a dam and reservoir on the West Branch of the Mahoning River. A generation earlier, near the beginning of World War II, hundreds of other families had been forced to sell their land for the building of the arsenal. I knew these facts as a boy, but I did not realize, back then, how much of America had been sacrificed for war-making or arrogant engineering, nor did I understand my own small loss as belonging to the history of displacement that began with the arrival of Europeans on the shores of the New World.

Soon after my high school graduation, our family trailed my father's job to Louisiana. By the time we left Ohio construction on the dam was well underway; soon, I knew, the river would begin backing up over the land where

I had come to consciousness. Instead of brooding on that loss, I focused on learning about the new places to which life carried me—the Deep South, then New England for college, then old England for graduate school, and then back again to the Midwest, to southern Indiana, where I became a teacher, a writer, and a father.

Yet I could not quit thinking about that Ohio landscape, and so I wrote a novel, two story collections, and a handful of essays that were set partly or entirely in Portage County. For many years I was content to visit the place only in memory, and thus avoid seeing how much the dam had erased. Then I was invited to give a reading at Hiram, a liberal arts college in Portage County. Why not have a look at the old stomping grounds? I thought. So I drove there from Indiana on a chilly gray November day in 1990. After I finished my stint at the college, I made a slow circuit of the terrain I had known from childhood, cruising along the rusted perimeter fence of the arsenal, closed to me now; through the crossroad settlement of Wayland, where the curving bulk of the dam rose above cornfields; past the land where our house had stood and on down the familiar road until a guardrail blocked the way and I could see the pavement dipping under the blank waters of the reservoir. I walked for an hour or so around Wayland, which looked scarcely changed from the place as I had known it; but I could not bear to get out of the car anywhere near the site of our house, where everything I remembered, except for a few old trees now surrounded by a burgeoning woods, had been swept away.

On the long drive back home to Indiana, I began imagining an essay that would recount my tour of Wayland, where as a boy I had first stumbled upon a few of life's great mysteries. Within a month I had written "Wayland," which appeared in the autumn 1992 issue of the *Gettysburg Review*, was reprinted in *The Best American Essays* 1993, and became the final chapter of my book *Staying Put: Making a Home in a Restless World*. Although "Wayland" alluded to the dam and reservoir, it was less concerned with the loss of place than with the persistent links between place and consciousness.

In January 1991 I faced the loss more directly by writing "After the Flood," which appeared first in Michael Martone's anthology *Townships* (1992) and which became the opening chapter of *Staying Put*. As in many of my essays, I used personal experience as an opening to collective experience: "If the loss were mine alone, the story would not be worth telling. My grieving for a drowned landscape is private, a small ache in a bruised world. But the building of the dam, the obliteration of that valley, the displacement of people and beasts, these were public acts, the sort of acts we have been repeating from coast to coast as we devour the continent." Later in the essay I cataloged some of those displacements:

> I think of the farmers who saw their wood lots and fields go under the flood. I think of the Miami and Shawnee who spoke of belonging to that land as a child belongs to a mother and who were driven out by white soldiers. . . . I think of the Africans who were yanked from their homes and bound in chains and shipped to this New World. I think about refugees, set in motion by hunger or tyranny or war. I think about children pushed onto the streets by cruelty or indifference. I think about migrant workers, dust bowl émigrés, all the homeless wanderers. I think about the poor everywhere—and it is overwhelmingly the poor—whose land is gobbled by strip mines, whose neighborhoods are wiped out by highways and shopping malls, whose villages are destroyed by bombs, whose forests are despoiled by chain saws and executive fountain pens.

Thus, I could view my own uprooting as merely a taste of a large and bitter history.

I was only too aware that grief over the loss of place could be dismissed as nostalgia. So I pointed out that the root meaning of *nostalgia* is "return pain," and I argued that such pain arises not from a superficial longing for one's youth but from "bone-deep attachment to place." The ache from severing that attachment sounds in the very cadence of the prose:

> There was no house in the hollow where the road dipped down, where the family of Seventh Day Adventists used to live with their stacks of apocalyptic pamphlets and their sad-eyed children. The spinster's white bungalow was gone, along with the battered bus in the side yard which had served her for a chicken coop. Yard after yard had grown up in brush, and the shade trees spread darkness over their own seedlings. No mail boxes leaned on posts beside the road, no driveways broke the fringe of weeds. The trailer park was gone, the haunted house was gone, the tar-paper shanty where the drunk mechanic beat his wife and the wife beat her kids and the kids wailed, that was gone, and so was every last trailer and cottage and privy and shack, all down the blacktopped mile to our place.

In chronicling what had been erased, I didn't seek to idealize this rural landscape or its people but only to show that even such a humble place can be saturated by human stories, can be cultivated and cared for, can be loved.

As I read "After the Flood" now, I perceive that the whole essay pivots around a central claim:

> One's native ground is the place where, since before you had words for such knowledge, you have known the smells, the seasons, the birds and beasts, the human voices, the houses, the ways of working, the lay of the land and the quality of light. It is the landscape you learn before you retreat inside the illusion of your skin. You may love the place if you flourished there or hate the place if you suffered there. But love it or hate it, you cannot shake free. Even if you move to the antipodes, even if you become intimate with new landscapes, you still bear the impression of that first ground.

Today I would not speak of "native ground" because the phrase suggests that only the place where one was actually born can hold such power over the heart and mind. In fact, one's primal landscape may be any terrain that one explores between ages five or six and twelve or fifteen, whether or not one happens to have been born there.

Hiram College invited me back for a week-long residency a year after the first visit, and so I returned there in November 1991. Again I made a circuit of my old home ground, only this time when I came to the site of our house I got out of the car and walked the land, and I was soon caught up in the bewildering experiences that I would later describe in "Buckeye." The force of my grief surprised me, for I had been living with the fact of my father's death for ten years, but what truly bewildered me was the sensation of meeting him in the guise of the red-tailed hawk.

For months after that encounter I tried to comprehend the merger of dead father and living hawk. Everything I knew from science, psychology, and common sense told me to dismiss the experience as a hallucination; yet I could not shake the conviction that what I had seen was real. Beginning from this episode, I tried, without success, to shape an essay about the conflict between material and spiritual ways of seeing the universe. I knew, of course, that the struggle is as old as science. Emerson spoke of it in "The Transcendentalist" as "this double consciousness . . . of the understanding and of the soul." Thoreau likewise spoke, in *Walden*, of "a certain doubleness," a split between flesh-and-blood existence and an awareness that is "not wholly involved in Nature." A materialist philosophy—which is implicit in science, if not necessarily embraced by any given scientist—holds that we *are* "wholly involved in Nature," that our sense of exercising free will or of tapping into a transcendent energy is an illusion. Unwilling to accept a simple dualism, which divorces matter from spirit, I thought of a Möbius strip, which seems to have two surfaces and yet has only one. Perhaps in the same way, I imagined, hawk and father—law-abiding matter and free-floating spirit—could coexist as twin facets of a single reality.

In spite of these reflections, more than two years passed before I could find a shape for my bewilderment. Even when I began work on "Buckeye" in January 1994, I did not set out to describe the encounter with the redtail, for I still could make no sense of it. Instead, I was aiming to write an introduction I had been asked to provide for an anthology of photographs and essays devoted to Ohio. Since the deadline was approaching, and the editors had not sent me any of the materials that would be included in the volume, I cast about for some way of introducing the book. Eventually, as I fidgeted at my desk, I lifted down that walnut box from a shelf, opened the lid, cupped the withered buckeyes in my hand, and the essay poured out.

Early in the writing, I found myself invoking the possibility of a spiritual dimension, as I gazed at the walnut box: "The top is inlaid with pieces fitted so as to bring out the grain, four diagonal joints converging from the corners toward the center. If I stare long enough at those converging lines, they float free of the box and point to a center deeper than wood." Then I backed away from that slippery ground and ventured somewhere safer, into the Ohio woods with my father, as he taught me the trees. The appearance and name of the buckeye set me thinking about deer, which set me remembering how, "if you were quiet, if your hands were empty, if you moved slowly, you could leave the car and steal to within a few paces of a grazing deer, close enough to see the delicate lips, the twitching nostrils, the glossy, fathomless eyes."

Once more I hesitated, drawing back from those unfathomable depths to lament the wounds everywhere visible on the surface of my Ohio neighborhood, injuries that culminated in the damming of the river. Only in writing the essay did I fully grasp that this land had been doomed not by our lack of affection but by our lack of imagination: "If enough people had spoken for the river, we might have saved it. If enough people had believed that our scarred country was worth defending, we might have dug in our heels and fought. Our attachments to the land were all private. We had no shared lore, no literature, no art to root us there, to give us courage, to help us stand our ground." The need for devotion to place called to mind Simone Weil's instruction: "Let us love the country of here below." No sooner had I quoted her words, however, than I questioned them, for I did not accept any division between "here below" and some superior realm: "How could our hearts be large enough for heaven if they are not large enough for earth? The only country I am certain of is the one here below. The only paradise I know is the one lit by our everyday sun, this land of difficult love, shot through with shadow. The place where we learn this love, if we learn it at all, shimmers behind every new place we inhabit." And thus I rephrased the claim I had made in "After the Flood," about the lifelong influence of one's primal landscape.

Only when I began describing my return to the home site, in the closing pages of "Buckeye," did I realize that I had been preparing a vessel to hold my encounter with the red-tailed hawk. Even as I described my mystifying vision, I acknowledged the arguments against it: "The voice of my education told me then and tells me now that I did not meet my father, that I merely projected my longing onto a bird." I was aware of the echo from D. H. Lawrence's poem "Snake," which describes the narrator finding a serpent at the water trough one morning: "The voice of my education said to me / He must be killed, / For in Sicily the black, black snakes are innocent, the gold are venomous." The education whispering in Lawrence's ear told him that sympathy with snakes is foolish, while mine told me that birds cannot embody the spirit of a dead father, indeed that all talk of spirit is nonsense. In the end, while I could not prove the truth of my vision, I could at least report it, and by setting it in this drowned landscape, perhaps I could keep both vision and place from being wholly lost.

"Buckeye" served as the introduction for John Moor and Larry Smith's anthology, *In Buckeye Country: Photos and Essays of Ohio* (1994). A revised version was published in *Orion* in spring 1995, and later that same year it appeared as the opening essay in my book *Writing from the Center*. Clearly, the emotional work I undertook in writing both "After the Flood" and "Buckeye" was to make my peace with places that had been destroyed—to learn to let them go, if only to free myself to put down roots elsewhere. At the end of "Buckeye"

I announced that I had been released from grieving over this flooded landscape, and yet it has remained a potent presence in my memory, drawing me back again and again—most recently in *A Private History of Awe*.

We're likely to flood, pave, poison, or otherwise abuse land if we think of it merely as property or as raw material for human designs. To think of land more intimately, more reverently, we need the help of art. Relatively few locations in America have been cherished by writers, photographers, filmmakers, or painters. The places where I lived as a boy, the place where I have chosen to spend my grown-up years, and many of the places I visit on my travels still await that cherishing attention. That's why I concluded "Buckeye" with a call to artists: "For each home ground we need new maps, living maps, stories and poems, photographs and paintings, essays and songs. We need to know where we are, so that we may dwell in our place with a full heart." To spare ourselves and our neighbors from further uprooting, we must defend the places we love, and we can begin that defense by filling our places with imagination.

After the Flood

A river poured through the landscape I knew as a child. It was the power of the place, gathering rain and snowmelt, surging through the valley under sun, under ice, under the bellies of fish and the curled brown boats of syca-more leaves. You will need a good map of Ohio to find the river I am talking about, the West Branch of the Mahoning. The stretch of it I knew best no longer shows on maps, a stretch that ran between wooded slopes and along the flanks of cornfields and pastures in the township of Charlestown, in Portage County, a rural enclave surrounded by the smokestacks and concrete of Akron, Youngstown, and Cleveland in the northeastern corner of the state.

Along that river bottom I gathered blackberries and hickory nuts, trapped muskrats, rode horses, followed baying hounds on the scent of raccoons. Spring and fall, I walked barefoot over the tilled fields, alert for arrowheads. Along those slopes I helped a family of Swedish farmers collect buckets of ma-ple sap. On the river itself I skated in winter and paddled in summer, I pawed through gravel bars in search of fossils, I watched hawks preen and pounce, I courted and canoed and idled. This remains for me a primal landscape, im-printed on my senses, a place by which I measure every other place.

It is also, now, a drowned landscape. In the early 1960s, when I was in high school, politicians and bankers and realtors ordained that the Mahoning should be snared. A dam was built, the river died, and water backed up over most of the land I knew. No city needed the water for drinking. The reservoir, named after a man who had never lived in that valley, provided owners of loud boats with another playground for racing and waterskiing, and provided me with a lesson in loss. If the loss were mine alone, the story would not be worth telling. My grieving for a drowned landscape is private, a small ache in a bruised world. But the building of the dam, the obliteration of that valley, the displacement of people and beasts, these were public acts, the sort of acts we have been repeating from coast to coast as we devour the continent.

Like many townships in farm country, remote from the offices where the fate of land is decided, Charlestown has suffered more than one erasure. Long before the building of the reservoir, the government had already sliced away the northern third of the township for an arsenal, a wild, murderous place I have written about elsewhere as a paradise of bombs. On current maps of the township that upper third is blank white, and most of the remaining two-thirds, flooded by the reservoir, is vacant blue. Merely by looking at the map, one can tell that here is a sacrificial zone.

Returning to one's native ground, always tricky, becomes downright treacherous when the ground is at the bottom of a lake. Unwilling to dive through so much water, I can return to that drowned landscape, as I can return to childhood, only by diving through memory.

I had just become a teenager when the government began purchasing the farms and trailers and shacks that would be in the path of the reservoir. (If there had been mansions and factories in the way, the politicians would have doomed a different valley.) Among the first to be unhoused was the Swedish family, old Mr. Sivvy and his two unmarried children, who had farmed that bottom land with big-shouldered horses, whose silage I had pitchforked in the steaming silo, whose cows I had fed, whose maple syrup I had savored hot from the vat. Uprooted, the old man soon died. The children bought a new farm on high ground, trying to start over, but it was no good, the soil too thin, worn-out, no black bottomland, no fat maples, no river pouring through it. All down the valley it was the same, people forced to move by a blizzard of government paper, occasionally by the sheriff, in a few instances by the arrival of bulldozers at their front door.

While gangs of men with dynamite and dump trucks tore down the condemned buildings, other gangs with earthmovers and cement mixers slowly raised a wall across the river. For a year I watched it rise, while I wooed a girl who lived on a ridge overlooking the dam site. Crooners purred love songs from the stereo in her parlor, against an accompaniment of chuffs and shouts and whistles from the valley below. I studied the contours of that girl's face while the river's contours were bullied into the shape of blueprints. The huge concrete forms, the Tinkertoy scaffolds, the blasting, the snort of compressors, the lurch of heavy machines, are confused in me now with the memory of damp hands and lingering kisses. The girl and I broke up, but the concrete held. Thereafter, I avoided that ridge and did not see the laying of the dam's final tier, did not see the steel gates close. By the time I graduated from high school, water was beginning to lap over the banks of the Mahoning, but I could not bear to go down to the river and look.

When I left Ohio for college, my family left as well, trailing my father's work to Louisiana. My childhood friends dispersed—to war, to jail, to distant marriages and jobs, to cities where lights glittered and dollars sang. I had scant reason to visit that flooded township and good reason to keep my distance. Why rush to see a muddy expanse of annihilating water?

Some years later, however, duties carried me through the northeastern corner of Ohio, within an hour's drive of my old neighborhood. I had not planned to make a detour. Yet the names of towns emblazoned on huge green signs along the highway tugged at me. The shapes of chimneys and roofs, the colors of barns, the accents in fast-food booths and gas stations, all drew me off the interstate onto the roads of Portage County, up the stream of recollection toward that childhood place.

The season of my return was late winter, after the last snow and before the first plowing, before grass resumed its green sizzle, before trees blurred with leaves. The shape of the land lay exposed. It was a gray day, a day to immunize one against nostalgia, a day safe, I supposed, for facing up to what I had lost. Surely I was prepared by now to see the great erasure. I was a man and had put behind me a boy's affection for a stretch of river and a patch of dirt. New places had claimed me, thereby loosening the grip of that old landscape. Still, to ease my way back, before going to the reservoir, I drove through the county seat, Ravenna, which had scarcely changed, and then through Edinburgh, Atwater, Deerfield, Palmyra, Paris, Wayland—tiny crossroad settlements where I had played baseball and eaten pie and danced—and these, too, had scarcely changed. Circling, I drew closer and closer to the blue splotch on the map.

The best way to approach the water, I decided, was along the road where, for half our years in Charlestown, my family had lived on five acres with horses and rabbits and dogs. Surely our gray-shingled house would still be there, safe on its ridge above the lake, even if most of the land I had known was drowned. So I turned from the highway onto that curving, cracked, tar-slick road, looking for the familiar. But at the corner, where there should have been a farmhouse, a silo, a barn, there was only a billboard marking the entrance to the West Branch Reservation. The fields where I had baled hay now bristled with a young woods. There was no house in the hollow where the road dipped down, where the family of Seventh Day Adventists used to live with their stacks of apocalyptic pamphlets and their sad-eyed children. The spinster's white bungalow was gone, along with the battered bus in the side yard which had served her for a chicken coop. Yard after yard had grown up in brush, and the shade trees spread darkness over their own seedlings. No mail boxes leaned on posts beside the road, no driveways broke the fringe of weeds. The trailer park was gone, the haunted house was gone, the tar-paper shanty where the drunk mechanic beat his wife and the wife beat her kids and the kids wailed, that was gone, and so was every last trailer and cottage and privy and shack, all down the blacktopped mile to our place.

I recognized our place by the two weeping willows out front. My father and I had planted those willows from slips, had fenced them round to protect the tender bark from deer, had watered and weeded and nursed them along. By the day of my visit those twigs had burgeoned into yellow fountains some fifty feet high, brimming over the woods that used to be our cleared land, woods that flourished where our house and barn had stood. I did not get out of the car. I could see from the road all that I was ready to see. The dense thicket, bare of leaves, was the color of rusty iron. Aside from the willows, no hint of our work or ownership survived.

I felt a fool. During the years of my absence, while my mind had suffered the waters to rise through the forest and up the ravines onto the margins of our land, I had preserved the gray-shingled house, the low white barn, the lilacs and forsythia, the orchard and pasture, the garden, the lawn. And yet, all the while, cedar and sumac and brambles, like the earth's dark fur, had been pushing up through my past.

Sight of the reservoir, surely, could not be worse. I continued down the road through the vigorous woods. Not a house, not a barn, not a plowed field. The first clearing I came to was half a mile farther on, at the spot where a man named Ferry had lived. He used to let the neighborhood kids swim in his pond, even after a boastful boy dived into a rock and drowned. We knew that when we knocked at Mr. Ferry's door, raising money for school or scouts, he would buy whatever we had to sell. He was a tender man. He loved his wife so much that when she died he planted a thousand white pines in her memory. The pines, spindly in my recollection, had grown into a forest by the day of my return.

In place of Mr. Ferry's house and yard there was a state campground now, encircled by the spiky green palisade of pines. The entrance booth was boarded up. A placard outside instructed campers to deposit their fees—so much for trailers, so much for tents—in the box below. There was no box below, only a slab of plywood with ragged holes from which the screws had been ripped. Nor were there any campers on this wintry afternoon. As I drove through the vacant lot, the only sounds were the crunch of gravel beneath my tires and the yawp of blue jays overhead and the shoosh of wind through the pines.

I pulled away from the campground and drove on. My mind raced ahead along the road as I remembered it, steeply downhill between fat maples and patchy sycamores to the river and the steel-girdered bridge. I had rolled down that hill in a school bus, swayed down on horseback, hurtled down on bicycle and sled, run down on foot. The slope and feel of it, fixed inside me, became my standard for all hills. From the bridge I had watched the river's current raveling over sandbars, minnows flickering in the shallows, water striders dimpling the surface. Now and again, when the sun was right, I had spied my own face peering up from the stream. In memory the road stretched on beyond the bridge, passing the tin-roofed shed where the maple syrup boiled, passing the Sivvy farm, rising up the far slope to a T-junction with a ridgeline road. Turn left from there, and I would go to the high school. Turn right, and I would go to the barbershop and feed store. As my thoughts raced ahead of the car, inside me the valley opened and the river flexed its long sleek muscle.

Rounding the curve, however, I had to slam on the brakes to avoid running into a guardrail that blocked the road. Beyond the railing, where valley and bridge and river should have been, flat gray water spread away toward distant hills. You know this moment from dream: you are in a familiar room, but when you turn to leave, where a door should be there is a wall; or you come up behind someone you love, speak her name, yet when she turns around her face is blank; or you find the story of the universe written on a page, but when you draw close to read it, the letters dissolve. Waters of separation, waters of oblivion, waters of death.

I got out of the car and pressed my thighs against the cold steel barricade and stared. Gray, flat, empty lake. Not even a boat to redeem the emptiness. A lone crow slowly pumped toward the horizon on glossy black wings. Along the shore a few sycamores still thrust up their mottled branches. Except for those trees, the pavement beneath my boots, and hills too high for water to claim, everything I knew had been swept away.

My worst imaginings had failed to prepare me for this. I stood there dazed. I could not take it in, so much had been taken away. For a long spell I leaned against the guardrail and dredged up everything I could remember of what lay beneath the reservoir. But memory was at last defeated by the blank gray water. No effort of mind could restore the river or drain the valley. I surrendered to what my eyes were telling me. Only then was I truly exiled.

Those who built the dam had their reasons. You have heard the litany: flood control, recreation, development. I very much doubt that more human good has come from that muddy, silting, rarely frequented lake than came from the cultivated valley and wild woods and free-flowing river. I am suspicious of the logic that would forestall occasional floods by creating a permanent one. But I do not wish to debate the merits of dams. I mean only to speak of how casually, how relentlessly, we sever the bonds between person and place.

One's native ground is the place where, since before you had words for such knowledge, you have known the smells, the seasons, the birds and beasts, the human voices, the houses, the ways of working, the lay of the land, and the quality of light. It is the landscape you learn before you retreat inside the illusion of your skin. You may love the place if you flourished there or hate the place if you suffered there. But love it or hate it, you cannot shake free. Even if you move to the antipodes, even if you become intimate with new landscapes, you still bear the impression of that first ground.

I am all the more committed to know and care for the place I have come to as an adult because I have lost irretrievably the childhood landscapes that gave shape to my love of the earth. The farm outside Memphis where I was born has vanished beneath parking lots and the poison-perfect lawns of suburbs. The arsenal, with its herds of deer grazing on the grassy roofs of ammunition bunkers, is locked away behind chain-link fences, barbed wire, and guns. And the Mahoning Valley has been drowned. In our century, in our country, no fate could be more ordinary.

Of course, in mourning the drowned valley I also mourn my drowned childhood. The dry land preserved the traces of my comings and goings, the river carried the reflection of my beardless face. Yet even as a boy I knew that landscape was incomparably older than I, and richer, and finer. Some of the trees along the Mahoning had been rooted there when the first white settlers arrived from New England. Hawks had been hunting and deer had been drinking there since before our kind harnessed oxen. The gravels, laden with fossils, had been shoved there ten thousand years ago by glaciers. The river itself was the offspring of glaciers, a channel for meltwater to follow toward the Ohio, and thence to the Mississippi and the Gulf of Mexico. What I knew of the land's own history made me see that expanse of water as a wound.

Loyalty to place arises from sources deeper than narcissism. It arises from our need to be at home on the earth. We marry ourselves to the creation by knowing and cherishing a particular place, just as we join ourselves to the human family by marrying a particular man or woman. If the marriage is deep, divorce is painful. My drive down that unpeopled road and my desolate watch beside the reservoir gave me a hint of what others must feel when they are wrenched from their place. I say a *hint* because my loss is mild compared to what others have lost.

I think of the farmers who saw their wood lots and fields go under the flood. I think of the Miami and Shawnee who spoke of belonging to that land as a child belongs to a mother and who were driven out by white soldiers. I think of the hundred other tribes that were herded onto reservations far from the graves of their ancestors. I think of the Africans who were yanked from their homes and bound in chains and shipped to this New World. I think about refugees, set in motion by hunger or tyranny or war. I think about children pushed onto the streets by cruelty or indifference. I think about migrant workers, dust bowl émigrés, all the homeless wanderers. I think about the poor everywhere—and it is overwhelmingly the poor—whose land is gobbled by strip mines, whose neighborhoods are wiped out by highways and shopping malls, whose villages are destroyed by bombs, whose forests are despoiled by chain saws and executive fountain pens.

The word *nostalgia* was coined in 1688 as a medical term, to provide an equivalent for the German word meaning "homesickness." We commonly treat homesickness as an ailment of childhood, like mumps or chickenpox, and we treat nostalgia as an affliction of age. On our lips nostalgia usually means a sentimental regard for the trinkets and fashions of an earlier time, for an idealized past, for a vanished youth. We speak of a nostalgia for the movies of the 1930s, say, or the haircuts of the 1950s. It is a shallow use of the word. The two Greek roots of *nostalgia* literally mean "return pain." The pain comes not from returning home but from longing to return. Perhaps it is inevitable that a nation of immigrants—who shoved aside the native tribes of this continent, who enslaved and transported Africans, who still celebrate motion as if humans were dust motes—that such a nation should lose the deeper meaning of this word. A footloose people, we find it difficult to honor the lifelong, bone-deep attachment to place. We are slow to acknowledge the pain in yearning for one's native ground, the deep anguish in not being able, ever, to return.

On a warmer day I might have taken off my clothes and stepped over the guardrail and waded on down that road under the lake. Where the water was too deep, I could have continued in a boat, letting down a line to plumb the bottom. I would not be angling for death, which is far too easy to catch, but for life. To touch the ground even through a length of rope would be some consolation. The day was cold, however, and I was far from anyone who knew my face. So I climbed into the car and turned away and drove back through the resurgent woods.

Buckeye

Years after my father's heart quit, I keep in a wooden box on my desk the two buckeyes that were in his pocket when he died. Once the size of plums, the brown seeds are shriveled now, hollow, hard as pebbles, yet they still gleam from the polish of his hands. He used to reach for them in his overalls or suit pants and click them together, or he would draw them out, cupped in his palm, and twirl them with his blunt carpenter's fingers, all the while humming snatches of old tunes.

"Do you really believe buckeyes keep off arthritis?" I asked him more than once.

He would flex his hands and say, "I do so far."

My father never paid much heed to pain. Near the end, when his worn knee often slipped out of joint, he would pound it back in place with a rubber mallet. If a splinter worked into his flesh beyond the reach of tweezers, he would heat the blade of his knife over a cigarette lighter and slice through the skin. He sought to ward off arthritis not because he feared pain but because he lived through his hands, and he dreaded the swelling of knuckles, the stiffening of fingers. What use would he be if he could no longer hold a hammer or guide a plow? When he was a boy he had known farmers not yet forty years old whose hands had curled into claws, men so crippled up they could not tie their own shoes, could not sign their names.

"I mean to tickle my grandchildren when they come along," he told me, "and I mean to build doll houses and turn spindles for tiny chairs on my lathe."

So he fondled those buckeyes as if they were charms, carrying them with him when our family moved from Ohio at the end of my childhood, bearing them to new homes in Louisiana, then Oklahoma, Ontario, and Mississippi, carrying them still on his final day, when pain a thousand times fiercer than arthritis gripped his heart.

The box where I keep the buckeyes also comes from Ohio, made by my father from a walnut plank he bought at a farm auction. I remember the auction, remember the sagging face of the widow whose home was being sold, remember my father telling her he would prize that walnut as if he had watched the tree grow from a sapling on his own land. He did not care for pewter or silver or gold, but he cherished wood. On the rare occasions when my mother coaxed him into a museum, he ignored the paintings or porcelain and studied the exhibit cases, the banisters, the moldings, the parquet floors.

I remember him planing that walnut board, sawing it, sanding it, joining piece to piece to make foot stools, picture frames, jewelry boxes. My own box, a bit larger than a soap dish, lined with red corduroy, was meant to hold earrings and pins, not buckeyes. The top is inlaid with pieces fitted so as to bring out the grain, four diagonal joints converging from the corners toward the center. If I stare long enough at those converging lines, they float free of the box and point to a center deeper than wood.

I learned to recognize buckeyes and beeches, sugar maples and shagbark hickories, wild cherries, walnuts, and dozens of other trees while tramping through the Ohio woods with my father. To his eyes, their shapes, their leaves, their bark, their winter buds, were as distinctive as the set of a friend's shoulders. As with friends, he was partial to some, craving their company, so he would go out of his way to visit particular trees, walking in a circle around the splayed roots of a sycamore, laying his hand against the trunk of a white oak, ruffling the feathery green boughs of a cedar.

"Trees breathe," he told me. "Listen."

I listened, and heard the stir of breath.

He was no botanist; the names and uses he taught me were those he had learned from country folks, not from books. Latin never crossed his lips. Only much later would I discover that the tree he called ironwood, its branches like muscular arms, good for axe handles, is known in the books as "hophornbeam"; what he called tuliptree or canoewood, ideal for log cabins, is officially the yellow poplar; what he called hoop ash, good for barrels and fence posts, appears in books as hackberry.

When he introduced me to the buckeye, he broke off a chunk of the gray bark and held it to my nose. I gagged.

"That's why the old-timers called it stinking buckeye," he told me. "They used it for cradles and feed troughs and peg legs."

"Why for peg legs?" I asked.

"Because it's light and hard to split, so it won't shatter when you're clumping around."

He showed me this tree in late summer, when the fruits had fallen and the ground was littered with prickly brown pods. He picked up one, as fat as a lemon, and peeled away the husk to reveal the shiny seed. He laid it in my palm and closed my fist around it so the seed peeped out from the circle formed by my index finger and thumb. "You see where it got the name?" he asked.

I saw: what gleamed in my hand was the eye of a deer, bright with life. "It's beautiful," I said.

"It's beautiful," my father agreed, "but also poisonous. Nobody eats buckeyes, except maybe a fool squirrel."

I knew the gaze of deer from living in the Ravenna Arsenal, in Portage County, up in the northeastern corner of Ohio. After supper we often drove the Arsenal's gravel roads, past the munitions bunkers, past acres of rusting tanks and wrecked bombers, into the far fields where we counted deer. One June evening, while mist rose from the ponds, we counted three hundred and eleven, our family record. We found the deer in herds, in bunches, in amorous pairs. We came upon lone bucks, their antlers lifted against the sky like the bare branches of dogwood. If you were quiet, if your hands were empty, if you moved slowly, you could leave the car and steal to within a few paces of a grazing deer, close enough to see the delicate lips, the twitching nostrils, the glossy, fathomless eyes.

The wooden box on my desk holds these grazing deer, as it holds the buckeyes and the walnut plank and the farm auction and the munitions bunkers and the breathing forests and my father's hands. I could lose the box, I could lose the polished seeds, but if I were to lose the memories I would become a bush without roots, and every new breeze would toss me about. All those memories lead back to the northeastern corner of Ohio, the place where I came to consciousness, where I learned to connect feelings with words, where I fell in love with the earth.

It was a troubled love, for much of the land I knew as a child had been ravaged. The ponds in the Arsenal teemed with bluegill and beaver, but they were also laced with TNT from the making of bombs. Because the wolves and coyotes had long since been killed, some of the deer, so plump in the June grass, collapsed on the January snow, whittled by hunger to racks of bones. Outside the Arsenal's high barbed fences, many of the farms had failed, their barns caving in, their topsoil gone. Ravines were choked with swollen couches and junked washing machines and cars. Crossing fields, you had to be careful not to slice your feet on tin cans or shards of glass. Most of the rivers had been dammed, turning fertile valleys into scummy playgrounds for boats.

One free-flowing river, the Mahoning, ran past the small farm near the Arsenal where our family lived during my later years in Ohio. We owned just enough land to pasture three ponies and to grow vegetables for our table, but those few acres opened onto miles of woods and creeks and secret meadows. I walked that land in every season, every weather, following animal trails. But then the Mahoning, too, was doomed by a government decision; we were forced to sell our land, and a dam began to rise across the river.

If enough people had spoken for the river, we might have saved it. If enough people had believed that our scarred country was worth defending, we might have dug in our heels and fought. Our attachments to the land were all private. We had no shared lore, no literature, no art to root us there, to give us courage, to help us stand our ground. The only maps we had were those issued by the state, showing a maze of numbered lines stretched over emptiness. The Ohio landscape never showed up on postcards or posters, never unfurled like tapestry in films, rarely filled even a paragraph in books. There were no mountains in that place, no waterfalls, no rocky gorges, no vistas. It was a country of low hills, cut over woods, scoured fields, villages that had lost their purpose, roads that had lost their way.

"Let us love the country of here below," Simone Weil urged. "It is real; it offers resistance to love. It is this country that God has given us to love. He has willed that it should be difficult yet possible to love it." Which is the deeper truth about buckeyes, their poison or their beauty? I hold with the beauty; or rather, I am held by the beauty, without forgetting the poison. In my corner of Ohio the gullies were choked with trash, yet cedars flickered up like green flames from cracks in stone; in the evening bombs exploded at the ammunition dump, yet from the darkness came the mating cries of owls. I was saved from despair by knowing a few men and women who cared enough about the land to clean up trash, who planted walnuts and oaks that would long outlive them, who imagined a world that would have no call for bombs.

How could our hearts be large enough for heaven if they are not large enough for earth? The only country I am certain of is the one here below. The only paradise I know is the one lit by our everyday sun, this land of difficult love, shot through with shadow. The place where we learn this love, if we learn it at all, shimmers behind every new place we inhabit.

A family move carried me away from Ohio thirty years ago; my schooling and marriage and job have kept me away ever since, except for visits in memory and in flesh. I returned to the site of our farm one cold November day, when the trees were skeletons and the ground shone with the yellow of fallen leaves. From a previous trip I knew that our house had been bulldozed, our yard and pasture had grown up in thickets, and the reservoir had flooded the woods. On my earlier visit I had merely gazed from the car, too numb with loss to climb out. But on this November day I parked the car, drew on my hat and gloves, opened the door, and walked.

I was looking for some sign that we had lived there, some token of our affection for the place. All that I recognized, aside from the contours of the land, were two weeping willows that my father and I had planted near the road. They had been slips the length of my forearm when we set them out, and now their crowns rose higher than the telephone poles. When I touched them last, their trunks had been smooth and supple, as thin as my wrist, and now they were furrowed and stout. I took off my gloves and laid my hands against the rough bark. Immediately I felt the wince of tears. Without knowing why, I said hello to my father, quietly at first, then louder and louder, as if only shouts could reach him through the bark and miles and years.

Surprised by sobs, I turned from the willows and stumbled away toward the drowned woods, calling to my father. I sensed that he was nearby. Even as I called, I was wary of grief's deceptions. I had never seen his body after he died. By the time I reached the place of his death, a furnace had reduced him to ashes. The need to see him, to let go of him, to let go of this land and time, was powerful enough to summon mirages; I knew that. But I also knew, stumbling toward the woods, that my father was here.

At the bottom of a slope where the creek used to run, I came to an expanse of gray stumps and withered grass. It was a bay of the reservoir from which the water had retreated, the level drawn down by engineers or drought. I stood at the edge of this desolate ground, willing it back to life, trying to recall the woods where my father had taught me the names of trees. No green shoots rose. I walked out among the stumps. The grass crackled under my boots, breath rasped in my throat, but otherwise the world was silent.

Then a cry broke overhead, and I looked up to see a red-tailed hawk launching out from the top of an oak. I recognized the bird from its band of dark feathers across the creamy breast and the tail splayed like rosy fingers against the sun. It was a red-tailed hawk for sure; and it was also my father. Not a symbol of my father, not a reminder, not a ghost, but the man himself, right there, circling in the air above me. I knew this as clearly as I knew the sun burned in the sky. A calm poured through me. My chest quit heaving. My eyes dried.

Hawk and father wheeled above me, circle upon circle, wings barely moving, head still. My own head was still, looking up, knowing and being known. Time scattered like fog. At length father and hawk stroked the air with those powerful wings, three beats, then vanished over a ridge.

The voice of my education told me then and tells me now that I did not meet my father, that I merely projected my longing onto a bird. My education may well be right; yet nothing I heard in school, nothing I've read, no lesson reached by logic has ever convinced me as utterly or stirred me as deeply as did that red-tailed hawk. Nothing in my education prepared me to love a piece of the earth, least of all a humble, battered country like northeastern Ohio; I learned from the land itself.

Before leaving the drowned woods, I looked around at the ashen stumps, the wilted grass, and for the first time since moving from this place I was able to let it go. This ground was lost; the flood would reclaim it. But other ground could be saved, must be saved, in every watershed, every neighborhood. For each home ground we need new maps, living maps, stories and poems, photographs and paintings, essays and songs. We need to know where we are, so that we may dwell in our place with a full heart.

◗ REG SANER

Reg Saner is a poet and essayist and emeritus professor at the University of Colorado at Boulder. He has published three collections of nonfiction, *The Four-Cornered Falcon: Essays on the Interior West and the Natural Scene* (1993), *Reaching Keet Seel: Ruin's Echo and the Anasazi* (1998), and *The Dawn Collector: On My Way to the Natural World* (2005). His first collection of poetry, *Climbing into the Roots* (1976), won the Walt Whitman Award for 1976, and *So This Is the Map* (1981) was selected for the National Poetry Series by Derek Walcott. His other two poetry collections are *Essay on Air* (1984) and *Red Letters* (1989). In 1997 he was presented with the Wallace Stegner Award from the Center for the American West. "Mesa Walk" was first published in the *Georgia Review* and appears in *The Dawn Collector*.

Over the Rainbow, My Kind of Place

Essays whose logic is associative rather than linear aren't for every reader. But isn't that a bit odd? For the past hundred years montage and jump cuts have been standard techniques in cinema and every art form except pottery and painting by number. I nonetheless admit my pole vault in "Mesa Walk" from an Italian monastery to mule deer bucks in Colorado is a stretch. At least I hope so. That was the plan.

Fact is, rereading the piece so as to comment on it for this anthology, I myself boggled at that six thousand–mile shift. "What on earth was I doing there?" Good.

You see, in the five years since "Mesa Walk," having forgotten my thinking in that regard made me something like an average reader of my own essay. That alone would have drawn me to read further, if only out of uneasy curiosity. Through the first half-dozen or so pages the uneasiness abated somewhat but not entirely. "Where was I going with all this?"

As long as I'm spilling my guts, I might as well also confess that the original impulse for "Mesa Walk" was as vague as simply wanting "to do something" with a walk I've been taking for years now, along trails near my house. To supply a body for that unfocused aim to inhabit, I had accrued lots of notes in the course of those walks. Writers use notes the way painters use quick sketches. An artist's sketchbooks are to her what journals and notes would be if she were a writer: indispensable. Not only that. They're a way of paying close attention, a way of keeping impressions you'd otherwise lose. As the saying goes, a short pencil beats a long memory. Nudged by a free-floating feel for how I wanted the essay to go, I doubtless made some sort of rough outline.

Or did I? In denying me any vestige of authorial direction or drift, a skeptical reader might well have said, "Maybe even he didn't know." In fact, I imagined one harrumphing as he pronounced such a judgment.

That stung. Despite this reader's being wholly fictitious, I decided to fight back, close the barn door after the horse had bolted, give myself some retroactive integrity. So I did what I've never done with any essay, before or after. I counted its sections by way of rediscovering my own strategy. Turns out, there are seventeen segments, of which nine bear either some allusion to religious belief or touch on it in explicit terms. Nine of seventeen? That many? I hadn't realized.

But what of the other eight sections, with their various critters and Colorado flora? What relation had they to the theologically tinged elements?

Well, those animal episodes enter into "Mesa Walk" for their intrinsic interest, always; but some also modify or contradict worldviews that set an abyss between us talking animals and the other kind, while projecting intelligent design onto the natural world. Such homocentric orthodoxy is teleological. It claims a divinely ultimate purpose for the existence of stars, rocks, trees, animals, down to March winds and July's mosquitoes. This pious way of seeing was once called "natural theology." Happily, Ogden Nash, that laureate of humorous verse, has spoofed it all in a funny couplet: "God in his wisdom made the fly, / And then forgot to tell us why."

(For the record, incidentally, I too dislike *theological*, a word glum as mud fudge. Unfortunately, the pussyfooting connotations of terms such as *devotional*, *faith-oriented*, *sacral*, and *spiritual* aren't any better.)

A bundle of notes lacks soul. If they're to have one, it must come in either of three ways: prior to beginning an essay, in the process of writing it, or by a combination of both. No matter how I start I always end up with the latter. Invariably, my first impulse undergoes a makeover through interanimation between me and my material. That's what creative writing is all about, the process of discovery. If discovery sounds like a fake name for drifting and dreaming, let me assure you it isn't. In writing, discovery is the real deal.

Having agreed that any work's vital principle is soul, we still mustn't underrate body. Because we all like something we can hold on to, any essay I write must convey a body of factual knowledge that in itself, at least partly, redeems the time it takes to read the piece. I have reasons for that preference. For one, I don't fascinate myself enough. Reality is infinitely more absorbing. Yet it's not as if I lack astonishing achievement. I was president of my high school's senior class, all twenty-six of us. The same year, as running back and placekicker, I scored twice as many points as the rest of our football team put together. (Owing to a coaching fiasco, we played only two games.) These feats notwithstanding, if someone offered to introduce me to the author of "Mesa Walk," I would be hit by a severe attack of ennui. What could I hope to learn? I already know everything he does, and a lot more. Five years' worth, remember? My main reason, however, is that I've better things to do, such as learning the world. I assume you do, too. Happily, there are scads of us.

As I've said, though, a hatful of notes isn't enough. More important to written coherence than anything else is ourselves, our core concerns and convictions. In short, our souls. They tend to order elements into a pattern the way a magnet organizes iron filings. My own internal magnet is a religious worldview, one that orthodoxy would call unreligious to a damnable degree. In the Middle Ages and considerably later they'd have made a bonfire of me.

Convictions are very well, but the magnet analogy has limits. One's core tendency needs plenty of help. Therefore, any writer who expects his unconscious to do the work for him is just lazy and deserves what he gets. As W. H. Auden once warned, the Muse likes nothing better than whispering nonsense into the ears of poets gullible enough to write it all down. To avoid becoming one of their number in prose, I didn't commence "Mesa Walk" expecting to take dictation from some voice in a cloud; nor did I, as Theseus puts it when describing a poet's way of working in *A Midsummer Night's Dream*, let my eye in a fine frenzy roll from earth to heaven and back to earth again, then dash off hot page after smoking page. As an Elizabethan maxim has it, "Easy writing is cursed hard reading."

In contrast to the teleological way of looking at this world, for me and surely a billion others, the global scale of human misery, disease, parasitism, floods, fires, earthquakes, and other catastrophes makes belief in some benign Sky Father flatly impossible. Darwin's cameo appearance in "Mesa Walk" illustrates the same thing. As an ancient Roman naturalist, Pliny the Elder, observed, nature behaves both like a mother and mother-in-law. Worse yet, any objective visitor of Earth reveals overwhelmingly more evidence for a diabolic Creator than for one divine. A quip by Woody Allen puts his comic spin on much the same outlook: "If there is a god, he's a terrific underachiever."

For my pious friends, explaining all that away is easy as pie. They do it in a breath. Alas, I lack their facility

That being so, how dare I say my worldview is religious? "Religion," admits the *Oxford English Dictionary* with lexicographical caution, "is of doubtful etymology." The OED goes on to suggest a derivation from Latin *religāre*, meaning "to bind or tie back." Or—so say I—to tie together, to connect. In that latter sense I am indeed religious.

Religions exist to explain the world, but then, in my fumblesome way, so do I. To see or try to see bonds, ties, links, connections between this and that and the other thing—and our ties to all that exists—is to move toward a wholeness, a unifying view of the world. The difference between orthodoxy and me is that I prefer seeing for myself. I can't peer very far or delve very deep, of course. And with no pie in the sky, my reward must be in the trying.

This being a thematic anthology, it's no coincidence that my sense of place was paramount to the inception and unfolding of "Mesa Walk." If its finished form were to be true to my initial impulse, it needed to fuse my joy in where I live with my awareness of how profoundly *where* I am defines *what* I am, both in a personal sense and as a talking animal keenly aware of mortality. In his *Theatetus* dialogue Plato declares, "The sole origin of philosophy is wonder." I'm no philosopher, but in my case he's wonderfully right. Inside my every deep moment of awe is a question echoing further questions.

Beneath my whims and opinions shifty as wind, there's this granitic fact: I'm so allied to my mountain setting that I don't feel who I am so fully anywhere but here. In a way that's scary.

Raised amid Illinois farmland, I'm no longer myself there. The prairies of my midwestern origin have fertile appeal, but they've been "rationalized" by section lines, fence lines. Their very soil is purposeful. Every furrow has an aim. Native grasses have been told, "Go 'way." Forests were felled and burned to get them out of the road. All of that has its reasons. How could anyone be against food? Nonetheless, it's no overstatement to claim that our western terrain—this country where enormous spans of time rise up tangible as stone—has changed me too radically for a life anywhere else.

Humanity's precarious situation isn't so pervasively present in Ohio or Kansas as it is everywhere in the West. Anyone stepping from a car in the Rocky Mountains knows the feeling. Summits, blue ridgelines, sagebrush expanses—they turn us into mayflies. In any novel with a western locale its places aren't mere background; they're a main character. Quite often these fictional plots show all the other characters reacting to and being acted upon by that terrain.

Then there's a truth I find endlessly interesting. Context changes content. Where we are interacts reciprocally with who we are, what we are. As a Wallace Stevens poem has it: "I am what is around me," wittily adding, "One is not duchess a hundred yards from a carriage."

In the same poem, he declares, "Women understand this." Which brings me to Anne, my wife, and our little in-joke, "over the rainbow to Gubbio." Each of us had known Italy before Italians had cars in a ratio of one per capita. Huge difference. Oh, through the years we had driven in London, Paris, Munich, Milan, Rome, but Europe changed, and so had we. Traffic, mazes of one-way streets to ease the overload on streets narrowly medieval, tourist hordes, groping for cheap hotels—all had opened our eyes to a crucial truth: our decades in the West had made us Coloradoans. We needed breathing room.

My inner-city road rage at Sienese congestion added the last straw. I headed our Peugeot well off the beaten path, up into the region of Todi, Gubbio, Montepulciano. No sooner had we entered their greenly forested and montane vistas than Anne told herself, "I'm home!" while I was spontaneously thinking, "Oh, yes, this is more like it." Back in Boulder after a five-thousand-mile summer in Europe (and thirty-six hotels), we laughed at our special fondness for those places most akin to what we'd left behind.

Just as the context of a zoo diminishes its captives, an Apache pushing a shopping cart at Wal-Mart is no longer an Apache. Feeling I can't really be who I am when out of the West makes me, in that respect, also a distant cousin of those ancestral Pueblo peoples called the Anasazi.

My mailing address lies nearly four hundred miles away from the Sleeping Ute, a low mountain whose skyline resembles a reclining man. Ute lore identifies him as an immortal. Yet each time I've once again caught sight of the Sleeping Ute, he has moved me so reliably, so repeatedly, as to impart some faint notion of how—among Anasazi people farming or hunting lifelong in the area—his shape became an inseparable part of their lives. For miles and miles across that part of Utah, anywhere you go, whatever you do, there he is.

In the play of sunlight and shadow across his deific torso whose laccolith, geologically speaking, is an uplift of igneous rock, those Anasazi would have seen many a sacred implication. So did the Utes, who came after. Even for whites currently living in the area, his changing appearance continues to center sky and earth just as inevitably. Through the grand wheel of seasons, from winter through spring to summer and back again, through red sun and blue shadow, the Sleeping Ute can't help becoming everyone's sundial, calendar, and compass to find your way by.

Well, if our lives were half so imbued with the spirit profoundly felt in local regions by Cherokees, for example, or the Lakotas, the Cheyenne, or Utes, deep depression and grief at being forced out of their home terrain could kill us too. But that doesn't happen nowadays. In our consumer culture a man's "center place" is money, whose other name is career.

Any eccentric billionaire goofy enough to imitate Diogenes could prove it, but instead of a lantern he'd carry a checkbook.

He'd simply wander around as the ancient Greek did, but rather than questing for an honest man, he'd rove in search of somebody who wouldn't swap his ancestral region merely for cash. Someone who refused to give up the daily, hourly, feel of that natal terrain. Someone who wouldn't leave his deepest allegiance for a price, at any price. In short, he'd look for a person whom dollars cannot uproot. Once upon a time, right here in the United States, there were whole nations of them. Many. But that was then. Nowadays, the search might take a while.

By way of considering what essays like "Mesa Walk" are about, we must consider creative nonfiction as poetry in the widest sense. We recall how Aristotle in the *Poetics* affirmed that verse isn't a necessary attribute of poetry. Even so, he seems to take it as self-evident that poetic content must be fictive. Despite his view that poetry needn't use verse, we can therefore easily imagine Aristotle excluding nonfiction on the grounds that poetry deals with the probable, with what happens, not with what actually happened in true-to-life detail.

Having no hotline to the Elysian Fields, I can hardly beg the Stagirite to reconsider by accosting him in person. "Oh, high-IQ Greek whom Dante called 'master of those who know,' have the patience to abide my question. Don't you agree," I might say if he weren't so illustriously defunct, "that your own former teacher, Plato, in his dialogues enacting Socrates' trial and his final day under sentence of death, wrote poetry? Would not the same hold true of his *Symposium*?"

If silence is consent, I may have won him over. Yes, those witty speeches on love in the *Symposium* are reported at greater length and in greater detail than human memory could have managed. At the very least, surely Plato fleshed them out with his own thought; perhaps made some of them up entirely. On the other hand, drinking parties were common in Athens's heyday, and Athens—intellectual center of the Mediterranean world—teemed with brainy types well able to discourse on a wide variety of topics. Those Socratic compositions sometimes called, collectively, "Socrates' Last Days," could—like the *Symposium*—be considerably less fictive than many of their readers assume. Proto-nonfiction or not, we'll never know.

As a writer, let me assure you that I don't prefer nonfiction to fiction out of any foolish belief that nonfiction is better. Each mode has its excellence. Me, I find reality more wildly strange than the baddest, way-outest, most hyper-bizarre fiction. One likes what one happens to like.

Even if for the sake of surmise we concede creative nonfiction's claim to be poetry in this broader sense of any well-wrought verbal object, how could that matter when weighing essays like "Mesa Walk"?

The relevance is simple. Poems aren't diplomatic couriers. The point of a poem is the poem itself, not something called its message. Franz Schubert, on performing a piano sonata, was asked by a puzzled listener, "Pray, what does it mean?" In answer he turned to the keyboard, played it over again, then announced, "That's what it means." So, too, any word or phrase summing up "the point" of an associative essay is beside the point.

The nearer an essay comes to that self-referential condition, the closer it comes to being poetry. The same can be true of essays generally but is most obviously true of the nonlinear kind. Not only do their physical descriptions and information refer to the tangible world, they also refer to elements of themselves. Dramatic poetry like *Oedipus the King* and *Hamlet* are self-referential in this way, and to an extreme degree.

Like elements in any poem, good or bad, sections in the "Mesa Walk" sort of essay converse with each other, amplifying, modifying, undercutting. If it works, the result is satisfyingly complex. If not, the result is a mess.

That said, provided creative nonfiction has a valid claim to status as poetry, asking what a coherent nonlinear essay is *about* implies, therefore, a wider perspective than the narrower sense in which some readers would understand the term. As for "Mesa Walk," every writer choosing a nonlinear structure expects readers to become cocreators. They enjoy a challenge, provided it isn't too insuperable. "A poem," said Stevens, "should resist the intelligence almost successfully." That is, it should resist the facile categorizing that leads to easy dismissal. Its structure keeps readers uncertain enough to stay attentive, not thrust it quickly into a familiar category labeled, "Ain't Nature Great," "Anti-Gun Guy," "Love Is Good," or what have you. Clearly, in Stevens's dictum, "almost" is everything, especially in the case of essays whose logic is associative. Writers choosing that mode are continuously wary of pushing its resistances too far. Yet far enough to intrigue, involve.

But how far is too far? Compared to the millions reading prose, fans of serious poetry are nowadays a coterie. Any member of their savvy and happy few is correspondingly more hip to complex language and its oblique ways of saying things than is the average bookstore customer. On the other hand, in both prose and poetry easily foreseeable development of themes is boring. Balance is all. The *Goldilocks* rule.

As we know, poetry, like music, says what can't be said, or at the least, can't be said in any words other than those of the poem, and in their exact sequence. Among much else "Mesa Walk" says, "I like it here," but I hope that doesn't sum it up.

For instance, where is *here*? What are its boundaries? The essay's concept of place is far from static. After all, as we've noted, the opening section features a Tuscan sunrise and the chanting monks of a Benedictine monastery called Monteoliveto Maggiore, to be immediately followed by a section foregrounding mule deer on a Colorado mesa. This hither-and-yon shift is one of many in the essay. Therefore, the implicit answer to "Where's here?" suggests that the writer's sense of place is interactively local and global. The sung Latin reminds him of his Illinois hometown. Again, that's merely one of several such interactions. Finally, although the assertion may seem grandiose, his sense of place is also cosmic. In addition, the essay reflects on its temporal dimensions. Monteoliveto Maggiore's walls of red brick were laid seven centuries ago, the essay's incomparably older mesa is made of alluvial epochs, its mule deer arrived there via evolution, and so forth.

But why do I find myself referring to *"the writer's* sense of place"? The writer. Ha! That critical figment has no relation to me; no eyes, either blue or brown, no forelock of hair, no baggy cargo pants, no "lean and hungry look," no copiously sun-crinkled skin. "Come off it," I tell myself. "Lose this germless objectivity."

Okay. So instead of leaping from a phone booth as The Writer, I hereby step out of a broom closet as just me. What's more, since I'm an alter ego to "the writer" I can tell you point-blank that "cosmic" isn't grandiose. When it comes to place seen in a wide-angle view, your underwear is cosmic. Willy-nilly, every reader and place whizzes at terrific speeds inside a cosmos, like it or not.

I do. That's why the world of "Mesa Walk" is both "my" world, unfolding as it does right where I live, at the foot of a Colorado mesa, and its larger context in space and time. Yes, the locus where we spend our days—that's our place to know the world in. But dawn is hardly a parochial event, and I'm one among its creatures, with ties to all that lives—as who isn't? Yet ties unbeknownst aren't the same. Even Jean-Paul Sartre might agree, y' gotta *be* there.

When it comes to reflecting on the world and existence itself, a short poem by the Colorado poet Thomas Hornsby Ferril bears a title worth keeping in mind: "Always Begin Where You Are." Originally, "Mesa Walk" was to lend its name to a book dwelling on aspects of where I am, my place. For setting the book would draw on creeks and critters within a short walk of my house and further develop topics foreshadowed in its title essay.

Soon, however, a piece exploring my delight in sunrises took over that lead spot, the better to emphasize the single facet of place I find most absorbing: being here. For me that's what dawns are about, as up from the Colorado plain east of me and "over the bent world," the sun rises. In becoming *The Dawn Collector,* the book widened its scope. Being briefly alive is the strangest thing that can possibly happen, and dawn brings that home. Nothing else even comes close.

All the same, seeing and being alive must have somewhere to stand, either chosen or imposed. The Colorado setting of "Mesa Walk" is mine, gratefully chosen, thus all the more freely espoused. Using my local setting to see this Earth truly, not as a waiting room for heaven but as the only heaven we'll ever have, is something like the direction "Mesa Walk" tries to explore.

Mesa Walk

The eyelids flutter open. The mind interprets . . . or tries. Undersides of leaves, coppery ones turning gold. Early light. Sky through thick branches. Sunup?

As if out of a life slowly trying to recall how it got here, I find myself lying on ground somewhat damp, looking straight up into an olive tree not far from a monastery I remember hiking toward. Arriving long after nightfall, unable to see any but large dark forms, I had flopped down on the most level spot I could find and—after legging eighteen rural kilometers through the Tuscan countryside to get there—had quickly dropped off, sleeping, not sleeping, all night, checking stars against rain cloud because I had no tent, just a U.S. Army war-surplus sleeping bag.

Then this awakening: the choral surge and lull of monks chanting matins in the monastery called Monteoliveto Maggiore, its walls and towers the chalky red of old brick, their upper courses showing patterns cunningly laid. Through August air still cool and laced with the resinous scent of cypress, the unisoned voices—rising, fading, rising again—lift a monastic answer to daybreak. For a while I lie snug in my bag, delighted to be looking up through olive leaves at blue sky, charmed by the rhythmic thrum and lull of that medieval invocation—like antiphonal waves lapping a sacred shore. In their chant I catch occasional Latin phrases as if from halfway around the world. Amid downstate Illinois prairie I grew up in the same faith as these Benedictines now intoning and on countless Sundays heard the same rhythmic recurrences of Gregorian singsong. So, among terraced groves on the volcanic *tufa* of a hillside miles from Siena, I loll half-here, half-home.

Monteoliveto's Benedictines, however, lift a collective voice of grown men far better practiced and with richer timbre than any farm town's motley choir. What's more, their sung devotion floats to me reverberated from the ogive arches and vaults of a chapel emitting the sound of concentric tongues and from a monastery founded in 1313 by one Bernardo Tolomei.

Breathing Colorado's high, frosty air of mid-February, I spot five large, fur-bearing mammals widening the context of my teenage past as I watch. Out for sunup, I come across them in a spacious meadow on the northwest side of our mesa, where they rehearse a routine so stylized it's virtually a rite, one that mule deer mostly perform in breeding season.

Dangerous as sharply pointed antlers can be, deer use them as we use hands in arm wrestling, for a firm grip on the other guy. The first challenge develops when a six-point buck with a couple of broken tines steps gravely among yucca and lichened boulders toward a four-pointer, thus his junior, who turns to face him. Their winter coats, unshed, aren't so thick that they conceal the lean ribcages of animals surviving on the tan meadow's skimpy browse. All the same, precisely like human wrestlers in a supervised contest, each buck lowers his head, chin almost touching the ground's straw whiskers, and each waits till his antlers fully engage those of the other.

Then, under that chilly sky's few stalled clouds they begin. The more mature six-point deer strains to force his opponent's head sideways, like a rodeo bulldogger twisting a steer's horns. As the other buck fights back, their heads wag to, then fro, antlers loudly clacking with the sound of rattled pool cues or walking sticks in a hallway stand. One Christmas morning I watched a bout between two so evenly matched it lasted several minutes.

Amusingly, although females are the ultimate prize of these sparring matches, three of them foraging nearby never once glance up at the display. So much for impressing the ladies. Maybe these contests well after the nominal end of rutting season help bucks cast their antlers, yet, for all the vigorous twisting, shoving, wresting, I see nothing break or come loose. On both the full-chested six-pointer and his rival the hindquarters are equally tawny, but fur on the year-older deer shows darker pelage along his shoulders; and, predictably, he outwrestles his junior several times running. As if to signal the end of each encounter, the younger animal scampers away, well beyond the three does, then circles back. After a nip or two of forage, his antagonist steps with the same gravely deliberate gait downhill toward him for a rematch. To my surprise, the loser accepts, facing about as before, lowering antlers, and yet another go-round begins. If nothing else, he gets bodybuilding out of it, since the isometric tensioning of those neck muscles alone—lasting from twenty to thirty-five seconds—must be considerable.

Their final have-at-it starts easy, then abruptly alters tone when the older buck lunges with a burst of power that shoves the other into fleeing quickly downhill as if alarmed. Message received? Apparently so. Content with his winning streak, the six-pointer extends no further invitation, and with nippy breeze ruffling fur on his withers goes back to raking at a patch of meadow with a forehoof. Nothing there. Then scrapes at a spot just under the naked twigs of clumped squawbush, in hope of turning up an edible rootlet out of February's slim pickings.

Fifty yards to the southwest, a couple of mature and fully racked eight-pointers start testing each other. Those two seem also to be "just fooling around," but soon get really into it, neck muscles straining, heads yanked now to one side and now the other, powerful haunches thrusting, rear hooves tearing straw turf from a soggy meadow not yet green. The buck on my left is at first slowly forced to give ground, then ups his effort enough to retard that momentum against him, then strains even harder, thrusting back till they come to a dynamic standstill. Through perhaps four visibly strenuous seconds their matched powers hold that tense, trembling balance. Then the leftmost animal goes on the offensive, pushing his antagonist back a very few inches, another few, forcing him reluctantly backward . . . backward . . . backward, one slow, shuddering, haunch-tensioned step at a time.

Great theater. And familiar as a locker room. From his peak testosterone years every ex-jock can recall the times when horseplay between two pals turned nasty. No wonder we use *young buck* in assessing late-adolescent aggressiveness. Always, the pre-adult studlings tell themselves, "We're just fooling around." They are, but doing something else as well. I can still hear my mother's alarmed outcry when, in our living room, the furniture's glue joints began to creak ominously: "All right now! If you boys are going to do that sort of thing you can just go on outside. I won't have you tearing up the house!"

Watching bucks enact so transparently the roots of my callow machismo—

back when I thought I was being me—brings a smile at closer kinship with mammalian behavior than vanity cares to admit. Not just boyhood vanity. Countless are the high-minded adults who, while wearing claws on fingers and toes, and tufts of fur in small personal places, hotly deny they're animals.

That chanted dawn at Monteoliveto was years ago. Even then, no idea what other mornings my eyes might open to, I doubted I'd ever again stir awake so deliciously. Wondered how many sleepers ever had. It was August, I was a twentysomething, mad-about-Italy Fulbrighter keen to explore a monastery founded when Dante, Petrarch, and Boccaccio were very much alive. Thinking of happiness, I've more than once thought of Monteoliveto.

Yet for me the deity those monks were invoking had already ceased to be anything but the name of an emotion, very real, even if I don't believe it, one more god among the innumerable gods begotten by our species' quest to know the what, where, and why of existence.

While footing it along Tuscan back roads, chatting with an occasional *contadino* unyoking his oxen or pitching hay, I was, therefore, far from a pilgrim drawing nearer the Lord. Was instead just another low-budget culture vulture roving Europe, yet impressed by the no-nonsense, unwimpish Benedictines whom I distantly glimpsed hustling to and fro in their robes of white linen. I was impressed, also, by as much as I could make out from my little campsite of their venerable monastery's rampart-like merlons and crenels, its turreted tower of red brickwork. Rather than offering prayer, however, I felt eager to pay reverence to its many inset wall sculptures, Della Robbia ware in glazed terra cotta, whose images—overlooking the garden's clipped hedges—were overlooked in turn by exotic palmettos and lofty cypresses. And I wanted to lay eyes on a fresco sequence of episodes from the life of Saint Benedict by the maverick painter frankly answering to the name Sodoma, whose work I'd seen only in art books.

Among it all—though rather oddly, because I now can't imagine why—I was specially curious to see the very choir stalls where monks were just then lifting their sacred song, stalls which my guidebook awarded two stars, saying they featured "notable intarsiatura by Giovanni da Verona." With fervently chanting monks worshiping in the very chapel I'd hiked all that way to admire as Renaissance woodwork, my affection for the monastic tradition and my secular motives made an uneasy couple.

True, my compendious Hachette guidebook with its dark blue binding looked sober and serious as the fat missals whose pages I used to turn so religiously during Sunday Mass, complete with a missal's little ribbons for place-keeping. I smiled at the likeness. Culture worshipers do go on pilgrimages, enact rituals. Art, too, has its sacral aspects, transcendence among them. Swapping prayer book for guidebook implied less interest in looking up than in looking around.

Throughout history approaches to "Where am I?" and "Why?" have been fenced off in a thousand and one different ways as sacred precincts by the world's thousand and one religions. Equally well-known is the fact that some orthodoxies have taken unamiable, not to say murderous, views of people who dare pursue their own answers—on pain of being set afire or torn into small pieces.

Trite as citing Galileo's trial may seem, his condemnation illustrates exemplarily well the reciprocity between context and content and, therefore, marks the Great Divide between thought control and science. With intuitive accuracy the Church sensed that a widened knowledge of *where* we are would change *what* we are, in ways making its dogmas problematic. And how.

Nowadays, instead of oppression by censorship or propaganda, curiosity is mainly quashed by dogma's opposite: information out the ears—and more coming in via Windows. So much stuff is so omnidirectionally dumped on us that we sag under its weight. Sound bites from the surreal domain of subatomic physics and orbiting sources like the Hubble telescope's successors become everyday's predigested and brief curiosities. Curiosity itself slowly loses any personal dimension, like a house cat expecting to be fed by others. After all, with such expertise probing nature, the savants will keep us posted. As they do, incessantly.

Indeed, many of my acquaintances stay well connected: cell phones, voice mail, e-mail, Palm Pilots, cable, and the Web. To them an old wish has been magically granted, the electronic gift of godlike omnipresence: here, there, and everywhere at once. Now nothing can escape their attention. Or is it the other way round? A sort of captivity?

Maybe yes. Amid a culture exhorting us to multiply experiences instead of deepening them, it's easier and easier to keep in touch with everything but yourself. As for linkups, one might ask, "Connected, yes, but connected to what?" A Microsoft researcher recently referred to the state of "continuous partial attention." If that doesn't make you shudder, what does? Therefore, no pager has ever touched my person, nor have I ever put ear to a cell phone.

Instead, my homemade response has been to mute—though by no means ignore—the static-like crackle of "input" and to stay in touch by often pulling on a stout, full-leather pair of hiking boots. In them I go forth to tacitly quiz animals, plants, skies, their weather, and the rocky terrain near my house. Maybe they know something. Doubtless my loss in late-breaking flashes on some 24/7 nature channel, or updates from the Internet, is great. As compensation, however inept or amateurish by comparison, taking the natural world personally earns you the quiet pleasure of seeing for yourself and coming tangibly closer to what you are.

I keep going round in circles. Yet our senses are dumb to how fast Earth travels, even when we know. What's more, the planet puts its own spin on those orbits by turning us in smaller, diurnal circles within that seasonal journey. One fine Colorado morning quite by chance I realized that my strolling round the mesa near my house roughly rhymes with those larger motions. And that, too, made me smile. At seventeen, musing on girls, the universe, and my chances in professional baseball, I'd have been incredulous if, say, within an abandoned grain elevator some oracular echo had prophesied, "One day, going for a walk will come to seem the luckiest thing in your life." What a downer that would have seemed!

My three-and-a-half-mile route, which lopsidedly circles back to where I start from, wasn't planned—just the happenstance of living across the street from open fields at the foot of forested mountains. Part of my luck is living at the interface of two diverse ecologies: grassland meadows rising to fir trees thick-sown on steep mountainsides half-conifer, half-rock. Tumbledown talus. Gray trunks lying windfallen and barkless over boulders bigger than my truck. And high above them, the angular jut of bare cliffs whose summits rise higher still.

Regionally, the area is known as "the foothills," which to an ex-flatlander seems absurd. My house sits at 5,600 feet above sea level, while the two nearest peaks rise over 2,500 feet above that. Some hills! After decades spent enjoying their steep terrain, so wild yet close at hand, the Illinois boy in me may halt, look way up, and chuckle while shaking his head: "I can't believe I actually live here."

So, along a rocky trail's circuit I'm at my happiest alone among friends— evergreen trees, rock, water, and sky—just following the turn of the year. In March our mesa slopes wear snow-mottled patches, burlap-colored where those aren't, then begin greening up into spring's resurrection, when streams seem a continuous birth. By late April gold-green buds of box elders lining Bear Creek begin leafing out. By May, amid the blurt and whistle of bird-song, chokecherry bushes and thickets of wild plum turn Bear Creek Canyon fragrant with blossoms, and sand lilies make white seem a new color. Under July's high cirrus clouds their bright petals shatter, morphing to fruit as August burns toward October. By mid-September, the air still busy with dust and insects, chickarees and jays scold me as I pass. Fall cottonwood foliage is the first to yellow and twirl away on wind. Soon after, I pause to enjoy the autumnal blush in a sumac leaf. Any September morning we may awake to first snow high up on peaks and mountainside conifers. By winter my circuit can take twice the time to complete because I'm knee-deep in drifts, with more coming down as I wade, and I love it. Off and on through February, snowy areas and long scabs of trail ice can become puddles, refreezing after sundown, but by midmorning—though the thawed trail is mostly too rocky for continuous quagmire—stretches of red mud here and there churn under my daytime boots like the muck of World War I. Followed, often as not, by a March blizzard or two, and more white weather in April. Nonetheless, outing added to outing carries me further ahead and back where I started: spring's green apparition and pasqueflowers poking up through pine duff.

I've always felt most at home when in motion, but some days are specially blessed. It's then that I tell myself, "This is the best thing you ever did. And you're doing it right now."

What's incrementally legible, therefore, in my day-to-day strolling over the same trail in this, my place to be true to, is the year cycle, our orbital story told by "great creating nature." And my story within theirs. Not mine as individual, but as one six or seven billionth of our kind now alive.

No sooner had I entered my teens than serious thoughts of the priesthood gave rise to the usual scruples. Were my hands worthy to touch the Lord's

235

body and blood in celebrating the sacrifice of the Mass? I'd been taught—and truly believed—that willfully entertaining certain thoughts was deadly sinful. Alas, every time I looked into my soul for the spotlessness a priest ought to have I found no such thing. Consequently, my testosterone-sodden being came to picture his mortal sins of impurity as so many USDA judgments on sides of beef, their bluish-purple impressions seeped into the fatty tissue. Despite sin-free patches, my soul's case history was grievously stamped with temptations stronger than I was. How could such a bedeviled mind dream of Holy Orders?

My long-standing fondness for dawn collecting isn't sun worship. By no means. More of that later. For now it's enough to admit that if going forth year-round to watch sunrise from a stance on the mesa does have a quasi-religious tint it's because, except for the nearest star, other gods refuse to appear. Strange to say, all religion is made credible through their refusal, which our human nature has turned inside out by deeming nonappearance the surest sign of divinity. Hence we've erected cathedrals and mosques, stupas and temples, monasteries and convents, to honor deity's utter transparence. Hence the countless stones carved and bronzes cast as moving images of the gods' strict invisibility. So, too, in that vaulted chapel of Monteoliveto, men's voices sounded all the more profound for echoes of the sacred absence.

Turns out, every deity lives at the far end of hearsay. A god is what you have to take somebody's word for. More than any syllable I know, "god" tends to become what it names. Gods have always led this strictly word-of-mouth existence—the mouths being ours, not theirs. Immortals made of words. That doesn't in the least deter endless generations of believers who demand that the deity of their choice exist. As in economics, where there's demand there *will* be supply. And how! Because the sacred's what nobody can see.

The exception to this rule of invisibility is *Helios*—to use the Greek for a sun spirit called *Tawa* by Hopi—because our species has always seen wheat, corn, and life itself as gifts of the sun. Thus it's the nearest star I begin with, that gorgeous horror to which we owe everything, and by whose light I read brevity as inscribed within the Book of Nature. A leaf, a stone, the sun. Theirs are the scriptures I believe in.

Growing up in a Midwest farm town I shot birds and trampled wild plants freely as "weeds," which is what to my eyes they were. Recalling my vandal past nowadays brings a sigh not so much of remorse as of regret for time lost to blindness. Yet boys being boys being little animals (because they are), that too is nature.

Natural as well, a youngster's ability to see better. At age eleven or twelve and holding my prize possession, a Benjamin air rifle, I stood looking down at a bright dribble of blood still glinting on russet feathers. (As I now know, the bird was a flicker.) Looked and told myself, "Why, it's beautiful. And you killed it. Just because you could." Through mindlessly scanning for something to train the sights of that BB-shooting pump gun on, I'd become a deed worse than dirty. I can still see those sleek wing feathers, the scapulars and primaries half-spread where their shot life had fallen. Also, like paint oozed from a tube, the red dab on a breast still warm.

All the same, guilt turned me into neither some youngest-ever member of the Audubon Society nor a general friend of the animals. It merely opened the mind's eye a *slight* bit wider. Ah, the years it takes to see anything, one's self included.

As it happens, Earth receives one-half of one billionth of our daystar's total radiation. (Less than one-half, actually.) If on some hot day in downtown Little Rock or in Utah's canyon country, that fact feels absurdly mistaken, think it over. Not being a disk but a sphere, our sun spews hyperfire with equally manic generosity in every direction.

Often, at dawn, I stand unscorched on the solar surface looking toward Earth's faintly discernible pinpoint of reflected glint all but lost in galactic vastitude. Seen thus, our "one-half of one billionth" explains itself. And does more. Shows me the size of my importance. How much of that star's half-billionth, I sometimes whimsically wonder, does an average human life receive?

No telling, of course. Yet our bodies and minds inherit solar inflections accrued all the way from the first living cell to this morning's toast. With retributive circularity any thought we have about the sun begins deep inside the solar core, taking millions of years to surface as electromagnetic radiation, thence into our minds by way of a leaf's photosynthesis and what the brain, thinking that very thought, does with sun sugar.

Back in my days as heroic stalker of rabbits and quail, had even the grasses tried to speak to me? If so, I didn't listen. Botanically blind, I didn't know that grasses have leaves, that wheat is a grass once among those very plants I thought of as weeds. How could they lift anything but themselves, much less my heart?

They can't unless seen by the mind's eye, not just retinal nerves. If insight happens, stories humble as dirt may grow to be a perennial encouragement. When I'm in a mood dull as asphalt, just stepping off pavement to walk among lives of the unimproved earth—whether those plants be husky as November or green as May sun—perks up my bloodstream so instantly that the immediacy itself feels like a blessing.

Perhaps in all this world that spontaneous rush of delight is the one thing it would kill my soul to lose, the one thing most mine. The solar narrative couldn't be cherishable without it, because a mind bereft of delight would drag around amid mere coagulations of atoms. Would be a mind with no ghost in its own machine. When you're blue—and who at times isn't—sudden joy is like returning from the dead. A millisecond of springtime, proving the soul's an event, not a thing.

Actual springtime brings a seasonal version of the same exuberant uplift. That's why any country enduring long visits from snow and ice celebrates it, and certainly where I live qualifies. In mid-December, around the winter solstice, our house sees the sun go behind Bear Peak at about 3:15 in the afternoon—at which time, if I'm outside, the ridgeline's eclipse of its rays is instantly felt.

For us northern Coloradans, however, spring is a very mixed message, more a calendrical event than one continuously seen on the ground. Our deepest snows fall from skies of March and April, with spring's advent a matter of waxing light as night wanes and fields often greening up at the fringes of drifts. It's then many a heart becomes a chamber of sighs. So everyone emerging from the dark of the year—whether at montane altitudes or sea level—gladdens to see skylight grow wider while nights shorten; as from its nadir to the south, the point of sunrise on our horizon advances, dawn by dawn, more to the east.

Unsurprisingly, "Easter" was the pagan name given a Northumbrian dawn goddess whose festival was celebrated at her spring return, surely a sacred event ever since humans grew happy to see snow and ice melting away, see the dead earth breathe again, twigs bursting their buds, sun climbing higher. In truth, the goddess they believed they were celebrating was their own joy.

Mile high and then some. Cold wind of 22 March whipping through the saddle between Boulder Mountain and Green Mountain. Defying bleak weather, along comes a coyote trotting past. Sees me, stops. Trots another ten yards, stops again, again swiveling his head around at me. Goes another ten, halts, takes a quick look, as with typical coyote circumspicuity his body points away while his head comes fully around in the opposite direction, staring exactly backwards at me. Limber indeed, and always keeping an eye out. His ancestors knew me of old. Traps, guns, poisoned bait. Any cruel thing our two-legged kind could inflict on a coyote, we have, and do, lately upgrading in some states to gunship helicopters.

Meanwhile, I'm stock still. As if to say, "Your move." Then here comes a mate or coyote pal. Windy raw as it is, icy and snow patchy as the mesa slopes are, it doesn't seem they'll find much—but I lack a coyote's sharp ear for critters under the snow. Once past and well beyond me, that second animal stops, looks around, stretches like a dog or cat with forepaws extended, yawns, resumes its trot, nears four grazing does and, pausing, looks toward them as if estimating prospects. A doe lifts her head, returns that gaze for a long moment, then steps slowly down the mesa's east slope straight toward it: "We can make this easy, or we can make it hard. Your choice."

The doe's approach is all it takes. She is bigger, faster, her hooves sharply pointed. She has friends. The coyote trots off after its companion.

"It ain't easy being no *Canis latrans*," a coyote might say. From years of sharing this locale with them, I agree. If you're a "prairie wolf," as some settlers called them, for all your poking and rambling around, for all your hither-and-yon trot, you log miles even to come up empty. Your pelt shows it. A kind of thrift-store, poverty-line fur, its color a sort of dirt-road tan with weedy touches of gray. Only when weather's fit for neither man nor beast do you get a day off, free to lie curled nose to tail, bad hungry.

Curious to see what this pair may try next, I hustle rock-stumblingly after them. With long practice in dodging my kind, they're masters at keeping a juniper, boulder, or hawthorn brake between us, when there is any, and soon lose me—as I knew they would—dropping from sight behind a ridge to nose out deer mice or voles without me kibitzing.

In any but a trained eye the meadow vole (*Microtus pennsylvanicus*) might as well be a big fat field mouse, though rounder, and wearing a coat rich as sable. So, except for dodging coyotes, snakes, hawks, and their sort, I'd enjoy paleo-recall enough to remember back when our species hadn't yet evolved from seed-eating rodents. Some Mesozoic time I was a down-to-earth vole myself. As it is, their prolific breeding makes them staple fare not only for those usual suspects but for foxes, owls, raccoons, cats, and town dogs as well. I've seen an Irish setter pawing frantically after one, scattering dirt from a burrow entrance; have seen house cats crouched and staring, staring, staring into grass for the next ever-so-slight, fatal stir. No wonder voles are forever atwitch with anxiety.

The vole who goes gnawing or skittering along a drift-covered runway is naturally unaware that its roof of snow doesn't keep a nearby coyote from picking up on the least squeak, scurry, or munching sound. Its audibility becomes suspenseful when a stalking coyote suddenly goes into slower motion, slower yet, freezes, cocks its head—then leaps upward, stiff-legged, to pounce with both forepaws, often fast rummaging the snow with those paws—like a cardplayer eager to see what hand he's been dealt. Comic if you don't take the vole point of view.

Out of nowhere this monstrous *thing* comes crashing through the roof of your life, like the beastliest dream you've been encoded to avoid. And far worse to follow. Toothy jaws gaping so wide that they swallow the sky, now zoom down to impale, then gulp you into an acid-filled cistern already holding others of your kind. Which is why all voles seem hyper-timorous. If winter doesn't turn you to stone, spring could drown you, and if neither a frozen death nor death by water should happen, fangs, beaks, talons, claws, paws, or jaws will.

Those whose lungs didn't fill with spring runoff find snowmelt has left their surface-level runnels called "runways" open to sky. Just below my dawn stance on the mesa, the drift created by squawbush has in great part vanished to reveal a maze of vole tunnels, really half-tunnels now that snow's gone from above them. Their labyrinthine little paths laid open to light and weather seem poignant, yet allow me to follow their winding ways through winter-killed herbage and green shoots of spring growth, all the while keeping to grassroots level in twisting hither and yon as seed-and-root feeding lead them.

I trace one such runway and estimate its meanders amount to over thirty-five feet, which implies prodigiously gritty gnawing. But of course all rodents must gnaw; otherwise, their teeth grow overlong and so prevent feeding or—

in rare cases—curving upward to penetrate the brain. Another runway wanders some twenty feet before I lose it. Certain stretches get filled in with very loose soil. Elsewhere thatched grasses cover their swerves intermittently so I can't tell where they go or guess their continuance without disturbing them, which I don't want to do; however, holes near some tunnels surely lead to their grass-lined hideaways deeper down.

Last summer I picked up from the trail a dead vole, surprised to find it still warm. As my forefinger, stroking fur, felt the last of its body heat, I studied the wide, dark eyes, the snub nose, the ears markedly smaller than those of a mouse. Then by its tail I held it over a clump of bluestem and let it drop back into tall grass . . . only to notice on my palm, where it had lain, a pair of red wetnesses, tiny dots of vole blood, same spaced as fangs. The snake, perhaps startled by my footfall's small quake, had slithered off and left its kill. Had any other voles of the litter, I asked myself, seen what happened? If so, what did they make of it? Glimpsed from their level, a snake striking with wide-open jaws must be quite a sight. And a last one.

Taking this victim's perspective scandalizes bioscience. Agreed, especially when it comes to "cute" little fellows with large dark eyes we shouldn't mistake our feelings for theirs. Nonetheless, facts of vole mortality can't help stirring some touch of kinship. Nine out of ten voles die young, so for them—imperiled on all sides—spring rarely returns because, on average, eight months is a lifetime. If you're reincarnated as vole, riding earth's orbit back to the month of your birth won't be likely. Twice round the sun makes you Methuselah.

In one study area semiferal cats alone accounted for 16 percent of vole mortality. It seems most unfair that lactating females should be especially vulnerable. Why are they? Studies suggest that their frequent need to leave the burrow and replenish themselves—thereby turning grass into milk for their litter—gives predators more shots at them. Or perhaps lactation makes them easier to scent. The cause isn't known.

Admittedly, to imagine a background of weepy violin music for vole "pups," as the young are called, is bleeding-heart sentimentalism, not science; nevertheless, to picture a litter of newborns back in the burrow, awaiting their gobbled-up mama's return, surely gives even the most austere zoologist a twinge, however vestigial. She or he would probably agree that if the teeny brain of *Microtus pennsylvanicus* could form an image of this world's design, it would look like talons or a fanged maw.

The coyote view begs to differ—if I may further scandalize cool reason by putting it that way. Not being voles or deer mice, we don't begrudge coyotes their need to vomit forth at the den an acid-soaked mess of small rodents for scrambling pups to re-swallow in turn, thus finishing the digestive process already begun. Lacking such daily prey, along with what scraps mountain lions leave on slain deer, coyotes would starve to death in a hurry.

Ho-hum. We're up on all that and find it quite bearable. We know also it's natural for mountain lions, in turn, to regard those shyly stepping, softly stepping, nearly voiceless cervids—with their brown eyes so wide and so wistful—as put on this earth for seizing by the throat. Some like it hot, *Felis concolor* foremost among them. To whom deer—lovely, vegetarian, peaceable deer—are what's for dinner. Not quite so ho-hum when it's my own backyard.

Watching our predatory side explained there with the candor of coyotes and big cats does complicate the face in my bathroom mirror.

Family on my mother's side having been farm people and therefore avid hunters of small game, the Christmas gift of a Remington twenty-gauge shotgun sent me out quail shooting with them. That wasn't like murdering songbirds, flickers, or my usual targets, those pesky little brown birds called sparrows. Game was another matter entirely. Any quail or rabbit we shot got eaten, recycled into our blood and bones like plowland into cornmeal or alfalfa into milk. In farm country back then, hunting came with the territory.

I loved roving fields, searching out coveys of quail, startling with an adrenaline thrill at their explosive *whirr!* up from brush into air. Misses were common. Bagging so much as a single quail out of a big covey wasn't guaranteed, whereas the quickness it took to get a double felt like a touchdown or home run.

Picking up shot game, the warm and wet-blood feel gave me pause. In skinning a rabbit, then noting the firm musculature as my blade laid its carcass open, certain thoughts occurred. Or in feeling a quail's delicate hones. Or when holding in my palm the minuscule heart that had fired it up from cover into air like a rocket. Or in plucking off each bird's head, the slight click, as of popping a knuckle. My fellow creatures, nimble and swift, that had wanted to live.

Yet quail, rabbit, even squirrel, were "mighty good eating." Family chat round the supper table agreed on that. Talk went, however, by fits and starts as my mom, dad, two sisters and kid brother, our farm grandparents, and I chewed cautiously, lest we bite into birdshot. An eater's sudden silence explained itself when we saw the front teeth mincingly isolate yet another tiny pellet. Shooting larger game we used shells with bigger pellets, so those nights when we ate fried rabbit our talk was punctuated by the plink of shot dropped onto the rim of a plate.

While a young man, Charles Darwin had—rather ironically—plugged away at theology, so as to take up the life of a cleric-naturalist in some country parsonage. Slowly, however, his religious faith underwent erosion by nature's workings seen up close and personal. What he discovered was a parasitized, predation-driven, tooth-and-claw world, whereas his middle-class England saw God's provident hand everywhere it looked and extolled the "divine" side of nature in pious tomes that bore titles like *Natural Theology*. Nature's works, religiously misunderstood, were deemed an especially fitting study for clergy. Given all their credulous pother about "lessons in limpets" and "sermons in stones," it's an amusing twist that "design" in the ichneumon fly's life cycle so revolted Darwin as to quench any lingering scintilla of belief.

That "fly" was a whole family of parasitic wasp, the Ichneumonidae. Among them, for example, species of the short-tailed genera *Ophion* implant an egg on a caterpillar, depositing that egg precisely where the caterpillar can't reach, enabling the hatched larvae to thrive by feeding on the host's living innards till they kill it. Wasps of the family Braconidae (genus *Apameles*) aren't so fastidious. They positively bejewel the hornworm caterpillar with eggs that hatch into larvae that burrow into their host—who, feeding itself, feeds them till they riddle its skin once more in burrowing back out.

Darwin had long known better than anyone else the creepy details of parasitism in nature but for some reason found this arrangement especially loathsome. It reinforced his feeling that pious fervor about providential design was overwhelmingly mocked by our world's sum total of misery. Ichneumonidae made a sick joke of cozy, after-dinner intoning about "a beneficent and omnipotent God."

What Darwin—whose patient tenacity staggers the mind—was too neurotically cautious to say, I now add: If evidence counts for anything, the Creator of a world with the global suffering of ours would have to be seen not as divine but diabolic. That doesn't leave me any whit less passionately grateful for the dazzle and range of nature's intricacies. It simply leaves me all the more aware of my luck. Sheer luck.

On the same blustery day of 22 March that brought a coyote past me, I saw them. The male of the pair, ground feeding, flew in low swoops barely above the still winterish slope, wings flaring with a blue whose verve always ravishes me. Though powder blue to some, turquoise blue to others, there's general agreement (among me, anyhow) that the mountain bluebird, *Sialia currucoides*, is the most beautiful of our avian species. Not far off, more bluebirds alit, flitted low and away again, nearly sweeping the ground with their quick wing-beats. One settled on a rock scarcely eight inches high, its lookout. Another half-dozen scattered to perch atop yucca stalks, cocking their heads this way and that for insects or grubs. Each repeatedly flew low and fed, while across the slope other bluebirds in the flock did the same, keeping a uniform distance so as not to compete for the same beetle.

As hinted, most northern Coloradans find themselves fed up with winter long before winter's through with us. And though I like nothing better than skiing through a white forest, snow-dolloped boughs and trails high in the mountains are one thing; the off-and-on freeze/thaw of March down here where our "foothills" meet the plains is quite another. Then—with many a winter-weary soul feeling gray as slush—these migrated birds one day return as if out of nowhere, and become for me more than they are. Intensely so.

When from the crown of a ponderosa one suddenly dives, brakes upward, wings flaring wide open, and settles onto a yucca stalk, its appearance feels like rescue; and that azure flash, the color of good luck, tells me spring has kept its appointment.

Years and miles from Illinois, I traded away my fine Remington twenty-gauge, valued less for its game bagging than for its knurled walnut stock, polychoke barrel, and engraved gunmetal; also for the receiver's smoothly automatic action; and, best of all, for the open-air rambling involved. I swapped it for a used Rolleiflex. The shotgun-into-camera metamorphosis was and wasn't symbolic, because I'm neither rigidly antigun nor antihunter, just procivilization.

As for hunting, I grew to realize it had been my male pretext for roaming fields with my golden setter. Besides, human population was growing, and game birds getting scarcer. I asked myself, "Why blow away what little is left?" Mainly, though, the mind's eye had widened. I no longer felt like drawing a bead on the bodies of living creatures. A shot flicker tried to tell me as much, but I wasn't yet ready to get the full message.

For tens of centuries false analogies between animals and humans pervaded Europe's pulpit rhetoric and literature, as to a lesser extent they still do, and shall. In crossing paths with mule deer, black-billed magpies, ravens, and other fauna on an everyday basis, I too see animals behave in ways tempting me to say, "Just like us." Which puts it backward. After all, they were here first, were in fact us before we were ourselves. Maybe that's why this urge to project our motives onto them, and the reverse, is old as *Homo sapiens* itself. Perhaps older. Thanks to ethologists, we're now aware that our animal-drawn inferences are in good part illusory, but certain turns of mind are too ingrained to change.

It's also true that my sense of kinship with them would feel more immediate if this were Africa and I were gazing at primates. On the other hand, a magpie's very difference from a marmoset makes any parallel trait pretty striking and, therefore, all the funnier—sometimes downright embarrassing.

For example, birds gregarious as magpies can be very gabby, announcing their affairs a half-mile off. As it happens, *magpie* derives from France and the name Marguerite, by way of Margot—presumably through a gender-biased view of the bird's chattering and squawking. The North American breed, *Pica hudsonia*, is loquacious all right, sharing its undulcet notes with others of the family Corvidae—ravens, jays, crows, and several cousins less raspy.

Sweet singers the corvids are not, though each species can be handsome in its way, and the magpie handsomest of them all.

In flight the black-and-white of a magpie's wingspan so flashes and catches the eye that visitors to the West invariably say, "What bird is *that*?" Seen ground feeding, the black of its head, breast, and folded wings isn't simple either. Owing to sunlight's refraction in preen oil, hints of midnight blue, emerald, even ruby and amethyst show how really fathomless their black-beyond-black can be. Yet at the same time alive. Those iridescent glints never prism the same way twice. Magpie white isn't common, either: too immaculate. A kind of perfection. When seen with folded wings the magpie's black beak, black head, and long tail over a spinnaker-like white belly make it seem a raven that has swallowed a dove. Other times I'm reminded of the black-and-white habits worn by Dominican priests or nuns, perhaps because I was taught by them. A quirkily personal association for so raucous a bird.

No use putting magpie calls into words. They won't go there. Authors of field guides know better than anyone that transliterating bird voices into al-phabetic combinations is hopeless, but that hasn't stopped them.

It certainly stops me. Having shared magpie territory year-round through dozens of seasons, I hear them simply as my reedy-voiced familiars, some-times talking to themselves or rasping away within a yakking flock of black-and-white others that I try to surmise what has set off the racket. Out looking round a few days ago surmising came easy.

At the highest elevation along my mesa walk, 6,200 feet, which gets signifi-cantly more rain and snow than just 500 feet lower, I was entering a conifer passage I always enjoy for its primeval effect. There on the north-facing side of the mountain, where snow lasts a long time, Douglas firs thrive, lining both sides of the narrow trail so thickly that they squeeze the view almost to a tun-nel, with the aspect of dense forest. While still within that evergreen corridor I heard quite a magpie to-do but couldn't see where or why.

Then I emerged. The scene was dramatic. Perched up and down limbs of a dead pine about two hundred yards away on Dakota Ridge, a parliament of magpies was razzing a red-tailed hawk. Interesting, to say the least, because red-tails can easily kill magpies, and do. And eat them.

Yet there it was, motionless, on an upper branch, looking—with the light behind it—darkly ominous and large. Even in my binoculars, except for a yellowish speck of beak and that hint of rouge in the tail feathers, it seemed a shadow made solid. Meanwhile, magpies flew in twos and threes to join those already perched on lower reaches of the same dead tree. When an occasional magpie did leave the group, its departure was more than offset by new arrivals that kept coming. Against dark conifers the white of their black-tipped wings flashed and winked in lively wise as they flew, till at one point twenty-eight of them jittered like nervous blossoms over the grayly skeletonic pine, giving the red-tailed raptor their unanimous opinion of him and his ilk.

What a to-do they were making! Small birds routinely mob larger ones, driving them away, but do so mostly in flight, and in far fewer numbers. I've watched four or five perching magpies nag at a hawk on lookout in the same pine till it got the message and flew. Never so many as this, though, and in a full squawking chorus whose unmistakable aim was to make that red-tail feel so outvoted, so unloved, so beset and scorned that it would say, "Who needs this aggravation? I'm outta here!"

Nothing doing. Didn't budge. Not so much as a feather. But for how long would the passivity last? Clearly, they were giving that raptor hell.

Throughout their clamor, fresh magpie arrivals fluffed down onto branches as others left them, but their numbers remained about the same: a gathering of yakkety hawk-haters voicing rowdy, abrasive criticisms at their natural-born enemy. I don't speak magpie, and didn't need to.

As before, the hawk sat there. Not a twitch. My human mind naturally projected all manner of attitudes into its look. "Me move? Aren't you forgetting something? Who you *are*, . . . who *I* am? Aren't you forgetting what I *do*?" It resembled an allegorical tableau: fell tyrant taking his ease as angry villagers seethe with resentment. The "little people." Underlings who make do on whatever. Seeds, insects, grubs. Shreds of carrion left by their betters.

As parallel, this is a stretch—yet not wholly so. Collective behavior is even more crucial to *Homo sapiens* than to magpies. Weakness confronting strength is nature's everyday news, from which our cooperative species emerged as, in times of crisis, each feeble "me" felt emboldened by adding itself to an "us."

Whether or not the red-tail "cared" about its low approval rating, it was certainly aware what all that noisy comment was about. The din was far too incessant, too indignantly in-your-face aggressive, to be misunderstood, either by hawk or human.

Not only that. From moment to moment one of the highest-perched magpies really pushed the envelope by hopping, branch to branch, upward, nearer and nearer its foe, with boldness that felt really dramatic. Close as eight feet, then hopping to a branch higher, maybe six feet from those talons. And another hop upward, closer yet. I thought, "Oh oh." But no. Upward even farther—to four feet from the red-tail, squawking right at it all the while: "And your mother wears GI shoes!"

Then, back to its own branch. Bird courage? Altruism? Risk taking on behalf of its species? Probably not, but we really don't know. An anti-altruistic view would see the "brave" bird as protecting in a diffuse way its individual genes, whose chances of survival are improved by vigilante action against predators. Furthermore, those genes can only be passed on via other magpies, presumably ones among that flock. If such sallies and hawk flouting seemed plucky, at times foolishly brave, the valorous magpie's "nerve" was more likely to derive from a predator-triggered molecular program. An encoded sense of maneuverability: "Close but not *too* close is OK. Your kind, nimbler than his."

Given a red-tail's four-foot wingspan, that's so, but the scene felt no less dramatic. This mobbing action of magpies, like that of some other prey species, makes a lottery of their bodies. "He may nail one of us, but while he's at it the rest can skedaddle."

What the hawk's sense was, who knew. Bored? This particular red-tail just sat there. For fully twenty minutes by my wristwatch the defiant jeering proceeded, full throat, same difference. Hawk unflappable.

Gradually, a few at a go, the raptor's critics flew away till those gray branches stood nearly emptied of birds—lightly reinforced, it's true, as some magpies returned, though ever fewer. Numbers dwindled, and so did that rackety, truculent din. Nice try that hadn't worked.

After little more than half an hour only three or four diehards were left. Then, about forty minutes after catching sight of the melodrama, I too gave up and resumed my walk with a touch of chagrin. The meek inherit the earth? Not this time. One heavily armed raptor had outlasted twenty-eight magpies, me along with them. There on its uppermost branch it perched, red-tail unruffled as ever. As if to say, "Any questions?"

In villa tamed hills above Florence, heady scents of springtime wisteria, jasmine, and broom mingle with whiffs of linden tree audibly abuzz, their bees briefly touching one minuscule flower after another. Despite those tiny chartreuse-colored blossoms stirring up my hay fever whenever I neared them, I find that their scent, remembered, fuses with an April/May still the most fragrant of all my Italian nostalgias. Time to time, however, as would any farmtown eager beaver "making the most," I eclipsed their dolce vita by ducking—like one of those dutiful bees—into and out of museums.

Especially when spring's in full flower, the last place any but "serious" types would go is into the abstruse rooms of the Museo di Storia della Scienza. Barely one tourist in Florence's daily thousands ever does. Its rooms and display cases offer *strenuously* educational arrays of antique stuff like armillary spheres, brass astrolabes and quadrants, and seventeenth-century adding machines with all sorts of dials, kooky chronographs, and orreries. Well, you never know when you'll get a thrilling surprise. There I stood, alone and suddenly spellbound, reverentially gazing upon this circular bit of clear glass as if at the Grail. Broken glass at that, and more than just somewhat.

Galileo himself had done it. Must have let it drop, or banged his telescope against something. But not before that very lens had shown him sights till then unimagined: mountains on the moon, the phases of Venus, Saturn's rings, and the moons of Jupiter. At the implicit significance of what he was the first human to see, every hair on his nape must have risen. Far reaching significance, as well he knew. Galileo was as smart as they come.

So a bit of cracked glass no wider than the bottom of a beer bottle had helped change awareness of the cosmos we're part of, therefore of our lot within it. Following the fiasco of his trial as one "vehemently suspected of heresy," the slow century-by-century shrivel of religion's thought police had begun. A homemade lens it was. Less wide than the palm of your hand.

Since "the world" isn't visible even to an astronaut, we see it only with the mind's eye, and for that we might—as one approach among many—embrace the protomonastic tradition practiced by certain early Christian ascetics of the Near East called "the desert fathers." We'd withdraw into austere terrain, live in caves, eat low on the food chain, and enjoy the rigors of doing without.

Much as I admire the communal ideal of monks, and paragons of Asian sagacity in far places, my soul leans away from cloistered living and exoticism for its own sake. The means can become an end. After all, neither the mind's eye nor the cosmos amounts to much without facts: the actual, the particular. That's why, for exploring crosscurrents between me and the world, I prefer setting forth from my own side door. If in Darwin's youth "the mystery of mysteries" was the origin of species, for me it's being alive while riding at unimaginable speeds amid the planet's millions of species making up life biological as we hurtle along.

So I peruse scriptures inspired by our daystar, and feel the oddly grand reciprocity of being enlarged by my own insignificance. But that happens best at first hand.

❖ NATALIA RACHEL SINGER

Natalia Rachel Singer has published essays and fiction in such magazines and journals as *Harper's*, the *American Scholar*, the *Iowa Review*, the *Bellingham Review*, *Ms.*, *Confrontation*, *Prairie Schooner*, and the *North American Review*, where she is a contributing editor. Her essay "Nonfiction in the First Person, without Apology" appeared in the premiere issue of *Creative Nonfiction*. She is the coeditor with Neal Burdick of *Living North Country: Essays on Life and Landscapes in Northern New York*. She teaches at St. Lawrence University. "In the Courtyard of the Iguana Brothers" originally appeared in the *American Scholar* and later as a chapter in her memoir, *Scraping By in the Big Eighties* (2004).

Views from the Desk

My view out my window as I write these words is of an uncelebrated river called "Grass" in the way-north of Upstate New York. The island just beyond it is part of a college campus, which means that for as long as I live here, when I look out the window above my desk, I'll see stands of white birch and beech and sugar maple and scotch pine and the river as backdrops to my backyard, with its grass and rocks and irises and poplar trees, chipmunks and squirrels, the blue heron that drops in now and then to stand in tree pose on the river-bank when my dog, Zoe, doesn't scare her away and, in October and April, transiting Canada geese. The Grass flows gently in summer and in torrents in April, when the icebergs break and flood our yards, the best time to take a canoe ride if you don't feel like paddling (and can arrange to have a car waiting some miles down the road). My partner and I were floating on our backs in this river when we decided to get married. Zoe fetches sticks in this water and barks at the dogs swimming on the campus side of the river. This view and my daily walk with Zoe along that same island path make me glad to live the life I lead teaching and writing in a rural outpost "far from the known world," as I often describe my home to friends in cities. This view is also the setting for my first novel, which I am just completing. After living in this town for fifteen years, I finally feel that I know it well enough for a character to feel it inside her skin, on the nerve endings, in her stomach's rumblings and heart's longings. It pleases me to write scenes in which the characters' views from the window sometimes please *them*, if only in a low-key, non-gothic, unromantic, nonexotic sort of way.

It wasn't always like this for me—my view of the outdoors, my settings in writing. For a long time the places in my work were toxic and noxious or else the romantic destination of a young narrator's great escape.

Although the Ohio River Valley, where I grew up, had parks and rivers and lakes, they were so polluted that when I was in grade school my hometown, Cleveland, was nationally known as "The Mistake by the Lake." The industrial Midwest was on fire back then, and I mean that literally. The Cuyahoga River self-ignited the summer before I turned twelve, the same summer that men walked on the moon. You could feel the city smoldering deep in your lungs, and sometimes when I take a deep breath even now I can hear Randy Newman droning his satirical song, "Burn on, big river, burn on." And yet, even as a child in that toxic setting, I loved the outdoors, especially at dusk as the sun sank into the river, painting the sky magenta and blood-orange— bright and tropical colors that I did not yet know were a result of the lingering sulfur in the air. Anything that diminished the town's ugliness was okay by me. Sometimes all one could do was avert one's gaze and look inward. My family took the Rapid Transit to get around—my mother, newly divorced, did not have a car—and from the platform while we waited for the train we watched a junkyard crane scooping and arranging piles of crushed cars. This was a good place, I discovered, to bury my face in a book.

Although my grandparents lived only two blocks away from our apartment building, we considered their home to be "in the country" because it was situated on a quiet, tree-lined street and because there were fruit trees growing in their backyard and beyond that, a large field where my sister and I ran with our collie to play I Spy and Red Rover with neighboring children or hunched low beneath wooly bushes playing a game we called "Olden Days," imagining the Big Outdoors where we would one day escape from the burning river and factory fumes and the adults in our lives, who were always fighting.

Sometimes Olden Days played like *Little House on the Prairie*. Sometimes, inspired by a TV show featuring seven handsome men looking for brides and the rather misleading theme song that began, "The bluest skies I've ever seen are in Seattle," Olden Days took us to the Northwest Gold Rush. Sometimes Olden Days could only be found in books, and the peace and quiet we needed for good reading could only be found high above the ground on the branches of those backyard fruit trees. My favorites fell into two camps: Brontë novels like *Jane Eyre* and *Wuthering Heights*, which were set in wet, gothic, wind-swept northern English landscapes, where rain was the objective correlative to the heroine's tears; and Twain novels, in which the protagonists, in their flight from Pa and church and school and enslavement, lit out for the territories, where the thrills outnumbered the dangers if you knew how to navigate the Mississippi.

Looking back on my life now, it doesn't surprise me that the first territories I lit out for after college were in the Pacific Northwest, which, after all, had the same weather as the British Isles. Politics also played a role. Because I grew up near urban ugliness and because I also felt myself to be the product of deep familial turmoil, my quest to find a home has always been connected to the question "Where can I go to find out who I am when I am not reacting to toxicity and discord and danger?" That quest has led me to what we now, in the great cultural divide, refer to as the "Blue States" of both coasts. It's not just that I crave a close proximity to forests and water, to parks and hiking trails; the ideal landscape for me is also a place where the citizens tend to be peaceniks, folks who care about social justice and the environment and like to read good books. As a product of Johnson's Great Society, I still need to see a few Democrats on the ground when I'm walking my dog or climbing a tree.

In my recent memoir, *Scraping By in the Big Eighties*, I chronicle my search for a low-budget utopian paradise in the last gasp of the cold war, a time of increasing economic division in our nation, as the New Deal came undone under Reaganomics and the very landscapes I sought for refuge were threatened by a full-out assault on environmental protection laws and the increased possibility of nuclear war. Here's a brief excerpt from the first chapter, "Soul Work in the Age of Reagan":

> Seattle was the perfect, moist setting to give succor to a young, romantic heart. A shopping expedition downtown through the endless stalls of produce and crafts at the Pike Place Market could take all day if you indulged yourself, letting your nose lead you from fresh crab to wild blueberries; to avenues of cheeses pungent with pepper or chives; to herb stands aromatic with lavender, sage, rose, and myrrh. You could relive the Gold Rush era in Pioneer Square, whose dark, wrought iron benches and handsome old saloons and shops had barely escaped the flames that demolished the city in the great fire of 1889. When your feet were tired you could sip lattés in the cozy café of Elliott Bay Book Company and

gaze at the shiny new hardbacks feeling happily agitated—so much to read, and so little time.

For nature lovers, there were countless mountains in the vicinity—the Cascades, the Olympic Range, Mount Rainier, Mount Hood, Mount Baker, and more—the only rain forest in North America, and lovely city parks and beaches. Whereas I'd grown up near a junkyard of rusting cars, our new digs were just a jog from a place where salmon swam upstream to spawn.

I loved Seattle's coffeehouses, the cappuccino and pastries. I loved the neighborhood diners. A late leisurely brunch might offer avocado omelets, cinnamon rolls as big as box turtles, and primo people-watching. You could seat yourself at the splintered counter or at wobbly tables with sticky chairs, while big, hairy, slow-moving men in aprons served up cheap hippie fare and braless women with jangly earrings wrote down the recipes if you asked nicely. The drone of flies and bees dive-bombing the honey jars were perfect accompaniment to the scratchy old Traffic tapes and conversations about silversmithing and the Dalai Lama. You could work all this atmosphere into your novel.

Newcomers in their twenties were arriving every day, all with their big backpacks and their clunky hiking books and their chewed-up poetry volumes and their journals and their big dreams. There was still a pioneer mentality at work, the belief that you could start over, live cheaply and well, and become a completely superior being to the anxious striver you'd been in the industrial wasteland you had fled. . . . As a girl who hailed from the land of white bread, all of these innovations seemed revolutionary. The *real* revolution of the baby boom—young people uniting to end an unpopular war, to bring down a villainous president, to declare equality among men and women of all colors and persuasions, and protect the spotted owls—well, that had all happened before I came of age and I was sorry I had missed it. Now it seemed like the best way to help the planet was to lead a thoughtful, balanced life in a peaceful place. I wasn't satisfied with the social progress we'd made but I could live with this worldview, in a pinch.

And that was the plan, until I began to realize that, peaceful place or not, I had moved closer to where the cold war's nuclear bombs were being built. I would eventually discover that there *is* no refuge or safety to be found on the globe in a time of military escalation, but I would need to immerse myself in a few more pretty landscapes before I called off the search.

"In the Courtyard of the Iguana Brothers" is set in 1983, a year when I felt more like an alien in America than ever. That year I loaded up my backpack, bought an electronic typewriter, and took a bus down to Mexico, curious to explore a landscape that bore no resemblance to the burning river and singing power lines of home, the wet cedar bark and screeching seagulls of the Puget Sound, or anything in between. San Blas, Mexico, was so unlike any place I'd ever been that it remains remote and mysterious to me to this day, which is perhaps why it still has something to teach me as a writer.

My goal was to spend four months writing fiction in a beach hut—stories set not in Mexico but in the toxic and noxious Cleveland of my childhood. My long-lost father had once spent a winter writing in Mexico, and I had always romanticized the place as a bohemian haven—and so affordable! As you will see toward the end of this essay, I discovered that while I was holed up trying to write about Cleveland on two dollars a day, I missed a lot of prose-worthy action going on right outside my hut. That's partly because I saw my expatriate neighbors—smugglers, aging hippies, casino workers doubling as hard-partying surfer dudes—as distractions from the task at hand. Near the end of the essay I write, "There had been a whole life around us, as corrupt, Dionysian, fecund, and dark as any writer could ask for, and I had tuned it out."

If I had it to do all over again, I would have studied more Spanish before I set out on my journey, and I would have kept a more detailed journal. I would have seen this journal writing not as a distraction from my "real" work but as *new* work in its preliminary stages, some descriptive "prewriting." But I was too young then to know that *everything* was my work, that every setting was going to weave its way into my work, that my life was my work. The good news is that I wrote a few letters. What I did daily in Mexico—swimming, eating, writing fiction, jogging, avoiding the neighbors—was not that interesting, so I told my friends about the setting itself: the roosters in our courtyard, the coconuts falling on the roof of the hut, the sombreroed men riding donkeys along the beach, the pink flamingos, the hilltop jungle. These notes to loved ones were, in the end, all I really had to go on when I decided to include the Mexico trip in my memoir. And while I very much enjoyed writing this essay,

I include it here in this anthology of landscape writing as an object lesson: a cautionary tale of how *not* to live and write while on location.

Perhaps Mexico is still very alive in my imagination all these years later simply because it was the first place I visited that felt entirely new. If Cleveland, the original zone of alienation, is at one pole and England and the Pacific Northwest are at the opposite pole of emotional affinity and romantic and literary yearning, very foreign landscapes like Mexico and, more recently, India and China are not inside this spectrum and are therefore places I have been able to see—to the extent that I can train my eye, via on-site crash courses and outside reading—without my usual geographical biases. Coconut trees, mangoes, and geckos still have the power to amaze me, to say nothing of dueling crickets, village elephants, seeping rubber trees, and litchi fruit. When I encounter landscapes with these elements, I know I am truly an outsider because everything I see is strange and I am a stranger to everyone who sees me. Remote settings provide me with what Edward Abbey called the "shock of the real," real because they contain nothing comforting or familiar, nothing that would allow me to project myself onto their vistas as I did when reading *Jane Eyre*. I am the Other, the outsider, the visitor, the tourist, the roving writer, and I have no choice but to do what Barry Lopez asks us to do when we encounter new places, "to listen." I wasn't very good at this when I was young, but I think I'm learning.

Having also read Edward Said on Orientalism, I have to be careful as well not to exoticize (and thereby eroticize) the Other, not to project onto the landscape and its natives some shadowy counterparts to the colonial grand narrative, a script I long to dispense with entirely, although I'm not sure that's ever possible for an American abroad, especially in our current political climate. (In Mexico, while escaping an America enthralled by *The Art of the Deal*, no matter how few pesos I possessed, I was, as a gringo, always taking part in a financial transaction, always a buyer angling for a bargain.)

Now, wherever I go, I try to keep a written or audio-journal of my impressions. I will always remember that I once saw water buffalo on the monsoon-drenched streets near the Taj Mahal and monkeys rapping at my hotel window in Dharamsala, to say nothing of those Tibetan monks hanging their saffron robes to dry in tall pine trees while they played badminton after morning meditation. I won't easily forget the elderly men in Beijing "walking" their birds in cages to the park to give them—the birds—a workout or the ancient coffins hanging out of caves inside fiords high above the Yangtze River or the lotus flowers and rice fields and limestone karsts along the Li, where the famous Chinese landscape paintings are set. But these images will fade in time, and I'll be glad I recorded them, however inelegantly. Ultimately, it will take time, distance, and research (historical, political, ecological, and more) for me to know what to do with these memories, and I'll be glad I have those modest notes to turn to when I'm ready.

The writer Bill Roorbach recently told me that on his trip to Australia in the fall an ornithologist took him to look at birds, a favorite pastime of his at home in Maine. He was astonished to discover that there wasn't a single bird that corresponded to a bird he knew in North America. He was fooled a few times; he thought he spotted a crow then some distant cousin of the red-breasted robin, but no, these birds were foreign across the board, utterly Other, every last one of them. He had to scrap his familiar and start from zero.

How lucky he was to experience this new place as a total beginner. I try to imagine that newness now, as I remember the crow that landed on the poplar outside my window yesterday, a bird in a landscape so ordinary and dear and familiar that I sometimes don't notice it at all. But tomorrow, when I gaze out the window above my desk, it will all click back into view: river, lawn, island path, trees, and probably more crows. I'll start right here, noting the shape and color of November clouds, the dead leaves floating in the river, the approach of winter: all harbingers of change that with any luck will lead me into yet another book deeply steeped in a place.

In the Courtyard of the Iguana Brothers

Shortly before he was caught, Ivan Boesky drew up plans to convert his mansion in New York State into a replica of Monticello.

—James B. Stewart

As above, so below.

—Paracelsus

Among the mysteries that I would never solve in Mexico—along with how to distinguish the gecko from the iguana, or and repel the advances of men— was the true story of how our landlord, Antonio, lost half his right arm. The version of events he advanced was that he had put himself in the path of a wayward firecracker that was headed straight toward a general's daughter. The gringo rumor was that he and a friend got wasted one night and played a game of catch with live hand grenades. I never asked Antonio myself. His alcoholic rages were legendary. Besides, my Spanish wasn't up to it, and the only words of English he knew were *money* and *dukes*, as in *The Dukes of Hazzard*, his favorite TV show, which came in dubbed on Wednesday evenings, the only time of the week the generator bringing power to our huts was guaranteed to work.

Money and *dukes*: these words were emblematic of what I was still running away from in America, and what I would be forced to confront even in the squalor of tropical exile. While the North of 1984 was all about real estate investment (even, suddenly, in Port Townsend), insider trading, hostile corporate takeovers, and the first Zippy rock videos, the South had its own torpid, electronically challenged equivalent to the money-for-nothing-and-MTV mentality. This much was true: if you had American dollars, you could live like a duke (or duchess) south of the border—as long as you weren't obsessed with personal hygiene. Twenty-four dollars a month got us a thatched-roof hut with a dirt floor, a saggy double bed, a hotplate with two burners, a table and two chairs, some aluminum cookware, and a rat that left bite marks in our papayas. Besides the rent, which was cheap even by Mexican standards, the main attraction of Antonio's was that despite his temper, he didn't care what you did as long as you kept him floating in tequila. You could be the ruler of your own kingdom, the CEO of your own shady business concern, or, in my case, a not-very-disciplined writer playing house with her new boyfriend.

Rumors about a cheap seaside courtyard like Antonio's had traveled all the way up to the Salal. As cold autumn rains fell, I heard a customer speak effusively of these unnamed, mango-and-palm-tree-lined beaches where I could wake to the sound of falling coconuts, breakfast on bananas from the vine, read from a hammock, and feast on homemade corn tortillas and shrimp, all without the presence of high-rise hotels, cruise ships, or any other evidence of American hegemony other than me and a handful of kindred spirits. After weeks of dark skies I yearned to see bright colors: purple bougainvillea, red hibiscus, blood oranges, the golden eye of an iguana.

I arranged a leave of absence from the café and stocked my backpack with books (*The Night of the Iguana* and *Under the Volcano*), natural cures for Montezuma's revenge, double-D batteries for my new electronic typewriter, a six-month supply of birth control pills (I wasn't looking but hey, you never know) and, despite a sudden windfall of $750 (my share of the sale of my dead grandpa's old rifles and gold), nowhere near enough travelers' checks. The herbs clumped in the heat, the typewriter wouldn't work (why? another mystery), and my literary models (penned by alcoholics) did not wean me from the romantic self-delusion I still needed to shed in order to write anything serviceable, but I did get some use out of the contraceptives with the aforementioned beau, whom I met en route. He looked like a young John Travolta minus the hair grease.

I had always savored my mother's stories about my father's bohemian days in Mexico, where he started his one-and-only published novel in some cheap hotel room overlooking a lively outdoor market. When his pesos ran low, he caught iguanas and rattlesnakes in the wild and roasted them over an open fire. When he drank tequila, he swallowed the worm. Although my mother was, as ever, an unreliable narrator, I had wanted to believe her when she told me in a letter (to my post office box in Seattle, where she thought I still lived) that an old friend of the family's had seen him before he headed through Tijuana that fall to write and paint. I found myself rehearsing what I would say if I ran into him.

When he asked me about my life, I would give him the impression that I had transcended all of the material and emotional needs that had no doubt been a burden to him (or else why would he have left?). When he asked about my sister, I would not mention her worries; I would tell him how she and her Chicago friends assisted Guatemalans and Salvadorans in the underground amnesty movement. My father and I would toast my sister's courage, but he would reassure me that it was also an act of resistance to use the symbols of his ex-father-in-law's patriarchal authority on a trip the old gangster would have called me a *whooore* for taking.

These fantasies (my father spouting feminism? me tucking into charred snake?) underscore what I hoped would happen on the trip: that I'd become a fearless adventurer, the protagonist of some implausible picaresque narrative. Although the placard above the dashboard of the vehicle that got me to Mexico said, "Wherever you go, there you are," I was still hoping to become someone else: that free spirit I'd moved out West to be.

Ethan and I met en route to Cabo San Lucas on the Green Tortoise, the hippie answer to Greyhound. After the tour ended, he went back to his brother's house in LA to financially refuel on a construction site, and I took a ferry to Mazatlán and made my way slowly, by local village buses, to Mexico City, where we were reunited three weeks later on New Year's Day. We played tourist for a month—Oaxaca, San Cristóbal de las Casas, Palenque, Chichén-Itsá, Mérida—but we were impatient to set up base camp. We tried the unfashionable sides of Cancún, Tulum, and Playa del Carmen, but they were crowded with people who had the same idea, except that they could afford the pseudo-rustic rentals. Not even the sight, one evening over fajitas, of two boars mating a few feet from our table altered our gloomy conviction that we may as well have been back in California for all the middle-aged Americans flashing plastic, college kids on a cheap drunk, and ex-pats who claimed to live like the natives but knew no Spanish except *dos cervasas, por favor.* And we were no better: Ethan only knew the words for "love," "room," and "hot water," and I, having never moved beyond the present tense in my studies (something I tried to see as a Zen virtue), remained focused on "I am," "I have," "I want," and "I need."

Desperation thrust us two thousand miles west to San Blas, a small town between Mazatlán and Puerto Vallarta that had failed to attract major developers thanks to the pesky sandflies that swarmed the beaches at dusk, covering the skin of unwitting tourists with itchy, angry welts that took forever to go away. I had liked San Blas when I passed through it briefly in December, but I had not investigated the super-cheap beach huts I kept hearing about because the paradise in my mind featured daily, insect-free sunset strolls. It was easy to be picky when I still had money and had not yet encountered a Cancún conga line.

Ethan sprang for the plane tickets.

Which is how, that February, after interrogating several taxi drivers for the scoop on where and for how much, we found ourselves on the overgrown path five miles out of town that led into Antonio's property. "This is the place!" we both exclaimed like Mormons first beholding the Great Salt Lake. The *cabañas* were arranged in a horseshoe around a courtyard of hibiscus and bougainvillea, chickens and roosters, sunbathing geckos and iguanas, and the occasional roving dog. Bright-colored birds called down from the trees, and coconuts did indeed fall onto the thatched rooftops. Only a hundred yards from where we stood was the pristine sandy ocean beach of my dreams (although you had to pass through a buggy lagoon and stinky garbage heap to get there), and behind us were hilltop jungle forests of deep green.

For plumbing we had to contend with a communal outhouse, a well, and a garden hose for "showers," but we weren't deterred: Ethan, a Catholic-turned-Quaker and avid outdoorsman, was big on "voluntary simplicity," and I was big on anything that kept down the price. There were only two foreseeable problems: one, that being this isolated would make it hard to get groceries, and the other, that we weren't isolated enough. Although communitarianism was still my bohemian ideal, we didn't exactly fit in with the neighbors.

We had already been warned that to get to Antonio, you had to go through Jim, a tall, slim surfer dude with a brown ponytail. Jim was the Duke of

Campo Antonio, the master of ceremonies, the cruise director. His girlfriend, Marilyn, a small, cold, watchful blonde, was the Duchess. Bill, a shy man with sad blue eyes and a bushy black beard, was Jim's best friend and court eunuch (although Jim, being the consummate host he was, kept an eye out for pretty gringas to invite to his Help-Bill-Get-Laid parties). The three were coworkers at a casino in Lake Tahoe, Jim and Bill as blackjack dealers and Marilyn a cocktail waitress. It was Bill's first visit to Mexico, but Jim and Marilyn were regulars; they had arranged their lives to spend six months each year at Antonio's and had, over time, acquired the seniority needed to snag the nicest place in the courtyard, a small, white stucco house with a functioning kitchen. Their status made it possible for Bill to jump the queue to the next best house, whereas Ethan and I would scrounge in one of Antonio's standard ramshackle huts *if* his gatekeeper decided we weren't duds.

We met him and the others that first morning. After we had gazed appreciatively at the beach, we followed the sounds of laughter to an open window, where three young people about our age sat rolling joints at the kitchen table. Ethan and I had been traveling without sleep for forty-eight hours, but when I asked Jim if he'd take us to Antonio, he laughed and said, "Relax. You have to wait until he's halfway through his first bottle of the day. Take a load off." We lowered our packs to the floor and joined them tentatively. We'd both intuited that being hyper over anything, even finding a home, wouldn't fly in these parts. "Some folks from Fresno just left," Jim said, when Ethan asked with feigned casualness what was available, "so you *might* get their hut, or the one next to it, but we've got some friends coming next week. So, do you like to party?" As Jim went through the complicated social calendar, we toked on command; Jim had made it clear that he had only derision for people who turned down his hospitality. People like Mark, a thirty-year-old Italian-American from New York who was actually higher than Jim in the gringo chain of being because of his money and his friendship with Antonio but was too "antisocial" to screen renters.

"The guy's gone native," Jim said. "He speaks fluent Spanish," which was somehow another negative, and although he was a loner, he was friendly with the local *federales*, who often dropped by to drink shots with Antonio. He owned a car *and* a pickup; very few gringos owned vehicles at all. And he had been living in Mexico year-round for almost a decade, which was difficult to pull off since tourist visas were for only six months. "If you need anything at all, Mark will know who to bribe and how much to pay," Jim said. "But if you want him to party with you, forget it. He seems to think he has better things to do." Weeks later, when I had something better to do myself, Jim asked me how much money I made from my writing. When I told him, he said, "You should find another hobby, man!"

Ethan and I were exhausted and stoned to the point of incoherence when Jim took us to meet Antonio, a tiny, toothless, wizened man who looked seventy, was maybe fifty, but had the high-voltage energy of a frisky teen. He poured us tequila shots, waving around his stump merrily. After we had offered our stash of liquor as a deposit, we were in. Despite my worries about getting along with the Campo royalty—*antisocial* being a word often applied to me—I felt incredibly lucky to live anywhere, let alone a rustic beach hut with a hunk.

Not that everything was hunky-dory with said hunk. There were moments when Ethan and I were fighting that I had visions of one of us leaving the other on the side of a road. We both knew we had no future together: I couldn't see myself settling down with someone who had never read Shakespeare or studied history, and he wasn't sure if he could handle someone so persistently "negative" about world affairs. He'd set out on this trip in search of a life-changing epiphany about the career path he should take: something, he hoped, that would get him away from construction work but would not require any college. He had never planned to stay in Mexico this long, and he blamed his lack of clarity about his direction on me. Even his passion for me scared him; he hated the loss of control. He was not as even-keeled as he'd seemed when we first met; his daily meditation was actually an attempt to find an equilibrium that seemed always out of grasp. And whenever I asked him what he was so mad about or why he had suddenly stopped being affectionate, he accused me of being needy, which became increasingly true as I felt lonelier in his company. Being financially dependent on him didn't help.

Our travels had annihilated my budget. With three months left until I was expected back at the Salal, I needed a minimum of five hundred dollars to see the season out. Obviously, hitting up family or borrowing from Ethan were not options. I was going to have to ask someone else for help, but who?

I consoled myself with the thought that by North American standards five hundred dollars was *nada*. This was the year Ivan Boesky would make sixty-five million dollars in profits from a single merger deal, the year *Newsweek* would proclaim "The Year of the Yuppie." I still did not want to join my fellow baby boomers on the fast track, but that didn't make it any less demoralizing to know that while some of my crowd owned Manhattan apartments in buildings with uniformed doormen, I was scrounging to afford a twenty-four-dollars-a-month hut with holes in the roof and a rat.

I settled on borrowing the money from my old friend from high school and college, John, the one my mother had once pointed a gun at. As teenagers together when he drove me everywhere in his white Pinto—the getaway-mobile—our friend Sandy always imitated me by saying, "John wouldn't mind driving me to Mexico." Now that I was actually *in* Mexico and in trouble, John—who was now a well-paid entertainment lawyer in West Hollywood, a city he'd helped incorporate—seemed like the best person to turn to. I would call him from San Blas when Ethan and I went on our first grocery run. And that was where we were headed, on a mission to get me solvent enough to forget the business of America for three more months, when we came across a trio of American would-be businessmen who would make me realize that such escape was impossible. The men I would nickname the Iguana Brothers made me understand the permeability of borders in a personal way.

It was already sweltering when, just after dawn, Ethan and I set out on the five-mile walk to town. The driver of a rusted pickup with Florida plates asked us if we wanted a ride, and I regretted our decision when a fat man about our age backed out to make room for us, revealing some hairy butt crack. He introduced himself as Chris, asked us our names, and sat with us in the bed of the truck, smiling in a kindly, almost reassuring way, but I remained on alert. He was guarding a giant white gunnysack that moved even when we didn't bump over potholes. I felt the contents of the bag squirming toward my knees, and I thought I heard a faint groaning. Something inside it was alive. Acutely aware of my bouncing breasts and the guys in front checking me out, I moved closer to the passenger side so that if I had to jump, I'd be able to roll onto the dense undergrowth and not the middle of the road.

When we got to town Ethan and I made evasive maneuvers. We weren't frightened of Chris, but the driver had the erect posture, mirrored dark glasses, and buzz cut of a CIA man, while his friend riding shotgun, a dark-haired, slit-eyed, skinny smirker, put me in mind of a snake. "We should shop together," the driver said when he noticed the direction we were walking so quickly. "We have to watch each other's backs so we don't get ripped off. It's a jungle out there." The latter was literally true—how this region got into the guidebooks—but when I laughed, I realized he wasn't making a joke. His was a script from a movie where people dress in camouflage. Then he began boasting of his exploits in the actual jungle, where he and Chris and Snake Man had spent the last month tracking snakes, geckos, and iguanas. "We're going to sell them to pet stores and theme parks."

"Is that what was rubbing against our legs in the truck?" Ethan asked in the fake mellow voice I now recognized as his San Blas persona. I could see the driver assessing him: *Pussy*, his eyes seemed to say. *I could take him.*

"Payload." He then explained how the "profit margin potential" for this enterprise was unlimited because the critters came to them free of charge—the word *poaching* was never used—and by camping out and eating light, their "overhead" was practically nil. "What's so innovative about us, and makes us attractive to the customer, is we've eliminated the middle man. We deliver the product directly and can vouch for where it's been. We're insiders. Who can beat that?"

I have forgotten this guy's name, but years later, when his unpleasant memory came to mind, I dubbed him El Gecko, partly in honor of his payload. By then I had learned that geckos, unlike iguanas, have suction cups on their feet that allow them to climb, which make them literally upwardly mobile. By then I had also seen *Wall Street*, in which Michael Douglas played Gordon Gekko, a character that was supposedly inspired by the real-life Ivan Boesky. "If you are not inside, you are outside," Gekko says to his young protégé as he counsels him to use insider information to buy up shares in companies targeted for takeovers.

"Imports are *in* now," El Gecko continued. We did not ask the inevitable—how he planned to get his payload across the border, or whether it had ever tried to bite them or escape.

Ethan gave my hand a tug and we attempted our own escape. We entered the covered market: the stalls of whole chickens and cow halves swarming with flies, peppers in every shade of red, green, and yellow, perfect avocados and tomatoes. The locals stepped out of our way as the five of us marched through, Ethan and I in front, trying not to seem like we were running, the Iguana Brothers close on our heels. "I'm an alpha male," El Gecko actually said over the din of vendors hawking meat, and I began to suspect that this man, boasting about his hunting prowess and business acumen into the privacy of my inner ear, was launching his own hostile takeover.

My fears were confirmed when El Gecko put his hand on my shoulder and asked for a taste of the mango and banana smoothie I ordered at the *licuado* stand. Ethan glared at me as though I had invited this forwardness, and I wondered what a spectacle we were making, five young gringos marking our respective territories with barely masked hostility and prejudices we had imported from *El Norte*.

We got away when Chris announced that he was hungry for a sit-down breakfast at a restaurant. "You boys are starving me to death," he said, which prompted El Gecko and Snake-Man to ridicule him for his "lard ass" and accuse him of eating up their overhead. Chris did not deserve this venom, but I was grateful for the distraction. I pulled Ethan into a nearby bakery, and then we slipped into an alley, feeling like we, too, were in a movie where people dress in camouflage. We spent the rest of the morning as we would for days to come: jumping through the bureaucratic hoops it took to get cash.

To make an international call in the small-town Mexico of 1984 you had to get squatter's rights to one of the booths in the phone shack, hoping one of your fifty attempts got through. No one I knew ever made a connection on the first visit. You just kept coming back, maybe half a dozen times. Then, once you finally made contact, there was the tiresome business of waiting in the telegraph office. This entailed second-guessing when it might actually be open and then standing in a long, slow-moving line for two hours or more only to learn that the money had not arrived, all the while hating yourself for becoming the vocal champion of America's efficient infrastructure and fighting your growing paranoia that the man behind the counter had not only pocketed your *dinero* but was laughing at you.

When everything shut down for the siesta, we took a taxi to our hut and slept off the morning's troubles. Sometimes we'd catch a ride back to town for an afternoon go-round with the bilingual Mark (who was not that antisocial, we discovered), but often we just stayed sacked out in our bed or at the beach, waking now and then to the sound of Jim and company surfing or a local man in a sombrero clomping along on his burro. I tried to motivate myself to jog or write in my journal, but with humidity, birth control bloat, and the *mañana* culture oozing through my body like knockout drugs, I felt like a three-hundred-year-old tortoise.

Now and then, as a special treat, we dined out. Half a mile down the beach was an open-air café called Las Roches, where the proprietor greeted us by hacking two coconuts from the branches above us with a machete and drilling in straw holes for us to drink the juice. After this aperitif, we jumped off the rocks into the ocean. The man's entire family prepared the meal—a grandmother with gray braids grilling corn tortillas, children carrying out our beers, their mother chopping garlic—and because this place was *exactemente* the unspoiled *ramada* I'd set out to find, I stopped worrying if the children ever did homework or played with other children. Our feast of locally caught shrimp, frijoles, sliced onions, tomatoes, and tortillas cost less than two dollars each, including the coconuts and cool Tecates with lime. Despite my panic about my rising debt to Ethan, I felt like a low-maintenance duchess.

Before sundown, when the dreaded sandflies came out, we returned to our hut and, as Jim and Marilyn suggested, burned coconut husks on the dirt floor to keep the insects away. Then we zipped ourselves inside our mosquito net, made love, and played cards. Only after all this would I try to write.

I never understood why the portable electronic typewriter I'd bought just for this trip wouldn't power up down here—with electricity, on batteries, *nada*. After our victory at finding a home, discovering I wouldn't be able to type was a serious blow. I still managed to produce two stories set in Cleveland and some notes about the market life in Mexico, but everything was raw and unpolished. If I had worked every day, I would have revised more, but I was worried Ethan would get bored. Whenever he sighed extravagantly at the phone shack or scratched his sandfly bites or spoke longingly of his childhood home in Maine and how its cool temperatures made it easier to think, I put aside what I was doing and took his hand.

When I had traveled by myself before Ethan could join me, I had been stroked and groped on almost every bus. I could not even buy bottled water without getting catcalls. In Mexico City, just as New Year's Eve was beginning, two men had tried to pull me into a black sedan full of their empty liquor bottles. I don't know what would have happened if I hadn't been rescued by an old *abuela* with gray braids who appeared on the tree lawn where one man was just opening his car door to try to yank me inside. The woman shouted at the men like they were children, wagging her finger as she would to two little boys torturing a baby iguana or using the name of the Virgin in vain. After we got away, I took a cab to my hotel, where I stayed up all night quaking in fear as men outside the bars of the cheap hotel room ushered in 1984 with drunken laughter. By the next morning, when I dragged myself to a taxi stand and made it to the airport to welcome Ethan, I had begun to think of him as my savior.

While I had waited for his plane, I called my sister to wish her a happy 1984. When I made a joke about Big Brother listening in, she told me it was indeed likely that her phone was being bugged. She was in shock because an important figure in the amnesty movement, a folk singer she'd seen perform, had been deported back to El Salvador, where the Reagan-backed secret police interrupted his concert and, in front of the audience, amputated his hands. I gasped and wept at this story. The threat of male violence was everywhere. As she spoke, I cracked my knuckles and swallowed hard, trying not to think of what the men in the car might have done to me.

Every part of life in Mexico—getting to town, shopping, negotiating the telegraph office, eating out, hosing off in our yard (with Ethan holding a towel around me), and fending off El Gecko—was less hassle with a male companion. Although I had set off on my trip full of pluck and bravado, I no longer believed I could remain in Mexico without a bodyguard.

Which is partly why our domestic rituals became more important to me than my writing, why my curiosity about the world outside our hut faded away. When John told me on the phone from Hollywood that he was satisfying his need to nest by painting the walls of his new condo cobalt blue, I could almost relate. I loved trying to see what I could make on the hotplate with yams, beans, garlic, and tomatoes. We even had a dog, a blond little puppy that followed us home from the beach, rolled on her back on our dirt floor, and demanded to be petted. She ate our table scraps and slept beside the bed, guarding us, I hoped, from the rat. I was discovering something about myself I hadn't known in the years I was climbing out the window of my mother's basement apartment—that I am, at heart, a homebody.

We could have seen more of the area with Jim and Marilyn, who invited us to join them for alligator boat cruises and picnics on remote islands. We wanted to be friendly—I hoped, in fact, that I'd become a regular at Antonio's, that I'd learn the geography and something of the culture—but their invocations to "party hearty" bordered on bullying. I think they finally gave up on us after we gagged up their prize peyote onto their white vinyl kitchen floor—"You two better stick to milk and cookies," Jim laughed. Dozens of their friends from Tahoe came and went, the courtyard pulsing with the music of Jimmy Buffet, Men at Work, and UB-40, and we began to feel that even in exile, we were in exile.

The Iguana Brothers, we decided, were stalking us. El Gecko, in line behind us at the telegraph office, announced that he was waiting for money too: a business loan from one of his "financiers." When he heard me tell Ethan that I was going to fast to cut my expenses, he decided to let us in on "another little secret" that kept down his overhead.

"It's something I picked up in the military. The food was so bad I couldn't stand it, but I found a way to go for weeks just eating one meal a day."

"Yes?" I asked. Ethan thought by being polite I was leading El Gecko on, and we would fight over this later.

"I don't go to the bathroom."

In other words, El Gecko was, by design, full of shit.

"You'd be amazed at the discipline I developed in the army," he added, giving me the once-over, implying, perhaps, that he could delay the outflow of other bodily functions too, if given the chance.

The Iguana Brothers were at the market when we were at the market, the fried fish stand when we were at the fried fish stand, the highway in their pickup when we were huffing it on foot. At least we were safe inside our hut. But then one afternoon in late March something terrible happened. The Iguana Brothers penetrated the courtyard.

We were naked, in bed, when we heard a loud knock at the door. We thought it was our new next-door neighbors, a hippie couple from Spokane who often dropped in to borrow rice or offer us something tasty they had fried up on the hotplate. Usually, if we didn't answer right away, they got the hint, and once, as a joke, they cranked up their boom box with some mood music for us. The knocking persisted. Finally, Ethan wrapped himself in a towel and swung the door open with undisguised irritation. El Gecko entered, taking in with a glance our disheveled bed and me in it, bare shoulders above the sheet, and plopped himself right next to me, pulling at the mosquito net with his weight. He didn't explain his presence, whether he was there to rape me or just wanted a chat. I told him with the fake courtesy that had become my San Blas persona that I was sick, and "not to be rude" but I'd feel guilty if I vomited on his khakis. Ethan told me later that the whole time of this encounter he was scanning the room for a makeshift weapon. We would fight over this incident too.

To our horror, the Iguana Brothers had become our new neighbors.

What happened was this: Chris, fed up with his buddies' insults, had jumped ship. One night while El Gecko and Snake-Man were out, he took off with the truck and the large tent the three of them shared. Now the two remaining Iguana Brothers had to sleep in the small pup tent that housed their critters. Still trying to minimize their overhead, they tried this for a few nights, and I must admit I took some delight in imagining the menagerie of reptiles squirming over their sunburned bodies. They had made their bed, and now they could lie in it, literally. That's where I would have liked the story to have ended, except that Jim, ever the host with the most, encouraged them to sack out at Antonio's in the one remaining hut, if you could call it a hut. This ruin had huge holes in the roof and an abundance of rats, but it was roomier than the tent and gave them something to feed the snakes, who moved sluggishly now and were dying by the dozen.

Our paradise now reeked of decomposing reptile flesh.

When my money finally came, we took a vacation from our vacation, hoping the Iguana Brothers would pack it in while we hid out further south. They did, but not without waiting to say good-bye. The day after we returned, we were in Mark's truck on a grocery run with half the courtyard when we saw them hitching on the highway with all their gear. They and their payload were off to the border while they still had some living payload left. Ethan and I sighed as they climbed in. "*Vamanos*? A woman like you could help us get rides," El Gecko whispered to me, looking down my tank top, and I pretended not to see or hear. Every now and then I felt a snake or an iguana behind the cotton rubbing against my leg, but it was a small price to pay for the knowledge that—finally—we were free of these creeps.

I have no idea how they got across the border, how they got through customs with the quivering white bag. Although it was unlikely that El Gecko retired to Miami before the age of fifty as a millionaire, as was his oft-stated aim, I would not be surprised if he made his mark in some other unscrupulous enterprise that was in keeping with the spirit of our age.

But Ethan and I would soon be contending with an object lesson of our own—this time about *our* greed.

Someone new moved into the hut made vacant by the Iguana Brothers. He was the only non-gringo who ever rented from Antonio in our time there, an itinerant worker who picked grapes and oranges in California in the summer, apples in eastern Washington in the fall, and wintered in his native Mexico. At the moment he was earning his living whittling broomsticks from the fallen branches of coconut and mango behind our huts and binding the straws together with Dos Equis caps and twine. The finished products were funky and handsome; they might have sold for thirty bucks in the ethnic-chic stores of San Francisco or Manhattan, and Juan was charging a dollar.

We coveted those brooms, thinking they would make great gifts for our friends and family up north. Ethan, being from a family of ten, was in the habit of buying in bulk. "We'll take a dozen," he told Juan without consulting me (which we would fight about), and without considering how we would carry them and our backpacks in and out of cars and buses in the weeks to come. Juan, delighted, became his own one-man cottage industry. Whistling songs and carving away with his knife from dusk to dawn, he had completed the job before we could cut back on the order.

When he was finished, Juan offered us a small token of his gratitude. "*Para ti*," he said to me, his eyes gleaming. In his outstretched hands was a dead iguana that he had cut open, a female. Inside her abdomen were a dozen small eggs, blue and slick. I could see from the way he held the carcass so reverently that the iguana eggs were a delicacy and that this gift was a sign of his high esteem for us. Perhaps we would have gotten to know our neighbor better if I hadn't been so squeamish; my father would have swallowed the raw eggs without hesitation, invited Juan in for shots of bourbon, and written him into his novel, trading on the man's kindness in this way. It was our Last Supper at Campo Antonio, our last chance to bridge the gap with the locals, and we missed it. As acid churned in my stomach, I thanked Juan profusely, then carried the dead iguana inside our hut.

"*Deliciosa*," Ethan said when we ran into Juan later that evening. He had cooked the eggs up and fed them to the dog, who sucked them down with *mucho gusto*. After weeks of eating our leftover mashed yams, this was undoubtedly the best meal of her life.

I liked thinking that this pregnant iguana had escaped from the Iguana Brothers' gunnysack. Her life may have been cut short, but at least she died more or less in the wild. For our part there was something poetic about this justice, about being offered the spoils of our enemy in the outstretched hands of the one person we thought had a right to live off the bounty of this land. But I know I'm idealizing our neighbor, making him into a kind of noble savage when that's not what I intended at all. The problem is that even without a language barrier there could be no escaping the paradigm that we, the gringos, were the ones buying and he, the native, was selling, which is why he probably looked at us and thought whatever the Spanish is for *payload*. If we had to be ugly, more-is-better Americans, I'm glad we helped a nice man pay his bills.

By now the mosquitoes had hatched in the swamp, and I was beginning to think longingly of the cool spring days in the Pacific Northwest, the blooming rhododendrons and lilacs and cherry blossoms. And as luck would have it, we did not have to hitch to the border with all the brooms. Mark had to renew his six-month visa, and Ethan and I were glad to accept his ride. I have a vague memory of everyone in the courtyard turning out for our departure—Jim and Marilyn and Bill, their visiting friends, Antonio, Juan—but all that I can bring to mind are the tears I shed for the puppy as she ran beside us in the road. I had looked into bringing her with us to Port Townsend, but there was no way to do it legally. It had been cruel for me to let her get dependent on us, and now I had yet another thing to chastise myself about.

I was afraid that when I looked back to my time at Antonio's I would not remember the ocean and all the beauty, but only the Iguana Brothers' invasion, my quarrels with Ethan, and my worries about money, which only magnified my ongoing quarrel with America. I had no idea how I'd repay my debt to John on three dollars an hour, and all I had to show for the trip was the journal and the two Cleveland stories, which could have been written anywhere. I didn't have a realistic understanding yet of how long it takes to write two publishable stories, so I felt like a failure. Ethan felt like a failure too. He blamed me and the brain-frying Mexican sun for keeping him as confused about his life mission as ever. In six months I would turn twenty-seven. How long could I live in this day-to-day way? I was sick to death of the present tense.

We drove through the Sierra Madre Mountains in silence, staring out at desolate buttes and dry hamlets where grandmothers sold warm Fanta and children sold peso-packets of Chiclets gum and mangoes on a stick. Outside it was one hundred degrees. Mark put on the air-conditioning and kept the window closed, but at the end of each day our skin was caked with dust. It got into our underwear and in between our toes—emblematic, I would ponder later, about how the outside always gets in, no matter how isolated you are.

America did not exactly welcome us back. The customs agents at the border went to town on us. They strip-searched us, examining every dust-coated orifice for drugs. They tore apart our dusty backpacks, questioning us about everything: the useless typewriter, Ethan's film cases, even his contact solution. My gummed-up herbal remedies for diarrhea were a project for the sniff dogs while agents pulled apart every inch of Mark's car. I worried that he might be carrying some pot on him since people were so loose about such things at Antonio's but, thankfully, his car was clean.

Several hours later, when customs finally let us go, I asked what it was about us that aroused their suspicion. Ethan was still as well-scrubbed as a matinee idol, our plumbing situation notwithstanding, and I had braided my long hair and put on my favorite embroidered sundress. Mark had short hair and glasses and was wearing a clean white shirt and khakis. I'd assumed the three of us would breeze through.

"The brooms," the man told us. I laughed. Did he think we were part of some witch's coven?

"No, it's just that they're made from tropical woods. Everyone knows you're not allowed to bring them in. We figured you were using them as a decoy for something worse." I half-hoped he would confiscate them and lighten our load, but I guess he felt guilty for giving us a hard time. We were stuck with them and, for the time being, with each other, and this slapstick would continue.

The three of us were replaying our ordeal with hilarity at the Holiday Inn bar in Nogales when Mark made a startling admission. For the last several years, he said, lowering his voice to a near whisper, he had made his living smuggling sacred Huichol artifacts to the States. It was a very lucrative business. He'd intended to bring up his latest acquisitions on this particular border crossing, and he had already packed them in his duffel bag and put them in the car when he changed his mind. He took them back in the house while we were arranging our brooms, and we were so preoccupied we never noticed.

In other words, Mark was also an Iguana Brother, another insider trader, another modern-day conquistador out to haul away everything that wasn't nailed to the ground. The only difference between him and El Gecko was that he was good at it.

"And you were going to smuggle this stuff with *us* in the car with you?" Ethan said. I was afraid they would argue, and I was too tired for more friction. I just wanted to finish my drink and go to sleep.

"You guys were going to be my cover," he said. "I was wondering if they were starting to get suspicious of me, and I thought the two of you, with your sweet and innocent faces, would get my loot through."

"Sweet and innocent?" I don't need to go into how I fancied myself quite the world-weary traveler by now and a bit of a sexpot or how I had also believed that Mark was just a nice, generous neighbor with no ulterior motives when he insisted on paying our hotel and dinner bills.

"Oh my word," Mark said. "Didn't you know? Everyone in the courtyard called you John Denver and Rebecca of Sunnybrook Farm!"

I realized then why Mark felt he could share his secret with us. He knew what I had only just admitted to myself, that our time at Antonio's had been the kind of adventure neither of us had it in us to repeat; he knew he would never see us again.

There was a lot more that we had failed to notice, and Mark decided it was time to fill us in. About the man who ran the fried fish stand with his daughter, how he had been raping this girl since she was barely old enough to walk and was now forcing her, at seventeen, to bring up their baby and live with him as his second wife. About how the *federales*, who visited Mark late at night after they drank shots with Antonio, got a cut from his smuggling business and provided him with the names of crooked archaeologists.

"Since you're telling us everything, what really happened to Antonio's arm?" Ethan asked. We'd heard other rumors that put our landlord in bloody, fight-to-the-death barroom brawls.

I don't remember what Mark said. It's possible that I excused myself from the table and went to bed, that's how uninterested I was. I have never liked hearing stories about drunken stupidity and male aggression. I thought back to a night early in our residency when Antonio invited us over to watch *The Dukes of Hazzard* with him: the highest honor to be bestowed on a Campo Antonio resident. He hooted and slapped his stump against his knee at every car chase, while we sat motionless and mystified. Neither of us had ever seen this show in America. We had no idea who the characters were, but I guess we weren't supposed to care. What stayed with me was the feeling of bewilderment, like we'd heard a punch line but missed the joke.

There had been a whole life swirling around us, as corrupt, Dionysian, fecund, and dark as any writer could ask for, and I had tuned it out as though it were just another dubbed episode of *The Dukes of Hazzard*. Tennessee Williams and Malcolm Lowry and my father had written their Mexican courtyards into their work, but I had seen ours as one big distraction.

So how *does* a writer remain engaged in and still critical of the current time and place? I had set out on my journey believing I could and should escape the phallic culture of Ronald Reagan and Rambo and Donald Trump by locking myself away in a hut in a landscape where life could be stripped down to the elemental: food, water, sex, bug repellant. To avoid the predators on both sides of the border, I had chosen to live with blinders. Rebecca of Sunnybrook Farm wasn't off the mark. As George Orwell wrote in an essay about Henry Miller, "Inside the Whale," "Exile is probably more damaging to a novelist than to a painter or even a poet, because its effect is to take him out of contact with working life and narrow down his range to the street, the café, the church, the brothel and the studio." My range, as a woman, was much narrower than that.

And I also had to acknowledge that I was an Iguana Sister myself, wintering on a beach where children served shrimp because it was the one place I could *almost* afford another sabbatical. What's more, the mindless hedonism I had detested in Jim and Marilyn looked a lot like mine on the surface, only with fewer books and more libations.

But exile comes with a cost, even if you're going for it on the cheap. If you are only looking for some R&R, the naïve outsider's oblivion may be soothing, but as a writer who hopes to make accurate observations about the world she lives in and her place in it, this kind of isolation is not—and I choose the following word thoughtfully—profitable. And if you're not careful, all that you've kept remote and foreign will rise up like a snake escaping from a gunnysack and strike you in the back.

•✦ DEBORAH TALL

Deborah Tall was an essayist and a poet as well as the editor of *Seneca Review*. She wrote three books of nonfiction: *The Island of the White Cow: Memories of an Irish Island* (1986), *From Where We Stand: Recovering a Sense of Place* (1993), and *A Family of Strangers* (2006). She also published four volumes of poetry, including *Come Wind, Come Weather, Ninth Life, Eight Colors Wide,* and *Summons,* winner of the 1999 Kathryn A. Morton Prize in Poetry. With Stephen Kuusisto and David Weiss she coedited *The Poet's Notebook: Excerpts from the Notebooks of 26 American Poets.* She taught at Hobart and William Smith Colleges in Geneva, New York. She died of cancer in October 2006. "Memory's Landscapes" was originally published in *Tikkun.*

Whereof

Keats, comparing himself to Byron, wrote, "He describes what he sees—I describe what I imagine—Mine is the hardest task." To be a writer of place one must, I think, do both: evoke the present actual in all its complexity, all its lush or brutal being, while also describing the invisible—the implied, the erasures of time, the hauntings. And that requires both research and imagination.

I've been drawn to write about places from the moment I began writing. My first adolescent creation was a love poem, not to a boy but to the Grand Canyon. This was probably because I was the product of a nomadic, suburban American upbringing in what James Howard Kunstler has dubbed the "geography of nowhere." The subdivisions where I spent the 1950s and 1960s were designed primarily for the convenience of cars and shopping, not for the adventures of childhood or the pleasures and responsibilities of community. They were the kind of homogeneous, spiritless places for which Gertrude Stein's oft-quoted description is lamentably apt: "When you get there, there is no there, there."

And so I decamped the first moment I could in search of a genuine "there" and landed on a tiny island off the west coast of Ireland, a dramatic lump of rock in the Atlantic beset by gales and downpours, dotted with cottages constructed from the local stone. There was no electricity, heating, or running water but a stark beauty and lively population of two hundred who were deeply enmeshed in the demands and joys of their home, surviving by fishing, subsistence farming, and storytelling. There were few buffers; we were governed by weather, the flux of northern light, and the agricultural rhythm of the seasons. The world finally felt viscerally alive.

I learned many important lessons on that island that would shape me as a writer. I learned to look and listen with full attention and how to be an inhabitant rather than a mere resident. In rural Ireland in the 1970s, traditional culture was colorfully vibrant and firmly linked to the local. Every turn of the road and noteworthy rock carried tales and lessons—ancient rivalries, revolts, pratfalls, crop failures, storms, murders, and miracles—all dutifully, ritualistically, retold to children and newcomers every time they were sighted. It was as if the past were still fully visible and very much relevant. I came to understand how such stories serve as a map to a place—they teach you how to survive and how to belong.

For instance, there was a craggy outcrop in the harbor named Bishop's Rock. It's what's called in those parts a half-tide rock—exposed at low tide, submerged and invisible come high. Bishop's Rock served as a daily reminder of a bitter piece of the island's history: it was where Cromwell, in the seventeenth century, had tied and abandoned the local bishop to carry out a slow-motion death sentence. Those grievous colonial politics were thus reignited for the islanders, centuries later, with every glance at the harbor. And the rock was also a vivid emblem of the dangers of the sea, routinely pointed out to tourists and the young—don't walk out there at low tide and get stranded like that poor bishop, and if you're taking out a boat, for God's sake stay away from that stretch of water at high tide—that rock will destroy you. All the lessons of the island were, like this one, implanted geographically. That way of thinking gave me an immediate structure when I later came to write about my five years there in *The Island of the White Cow*.

In many indigenous traditions, of course, the landscape is a tableau of history and myth, often carrying a spiritual dimension. The land may be regarded as God's handiwork, or it may embody the presence of multiple gods and ancestors. So a peak becomes a reminder to worship, a lake evokes a myth of origin, a hillock an elder's sage advice, a gully a defeat or error. The landscape thus delineates a moral, religious, and practical map. It is text, full of visual mnemonics that speak history, lore, and values. In that sense it can speak a people back to themselves, cohere their identity.

These are the kind of texts a writer of place has to learn to decipher, to imagine one's way into.

279

Palimpsest is another useful metaphor. When we look thoughtfully into the world around us, we're apt to find festering wounds and lessons beneath fine scenery. We can learn to view the land vertically, through layers of the past: the literal past of the land itself, geologically, how successive human cultures have altered it and left traces of their presence and ideologies; the place's history of agriculture, transportation, economics, hunting laws, extinctions, zoning, religion, architecture, art, legends, and lingoes. The vertical plane of history eventually dips into the realm of folklore and myth as we recognize the archetypal dimensions of people's relation to places. All these elements can shape our experience of the place in the present.

The voice of place is thus polyphonic, and our literary forms need to accommodate and reflect this interdisciplinary richness. That's why books about places are so often adventurous hybrids in which physical description, character portraits, statistics, analysis, personal narrative, dramatic event, argument, meditation, and flights of fancy can happily coexist. Books of place are geographical, ethnographic, environmental, political, spiritual.

They are also memoiristic. Richard Wilbur asserts that all artists "approach the landscape self-centeredly or self-expressively, looking for what agrees with their temperaments." The lens through which we look at the world is unavoidably both cultural and personal, and so are the books about the places we immerse ourselves in. Though the two books I've written about places were written primarily out of passion for those places, they are also inevitably about myself, about two phases of my life.

From Where We Stand: Recovering a Sense of Place is about returning to America after my years in Ireland, seeking to make a home in the Finger Lakes region of upstate New York, a place I knew nothing about and came to by the accident of a job offer. I was an outsider trying to transform myself into an insider, and I carried the lessons of Ireland with me. But, alas, there were no convenient guides standing by in the woods or on the lakeshore with ready stories, no maps by which to read the subtle messages of the land. So I had to rely on history books, fragmentary archives, interviews, eavesdropping, ephemera like tourist pamphlets and roadside historical markers. The book itself came to mirror the purposeful process of discovery, a tale of how one becomes a citizen of a place. It was not about flight into an exotic "other," as Ireland had, in part, been for me, but about how to root oneself in one's own flawed world. In that sense, a book of middle age, as well as a portrait of a fragile region.

Knowledge of place imparts self-knowledge and an ethics of conduct. As Wendell Berry puts it, "If you don't know where you are, you don't know who you are." In that way place is reciprocal, a teacher of how to live on earth, of how to give back.

Though I felt very settled by the time I finished that book, the problem of the human connection to place continued to haunt me. Something still felt missing, and it was more than nostalgia for the vibrant community in Ireland I'd been transformed by. Over time I came to realize that the lack of an ancestral place had left a needy gap.

I had never known three of my four grandparents or where exactly they were from. My father was orphaned while still young and thought his parents might have been born in Kiev and Odessa; my mother called her parents English, but they had only stopped in London on their way to New York from some unknown shtetl in Poland. They had all fled the pogroms of the early twentieth century and were happy to leave the past and the places they were from unnamed, unremembered.

Place is mnemonic, even in our idioms. When we can't "place" someone, it means we can't remember them. I could not place my grandparents. And so a part of myself felt misplaced.

I have been thinking about how places we've never been might somehow influence us—their topography, politics, wars, hunger, weather—how I might have inherited something from my unknown grandparents and the places they were from. For instance, though I have never faced the kind of bigotry and terrors my ancestors did, I seem to carry their wariness and generalized anxiety. History's dark lessons must seep down through generations, even when children are intentionally shielded from past horrors, even when changed circumstances have eliminated the need for protective coloring and guardedness. Transplanted to new worlds, these responses may appear grotesque, pathological. It takes an act of psychic archaeology to know their source, to slough them off.

I think of it as geographical genealogy, a quest for the provenance of temperament. To discover *where* we've come from is to understand ourselves as a consequence of a particular history in a particular place. It is to acknowledge the DNA of place.

In America to seek familial roots used to be seen as resisting the "melting pot," the national aim of assimilation. Now roots are chic. The popularity of genealogical research (second only to gardening as a hobby) must, in part, be a compensation for our geographical rootlessness. A nation of wanderers, we seem to be looking, instead, for portable roots—the family tree rooted in time rather than soil, genealogical stability in lieu of the stability of place.

But it was the places I wanted much more than simply the identities of my extended family.

The essay included here, "Memory's Landscapes," is a glimpse of my search for ancestral place, part of my book *A Family of Strangers*. Traveling to Eastern Europe, I knew I was carrying preconceptions and a degree of longing that could stand between me and the place. I feared my sense of its sorry history would overwhelm my ability to see its present. And as Susan Sontag has warned, devotion to the past is "one of the more disastrous forms of unrequited love."

I also knew that what I was looking for was largely missing, deleted. The ravages of the war and the deliberate obliterations of Jewish communities meant I would be seeking the invisible. Whatever I came back with would be made of shards, wisps, intuitions.

But I felt compelled. As Walter Benjamin puts it: "There is a secret agreement between past generations and the present one. Our coming was expected on earth." I felt obliged to reverse the steps of my unknown grandparents, to make a pilgrimage out of the route of their escape, to document the aftermath of where they had come from and incorporate it into my own sense of place and self.

In fact, I found in Eastern Europe a place even more in thrall to its history than I was. As I'd experienced in Ireland, there was no barrier between past and present: everything coexisted, cried out, required heeding. The invisible was signposted, the imagination invited at every bend. I found myself mirrored. The place was part of me, and it was not-me. But it was a kind of poultice.

Memory's Landscapes

Every hour on the hour, every day of the year, the "Trumpeter of Krakow" appears in a high tower window of the Mariacki Church in Krakow's central square to blow a mournful call-to-arms known as the *heynal*. He plays the tune four times, once in each direction of the compass, beckoning the entire city.

Were this ritual just a live performance to mark the hour, it would be merely charming. But, in fact, the playing of the *heynal* is a rare instance of living history; for at the same moment in every rendition, the *heynal* is abruptly broken off mid-bar with a wobbly gulp. This melodic amputation has poignant meaning for natives of Krakow: it represents the moment in the year 1241 when, during a Tartar invasion, a trumpeter calling the sleeping city to alarums was shot through the throat with an enemy arrow, his song cut off mid-note. To memorialize his sacrifice and the trauma of that invasion over seven hundred years ago (and by extension the numerous invasions since), the *heynal* has been reproduced daily in its truncated form for centuries. It is even now played nationwide on Polish radio every noon—a national mnemonic of vulnerability.

It is commonplace to say that we Americans have a short memory, a shallow sense of history. But it is in contrast to other cultures that this feels truest. Living in Krakow for four months this autumn, traveling a portion of Eastern Europe, I've felt the ground's memories repeatedly erupting beneath my feet. History cannot be ignored here, here at the epicenter of World War II, in a country repeatedly carved up, wiped off the map, reconstituted, tyrannized. Poland's generalized sorrow and anxiety hold even the tourist in its grip.

But these are feelings, I admit, I fall prey to readily. As a child of the 1950s, granddaughter of Jewish immigrants from Poland and Ukraine, the traumas of this territory were inscribed in me. It was as if, to use Carolyn Forché's apt phrase, I was "haunted by memories which [I] did not have"—pogroms, poverty, roundups, gas chambers. In my family, as in many, these matters— once bequeathed—were not to be spoken of; it was vital we get on with the American dream. However, I knew that at heart I was a citizen of my Eastern European past even as I was groomed for my American future. When I chose to study Russian in college, I was already quietly preparing for this journey, my need to return to the "site of the crime," to decipher the genealogy of my character.

Now that I've finally come, I know I am carrying the baggage of my longing and expectations, my myths, my fears. But even had I come with no preconceptions, I've arrived in a place in thrall to its history, where the past insists on being met at every turn.

The landscape is spackled with plaques and monuments, turning city streets into the open-air corridors of a museum. In downtown Warsaw virtually every corner has its story, its hero, its death count—sculpted fighters rising out of sculpted sewer holes, lists of murdered children. The city's very architecture reveals its story: Warsaw, utterly destroyed during World War II, meticulously recreated its historic center in pre-War form from drawings and photographs—a tender gesture of loyalty to the past. Thanks to five decades of city grime, "Old Town" once again looks "old," but visitors are constantly reminded that what they're seeing is not historically original but a defiant reproduction. Postcards at every souvenir stand juxtapose 1945 photos of bombed-out buildings and squares with their elegant reincarnations. We are not allowed to let touristic pleasures distract us from the hour of devastation.

Elsewhere we are invited to reconstruct the invisible ourselves. In cities like Bialystok, where one is hard-pressed to find a pre-War building, we are offered instead a shadow cityscape scripted by plaques: site of the Great Synagogue where three thousand Jews were locked up and burned alive; birthplace of the creator of Esperanto, whose aspiration was world peace; site of the first ghetto uprising of the war—each site cited, a basso continuo droning beneath the cacophony of the now.

Outside of the cities there are fewer clues to guide us. For American Jews like me, seeking the towns their families fled, the strongest sensation of return may be the hollow of absence, the recognition that one culture has supplanted another. Signs of shtetl life, such a vibrant cultural fact only sixty years ago, are almost entirely missing in Eastern Europe. An echoing synagogue here and there, a desecrated cemetery, and everything else new. How can one find roots when the stalk has been severed?

In Krakow, on the other hand, one meets a city beautifully intact. The survival of its medieval streets, of course, carries its own history lesson: Krakow, unlike Warsaw and Bialystok, chose to surrender itself to the Nazis without resistance in order to spare the city destruction. Luck saved it later, when the Nazis, fleeing the quickly advancing Soviet army, had no time to dynamite it. Consequently, Krakow contains a haunting relic: an extensive, undamaged Jewish quarter—Kazimierz—dating from the fifteenth century.

Once home to over sixty thousand, Kazimierz is one of the few places in Eastern Europe where one can visualize a pre-War Jewish community. The Nazis stabled horses and stored weapons in its synagogues and halls but left them standing, as did the Communists. Though dilapidated, there are still beautiful squares and narrow winding streets here, portals of prayer houses engraved with Hebrew, doorposts still shadowed by the outlines of mezuzahs, two surviving cemeteries, schools, homes. An entire landscape of elegy.

But a landscape coming back to life in an eerie way. With the loosening of the Communist stranglehold and a curious revival of interest in things Jewish (a biennial festival of Jewish culture was established in 1988), cafés and nightly klezmer concerts have cropped up in Kazimierz, giving it stage lights and soundtrack. Deferential politicians and the hip, along with foreign tourists, crowd its restaurants. Kosher vodka, beer, and even kosher water are consumed in huge quantities, as if somehow "purer." When Spielberg chose to film *Schindler's List* here, the marketing of Jewish history intensified—one can now tour the sites of the film along with the synagogues and the mikvah.

Much of Kazimierz's boom can be ascribed to the post-Communist influx of American and European tourists. Yet with mementos of Polish Jewish culture having become chic in Krakow, there is a larger nod to history going on. Some see the current simulation of Jewish culture in Polish cities as evidence of guilt or a genuine sadness at the loss of a culture that was, for centuries, deeply entwined with Polish culture. But it isn't just Jewish culture that's being staged—Ukrainian and Gypsy music are trendy, too. Anything "ethnic," I'm told, is welcomed by many Poles as a relief from the long decades of Communist blandness and the postwar fact of the country's ethnic and religious homogeneity.

But what are Poles remembering in their dinner theater gatherings? (The film version of *Fiddler on the Roof* seems to be their major source of information about Jewish life.) And what are Jewish tourists remembering when they come here? In Kazimierz the search for history is beset with contradictions.

There are fewer than two hundred Jews left in Krakow, most of them elderly. The klezmer musicians in the cafés are young Catholics. When I go to Yom Kippur services at the only synagogue functioning in Krakow, the congregation is almost entirely composed of foreign visitors—a fascinating international hodgepodge—and services are led not by a Polish rabbi but by the Jewish scholar Jonathan Webber, come from England for the occasion.

From the first, Kazimierz caused me profound ambivalence. Wandering its streets initially, seeing Hebrew words carved onto buildings now empty or secular, I felt a palpable ache. To steady myself I stopped at the popular Ariel Cafe, with its menu in Yiddish, Polish, and English. Sitting outside, looking at the old market square, I felt genuinely pleased that this place still existed, that I could pay my respects here. A couple of musicians wearing dark suits and yarmulkes began playing appropriately mournful Yiddish tunes. I allowed myself my tears. But when the musicians stopped to smoke and chat, I noticed their boredom. They are hired actors, I had to remind myself, part of an engineered ambience that I had been more than susceptible to. To prove my point, a bus pulled up with thirty American Jewish tourists on board, and the musicians on cue broke out into "Hava Nagila." The tourists gleefully danced their way into the restaurant, teary-eyed. I bristled.

What does history require of us here? What if the musicians aren't Jewish—should they be allowed to wear yarmulkes, present themselves as the authentic article in this ghostly, authentic place? And what of the forty German tourists come to hear klezmer music another night at the Ariel? As I sing along, I feel as if I'm on display, a living remnant in the museum Hitler planned to build when it was all over, artifacts of an extinct, exotic people. Where does remembrance draw its battle line here?

Eva Hoffman's warning, in an essay on Jewish-Polish relations, illuminates the challenge: "At this point, the task is not only to remember, but to remember strenuously—explore, decode, and deepen the terrain of memory. Moreover, what is at stake is not only the past, but the present. . . . In memories, too, begin responsibilities."

The commercialization of memory is most painful when the memories are one's "own" and feel inviolable. Someone else's souvenir kitsch—such as the carvings of Chasidim and klezmer musicians sold in shops—feels like an offensive rip-off when it's your own culture being commodified. As well, the memory that's selected for touristic consumption out of the mass of available memories is inevitably a sentimental one. It spotlights only the surface representations of a complicated history. For instance, that Kazimierz was home mostly to poor Chasidim, whose orthodoxy would be at odds with the majority of visitors' values, is not something we're invited to think about. There is a distilled version of Jewish history for sale here, refined as kosher vodka. This is a place where one can easily cling to a vision rather than explore a historical reality. And it is hard, in season, to even find the silence to absorb this place.

My most resonant moments in Eastern Europe have been my loneliest ones. When I travel to my ancestral territory in Ukraine, I confront a place, unlike Kazimierz, utterly ungeared to tourism, where it is impossible to buy a catalogue at a museum, hard even to buy a postcard, where my footsteps echo in the long, dim hallways of hotels emptied of business. Arriving in Kiev from Poland, where Communist symbols, names, and memorials have been wiped off the landscape, it's a shock, first of all, to see hammers and sickles still adorning buildings. It's even more of a shock to see a statue of Lenin still standing, fresh red flowers at its base. Maybe the country can't afford to topple and rebuild its public spaces, or maybe such symbols reveal its political ambivalence and explain the ubiquitous police.

What's indisputable, though, is that Ukraine is still deeply entangled in its past. Even the casual tourist can see it in the countless memorials. The country is struggling to survive economically, yet hothouse flowers adorn its monuments, even tiny roadside shrines to heroes and past atrocities. Outside the cities, in small towns devoid of commerce or distraction, it's as if the monuments are all people have to tend to, to occupy their communal attention.

My people's memories have been excised, of course. When I journey to my grandfather's village, now a town with a rotting concrete center of high-rises, it seems it will be impossible to visualize his life there. But eventually, directed to the old Jewish section, I recognize the terrain, ravaged—the graveyard largely destroyed, goats grazing its grasses, synagogues gone, records gone, a dirt lane leading to nowhere. Along this lane stand small houses built with Jewish tombstones after the war. I glare at them as my footsteps raise ancient dust. It is even harder than in Poland to reconstruct the shape of Jewish life from what's left here. I apply the bits and pieces of reminiscence I've carried with me, images from photos, my imagination. The river still flows beneath the hillside as it has for centuries. Water is raised from the well. I touch the ground my family touched, but no stories come away in my hand.

That Jews are so little remembered here intensifies my sense of loss. Yet other losses resonate and shadow the landscape with mourning, a permanent elegiac fearfulness that, disoriented as I am, I recognize as my own, the place's legacy to a distant grandchild.

In this season of frantic harvest, I visit a number of memorials to the seventeen million Ukrainians who died during the Soviet collectivization of farms between 1932 and 1933 (a colossal catastrophe not much remembered in the West)—memorials festooned with flowers, nuts, and berries, bouquets of autumn leaves. In Kiev's historical museum an agonizing sculpture of hacked branches entwined with barbed wire, propped up by a fence splashed with red paint, commemorates that famine and World War II. A sign has been added to include the victims of Chernobyl.

There is no shortage of agonies to recall. The very landscape of huge borderless fields bespeaks history's scavenging hand. The land itself has been rendered Communist, even the cities with their communal systems of heat and hot water (everyone shall have heat or no one shall, and given the fuel shortages during the eight cold October days I spend in Ukraine, it is no one). The land tells its story on its body—the past won't soon be forgotten or physically transformed.

Formal gestures of memory can be less honest, though. By chance I am in Kiev on the fifty-fifth anniversary of the massacre at Babi Yar. During two days in the fall of 1941 the Nazis marched an estimated 150,000 residents of Kiev, three-quarters of them Jews, to a ravine on the edge of the city, site of an old Jewish cemetery. Stripped naked, lined up at the ravine's rim, they were machine-gunned to death and tumbled over the edge—one of the war's first mass murders of civilians. Two years later, with the Soviet army approaching, Jewish prisoners were forced to exhume and burn the thousands of bodies to hide the atrocity. But the memory held.

It was the Russian poet Yevgeny Yevtushenko who brought the grim name of Babi Yar to my generation's consciousness with his 1961 poem that lamented and accused: "No monument stands over Babi Yar." Today there are two monuments to the victims of the Babi Yar massacre, and they offer an interesting contrast. The Soviet monument, finally built in 1976, is located in a park over a mile from the actual site of the murders. It is a grandiose, oversized affair, with eleven bronze figures stacked up on a stepped pedestal. Its plaque makes no mention of Jews; rather, it proclaims itself a tribute to Soviet citizens who were victims of fascism. The actual site of the murders had already by then been encroached on by a highway and the huge headquarters of Ukrainian national television. There is only a thin strip of land left open at the edge of the ravine and the desecrated remains of the old cemetery. There, in 1991, the Israeli government was permitted to erect a memorial, a simple ten-foot-high menorah with a small plaque.

The anniversary of the massacre on the Jewish calendar had fallen a week before my visit, and a small religious ceremony had taken place at the Jewish monument. This week was the government's official commemoration, and it took place at the Soviet monument, out of sight of the killing grounds. A few hundred people and a few television cameras watched a platform of ambassadors and officials make their polite, redundant speeches, the flammable past at a safe distance. A Russian Jewish rock star—long censored, now idolized—who was to perform for free in Kiev's central square that evening, appeared with his entourage, briskly climbed the monument to deliver a bouquet of flowers, and then swept off, all caught on film, while the speeches ground on.

I left for the ravine. Here handfuls of people silently drifted in and out, some laying flowers, some lighting memorial candles at the edge of the abyss. I walked to the rim, looked into its alarming depths, saw some broken, tumbled tombstones, a creek quietly pushing its way through. The landscape swayed in vertigo.

Why hadn't the Soviets built their monument here where the murders happened, here where the landscape so dramatically sets the stage for an imaginative recreation of the terror? My guide, a Jew who had lost friends and family here, tells me the real reason behind the official excuses was that the ravine was being used as a garbage dump and the authorities were embarrassed. What's more, he says, it was later discovered that the garbage was polluting the city's water supply; one thousand residents of Kiev died as a result of toxic drinking water. There is no monument here to them. The ravine's been cleaned up, all evidence removed. A breeze exhales and gutters the candles.

Ceremonial commemorations like the ones for Babi Yar pose special challenges to history, as they so often feel canned, an occasion for platitudes. Solitude at the ravine is much more conducive to reflection, but—here's the rub—such places are only evocative given prior knowledge, historical background. You have to have done your homework or come with someone who knows the territory. Otherwise, you'll just see trees.

I happen to be writing this on All Souls' Day. The streets of downtown Krakow are deserted; the population has gone off en masse to the cemeteries with huge sprays of flowers and bagfuls of memorial candles in an extravagant annual ritual of commemoration. By dusk the cities of the dead will be ablaze with thousands of flames. We will walk in the smoky heat of it, sorting the graves of Solidarity heroes from Socialists; recalling painters, actors, grandmothers, and infants. We will follow the crowd to a new memorial in honor of communism's local victims—a cross clung to by a dozen severed hands, tonight flooded with candlelight.

Every day this autumn memory has encroached, tugged me down. For weeks I sat at the dining room table I'd transformed into a desk in our small apartment, unable to find words adequate for Auschwitz or the vanished landscapes of my family's past. I'd come here to connect myself to this landscape and its horrors, but instead I felt more hopelessly separated, silenced by its denials and reinventions, by its magnitude of pain.

As it happened, halfway through our stay in Krakow, we decided to move to another apartment, more central. The day before we left, while drinking a farewell cup of coffee with our landlady, I asked about the history of the apartment house where I'd felt so increasingly disquieted. She told me then the memories of its walls: it was built in 1933 by her uncle, an architect, and he had chosen for himself the second-floor apartment where we'd been living. But when the Nazis occupied Krakow, they had seized this neighborhood, one of the then-most elegant in the city, to quarter officers. The entire house had been commandeered and her uncle consigned to the basement as housekeeper.

When the Nazis invaded Russia, he finally got his apartment back (impeccably cleaned the night before their abrupt departure), and eventually, after decades of loss of ownership under communism, our landlady had legally reacquired her longtime home.

The dining room is still graced by the ornate table, sideboard, and twelve carved chairs that her uncle had had made for the place in 1933. It was at that same table, where Nazis had dined, that I'd been trying fruitlessly to write. I am not a superstitious type in general, but there's no denying this country is haunted.

The next day, in a strange piece of symmetry, I find a plaque on our new apartment building marking it as the secret headquarters of a wartime resistance group. I decide to take this as a kind of benediction to make my peace with the past I've unearthed, to carry home its thin cry. Here at my makeshift desk, two blocks from Krakow's central square, I can hear the *heynal* played every hour. Some days the trumpeter on duty plays it heart-wrenchingly slowly, a hopeless lament. Other days it's played with brisk verve, a robust optimism. Memory can pull us in either direction, dizzy us, set us straight again. With an ear cocked to the past, the city bustles in its busy present. The cobblestones in the sturdy streets resound.

Source Acknowledgments

Commentary, "On Place" by Kim Barnes © 2007 by Kim Barnes. Used by permission
of the author.

"Almost Paradise" by Kim Barnes was originally published in *High Desert Journal* no.
1 (Fall 2005): 12–15. Reprinted by permission of *High Desert Journal.*

Commentary, "Where Time and Place Are Lost" by Alison Hawthorne Deming ©
2007 by Alison Hawthorne Deming. Used by permission of the author.

"In the Territory of Birds" by Alison Hawthorne Deming is reprinted from *The Edges of
the Civilized World: A Journey in Nature and Culture* © 1998 by Alison Hawthorne
Deming. Reprinted by permission of St. Martin's Press, LLC.

Commentary, "Call and Response" by Elizabeth Dodd © 2007 by Elizabeth Dodd.
Used by permission of the author.

"Fragments" by Elizabeth Dodd was originally published in *The Georgia Review* 59,
no. 3 (Fall 2005): 514–34. Reprinted by permission of the author.

Commentary, "Why I'm Sick, and What I'm Sick Of" by David Gessner © 2007 by
David Gessner. Used by permission of the author.

"Sick of Nature" by David Gessner is reprinted from *Sick of Nature* © 2004 by David
Gessner. Reprinted by permission of the University Press of New England,
Hanover NH.

Commentary, "Tipping the Balance" by Barbara Hurd © 2007 by Barbara Hurd. Used
by permission of the author.

"Derichment" by Barbara Hurd is reprinted from *Entering the Stone: On Caves and
Feeling through the Dark* © 2003 by Barbara Hurd. Reprinted by permission of
Houghton Mifflin Company. All rights reserved.

Commentary, "Writing 'A Salt Marsh Reclamation'" by Lisa Knopp © 2007 by Lisa
Knopp. Used by permission of the author.

"A Salt Marsh Reclamation" by Lisa Knopp is reprinted from *The Nature of Home* ©
2002 by the Board of Regents of the University of Nebraska. Reprinted by permission of the University of Nebraska Press. The essay was also published in *Southern
Indiana Review* 8, no. 1 (2001): 55–67.

Commentary, "Scratch Flat and the Invention of Place" by John Hanson Mitchell © 2007 by John Hanson Mitchell. Used by permission of the author.

"The Kingdom of Ice" by John Hanson Mitchell is reprinted from *Ceremonial Time: Fifteen Thousand Years on One Square Mile* © 1984 by John Hanson Mitchell. Reprinted by permission of Perseus Books, PLC, a member of Perseus Books, LLC.

Commentary, "Writing about Place" by Simone Poirier-Bures © 2007 by Simone Poirier-Bures. Used by permission of the author.

"The Shepherds" by Simone Poirier-Bures © 2007 by Simone Poirier-Bures. Used by permission of the author.

Commentary, "Discovering Place" by Robert Root © 2007 by Robert Root. Used by permission of the author.

"Anasazi" by Robert Root was originally published in *North Dakota Quarterly* 59, no. 4 (Fall 1991): 145–54. Reprinted by permission of the author.

Commentary, "On 'After the Flood' and 'Buckeye'" by Scott Russell Sanders © 2007 by Scott Russell Sanders. Used by permission of the author.

"After the Flood" by Scott Russell Sanders is reprinted from *Staying Put: Making a Home in a Restless World* © 1993 by Scott Russell Sanders. Reprinted by permission of Beacon Press, Boston.

"Buckeye" by Scott Russell Sanders was originally published in *Orion* (Spring 1995), and also appeared in the author's book *Writing from the Center*. Reprinted by permission of the author.

Commentary, "Over the Rainbow, My Kind of Place" by Reg Saner © 2007 by Reg Saner. Used by permission of the author.

"Mesa Walk" by Reg Saner was originally published in *The Georgia Review* (Summer 2001), and also appeared in the author's book *The Dawn Collector: On My Way to the Natural World*. Reprinted by permission of the author.

Commentary, "Views from the Desk" by Natalia Rachel Singer © 2007 by Natalia Rachel Singer. Used by permission of the author.

"In the Courtyard of the Iguana Brothers" by Natalia Rachel Singer is reprinted from *Scraping By in the Big Eighties* © 2004 by the Board of Regents of the University of Nebraska. Reprinted by permission of the University of Nebraska Press. The essay was also published in *American Scholar* 73, no. 1 (Winter 2004): 95–97.

Commentary, "Whereof" by Deborah Tall © 2007 by Deborah Tall. Used by permission of the author.

"Memory's Landscapes" by Deborah Tall was originally published in *Tikkun: A Bimonthly Interfaith Critique of Politics, Culture & Society* 13, no. 5 (Sept.–Oct. 1998): 17–20. Reprinted by permission of *Tikkun*.